HUMAN SPACEFLIGHT
Rockets and Rivalry

T0286317

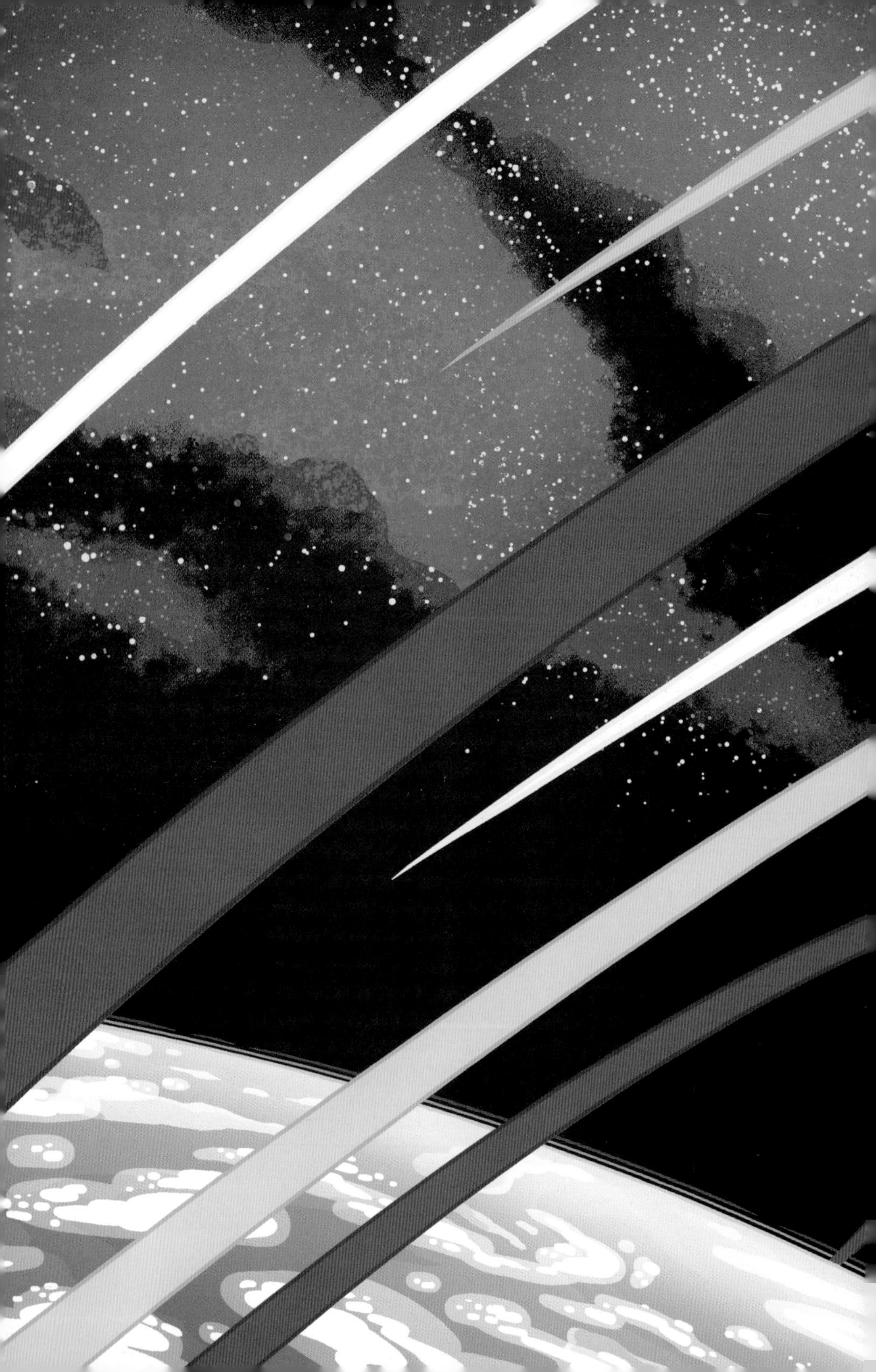

HUMAN SPACEFLIGHT

Rockets and Rivalry

Andy Hirsch

:01

First Second

New York

First Second

Published by First Second
First Second is an imprint of Roaring Brook Press,
a division of Holtzbrinck Publishing Holdings Limited Partnership
120 Broadway, New York, NY 10271
firstsecondbooks.com
mackids.com

Library of Congress Control Number: 2023940626

Our books may be purchased in bulk for promotional, educational, or business use.
Please contact your local bookseller or the Macmillan Corporate and Premium Sales Department
at (800) 221-7945 ext. 5442 or by email at MacmillanSpecialMarkets@macmillan.com.

First edition, 2024
Edited by Tim Stout and Benjamin Wilgus
Cover and interior book design by Sunny Lee and Casper Manning
Production editing by Avia Perez
Expert consultants: Leah Crane and Asif A. Siddiqi

Drawn in Clip Studio Paint. Colored in Adobe Photoshop CC. Lettered digitally with the Soliloquous font from Comicraft.

Printed in China by Toppan Leefung Printing Ltd., Dongguan City, Guangdong Province

ISBN 978-1-250-84654-9 (paperback)
10 9 8 7 6 5 4 3 2 1

ISBN 978-1-250-84653-2 (hardcover)
10 9 8 7 6 5 4 3 2 1

Don't miss your next favorite book from First Second! For the latest updates go to firstsecondnewsletter.com
and sign up for our enewsletter.

When I was five years old, I was an antenna engineer. My family's Sylvania black-and-white television set's reception was sometimes grainy with waves running through the picture. I would learn later about the atmospheric phenomenon that could cause the radio waves carrying television broadcasts to be disturbed, therefore requiring my services. If you're an antenna engineer, you are the person who holds the antennae on the back of the television set. My dad directed me, like the conductor of a choir, on which hand to move and where and when to stop. He used me to optimize the picture so the family could watch the first time human beings would set foot on the moon. On July 20, 1969, at 10:56 p.m. ET, a little past my bedtime, I was hearing but not seeing—because I was behind the television set—the words "one small step for a man, one giant leap for mankind," spoken by astronaut Neil Armstrong. The United States had just won the Space Race, beating the Soviet Union to the lunar surface. My five-year-old brain was still not impressed.

At five, I was present for one of the most incredible things ever accomplished by human beings, walking on the moon, but I never imagined in my wildest dreams that being an astronaut was something I could do. When I was in the sixth grade, my mother gave me a chemistry set, and I mixed some chemicals together and blew up our living room. There was fire and smoke everywhere, and I thought that was the coolest thing; it fueled my curiosity to be a scientist. I even went to college and majored in chemistry because of that young scientific misadventure. I studied chemistry, then engineering, and eventually I ended up working for NASA as a research scientist, where I developed sensors to help planes and space vehicles detect their own damage, similar to how our nerves alert us to damage in our bodies. While at NASA, a friend told me I would be a great astronaut and gave me an application to fill out, but I didn't. That same year, another friend filled out the astronaut application and got in. When he came back to visit me, he flew in a sleek white-and-blue military-style training jet that could go over 800 miles per hour. I told myself if he could get in, I could get in. And if he was flying jets like that . . . I could too. I applied this time and was accepted into the Astronaut Corps.

Three, two, one, liftoff, and the thrust of the main engines tilted us forward and back, a motion we NASA folks call the twang. Suddenly, there was the wondrous thunder of the solid rocket boosters roaring to life. Imagine you're in a sports car going about 100 miles per hour. Our acceleration was many, many times more intense. We were pinned in our seats, feeling three times our weight on our chests. I remember it being hard to breathe during the two minutes before the solid rocket boosters were finally jettisoned. At that point, I thought, *Okay, we're heading to space.* A minute later, we reached 10,000 miles per hour, rocketing over the East Coast of the United States with the Atlantic Ocean shimmering in the background. Another five minutes passed as we reached 17,500 miles per hour, fast enough to shut off the engines and jettison the external tank.

When the main engines cut off, I felt like I was no longer chasing space. I had arrived. I had made it to that "spacious habitation"—the phrase that came to mind when I first looked down from space and saw our home, Earth. A reporter asked me after the *Atlantis* mission what it was like to be up there. I initially spoke about being weightless and seeing things that weren't attached to anything in the shuttle floating around us. The talk quickly turned to that magnificent view of Earth. *Azure, navy, turquoise, indigo,* and *cerulean* were the few words I knew to name the colors of the Caribbean Sea. I needed thirty more words to define these vivid hues as my brain tried to comprehend the blues in this one sea. We circled the earth every ninety minutes and saw deserts, rivers, mountains, plains, and humanity. There was a sunrise and then sunset every forty-five minutes, and at night, the lights below showed the footprints of humanity all connected on our home planet. I was seeing the planet for the first time without borders. I thought about all the places on Earth where there are unrest and war, and here we were flying above all that, working together as one team to help advance our civilization.

—Astronaut Leland Melvin,
author of *Chasing Space: An Astronaut's Story of Grit, Grace, and Second Chances*, who traveled off-planet on Space Shuttle *Atlantis* to help build the International Space Station on flights STS-122 and STS-129

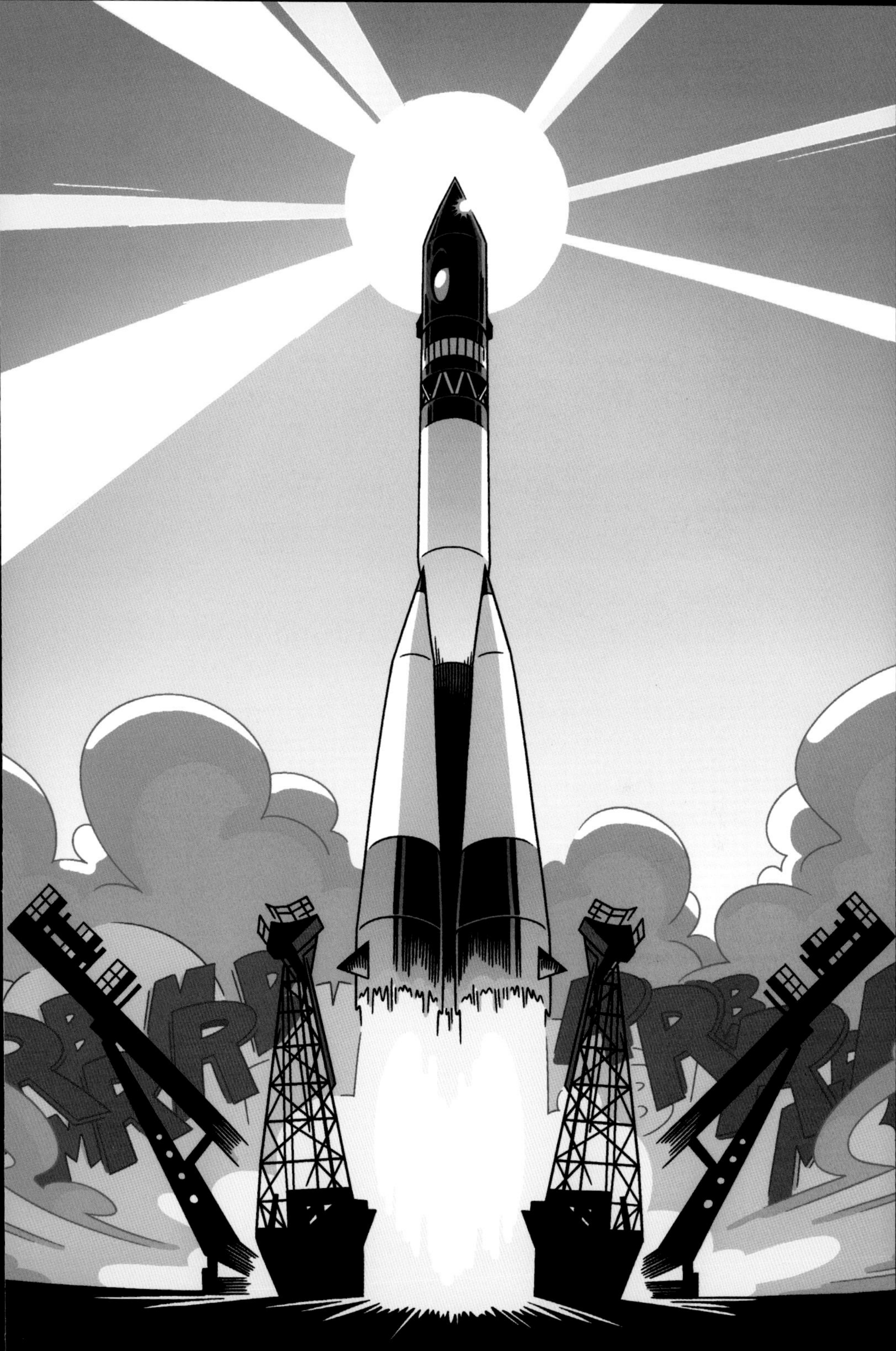

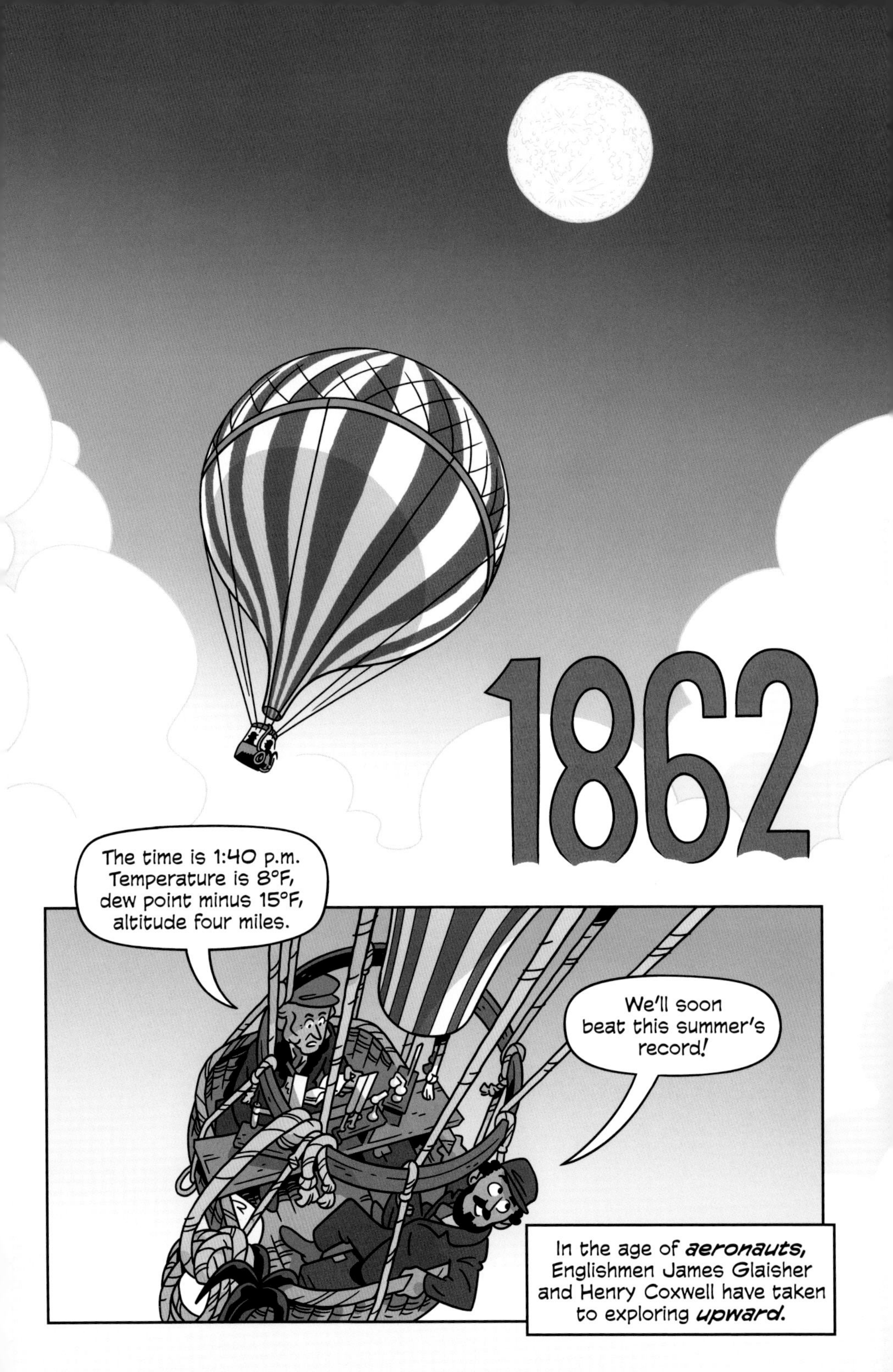
1862
The time is 1:40 p.m. Temperature is 8°F, dew point minus 15°F, altitude four miles.
We'll soon beat this summer's record!
In the age of *aeronauts,* Englishmen James Glaisher and Henry Coxwell have taken to exploring *upward.*

Within an hour of launch, they're miles above the tallest peak in Europe and still climbing.

The time is 1:50 p.m. Temperature -2°F, dew point... indeterminate.

It is very dry above the clouds. Altitude five miles.

The time is...

blurry.

Henry, can you read this?

A moment, James. We may have trouble.

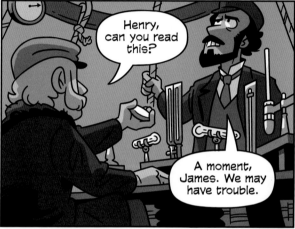

Altitude... altitude is... we are approaching *6 miles*, Henry.

They're higher than Mount Everest's peak and will soon find that the world's tallest mountain is uninhabited for very good reasons.

Earth's *atmosphere*, the air all around us, is a busy mix of various gas molecules.

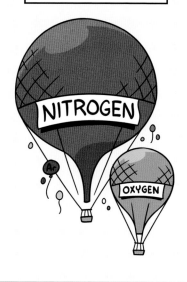

Gravity holds them near the surface, where you *feel* those molecules, tiny as they are, as *air pressure*.

Ack!

At higher altitudes, there are fewer molecules and *lower* air pressure. That doesn't sound so bad, does it?

Whew!

Oh, but thin air has fewer molecules of all types, including *oxygen*. People breathe that!

GASP!

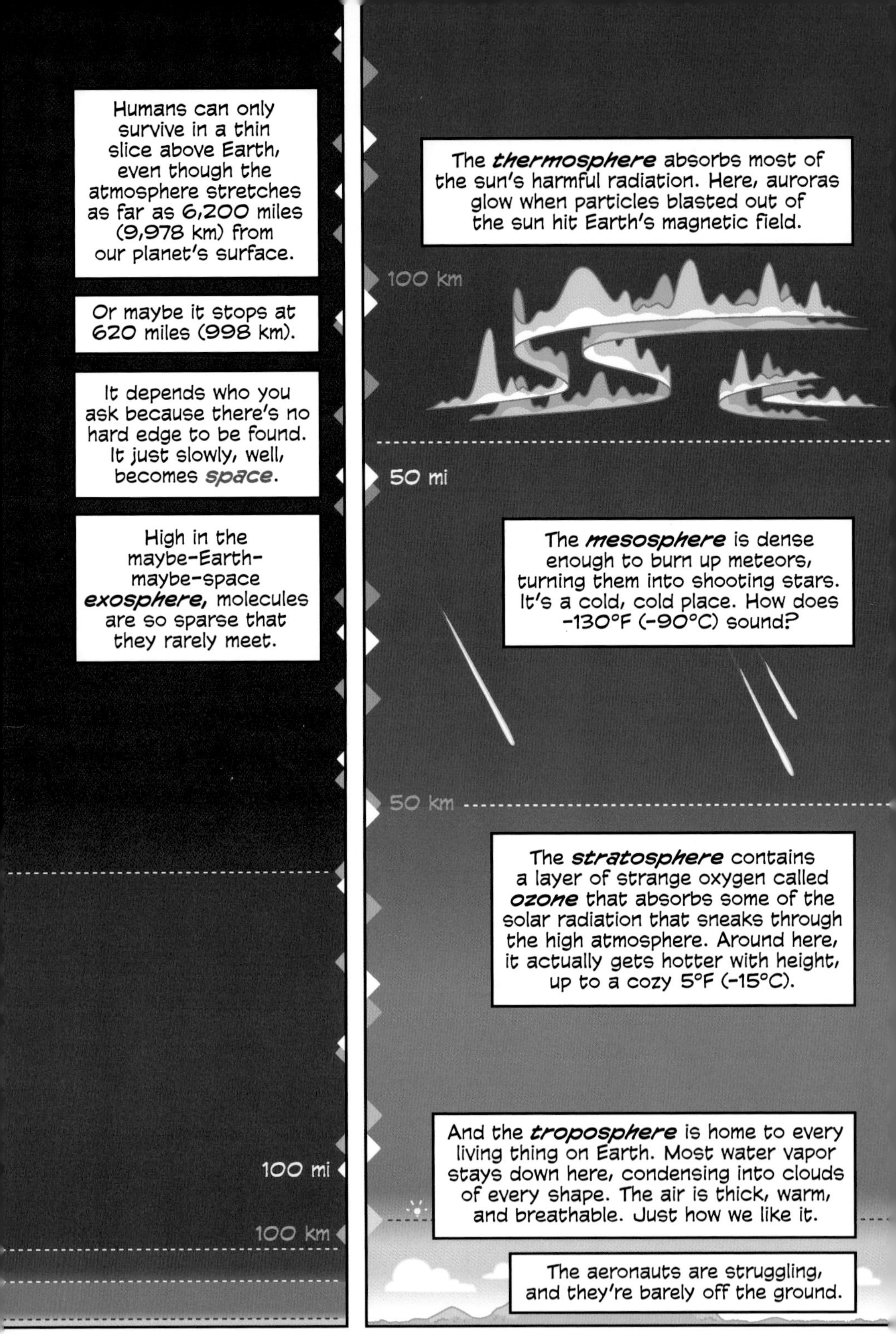

Humans can only survive in a thin slice above Earth, even though the atmosphere stretches as far as 6,200 miles (9,978 km) from our planet's surface.

Or maybe it stops at 620 miles (998 km).

It depends who you ask because there's no hard edge to be found. It just slowly, well, becomes *space*.

High in the maybe-Earth-maybe-space *exosphere,* molecules are so sparse that they rarely meet.

The *thermosphere* absorbs most of the sun's harmful radiation. Here, auroras glow when particles blasted out of the sun hit Earth's magnetic field.

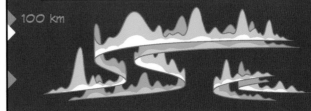

100 km

50 mi

The *mesosphere* is dense enough to burn up meteors, turning them into shooting stars. It's a cold, cold place. How does –130°F (–90°C) sound?

50 km

The *stratosphere* contains a layer of strange oxygen called *ozone* that absorbs some of the solar radiation that sneaks through the high atmosphere. Around here, it actually gets hotter with height, up to a cozy 5°F (–15°C).

And the *troposphere* is home to every living thing on Earth. Most water vapor stays down here, condensing into clouds of every shape. The air is thick, warm, and breathable. Just how we like it.

The aeronauts are struggling, and they're barely off the ground.

100 mi

100 km

The trouble is that the pressure on their bodies and the amount of oxygen they inhale with each breath are about a *third* of what each would be at sea level.

Thin air pits the explorers against...

💀 HYPOXIA

Lack of oxygen results in blurred vision, poor coordination, and difficulty thinking. It sneaks up on a person, and they'll pass out before long.

Ooh...

DECOMPRESSION SICKNESS 💀

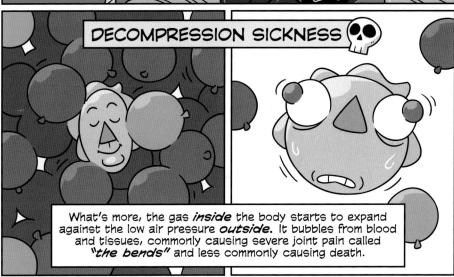

What's more, the gas *inside* the body starts to expand against the low air pressure *outside.* It bubbles from blood and tissues, commonly causing severe joint pain called *"the bends"* and less commonly causing death.

CHATTER CHATTER

HYPOTHERMIA & FROSTBITE 💀

Don't forget shivers, confusion, and eventual tissue damage from temperatures *far* below freezing.

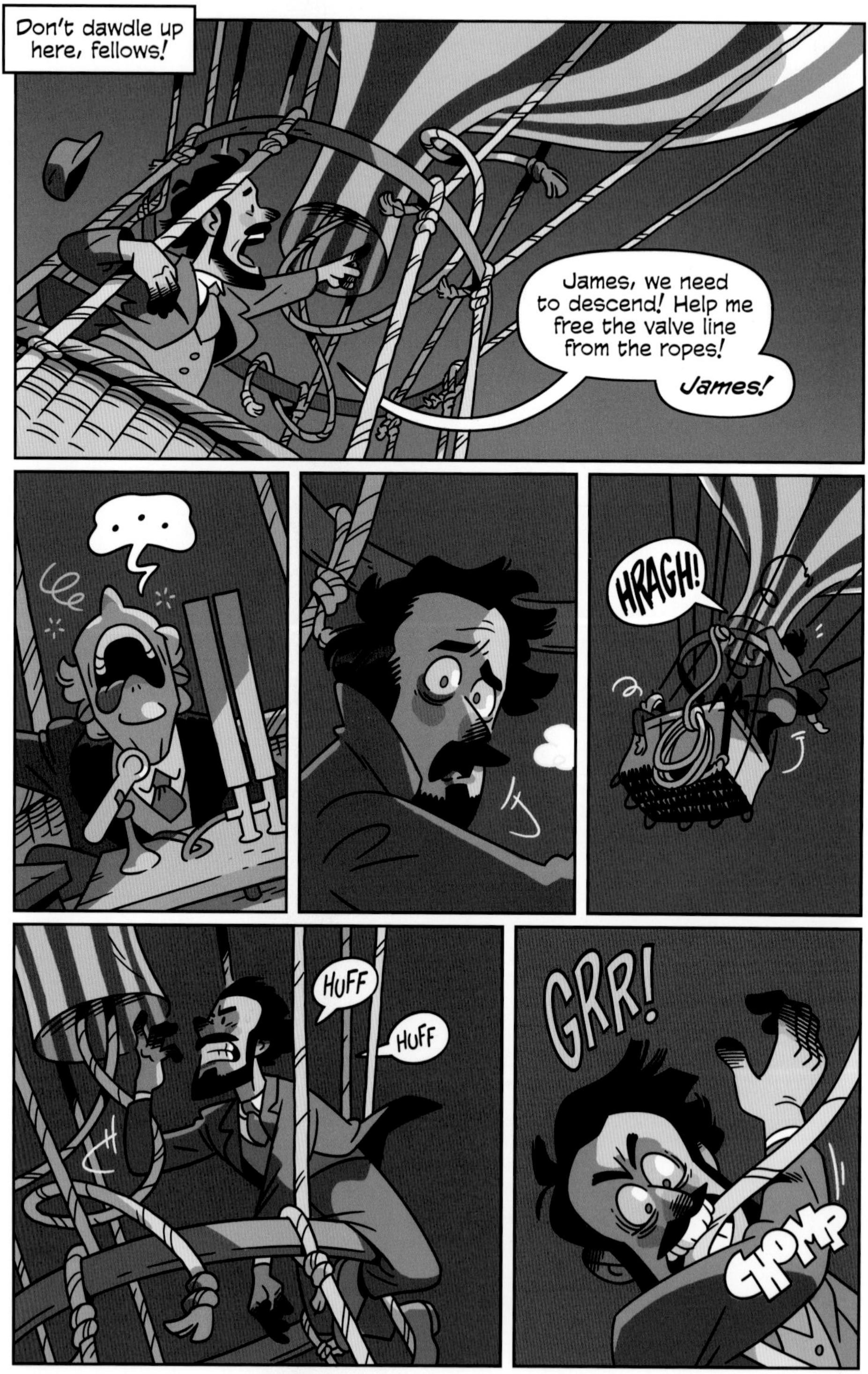
Don't dawdle up here, fellows!
James, we need to descend! Help me free the valve line from the ropes!
James!
...
HRAGH!
HUFF
HUFF
GRR!
CHOMP

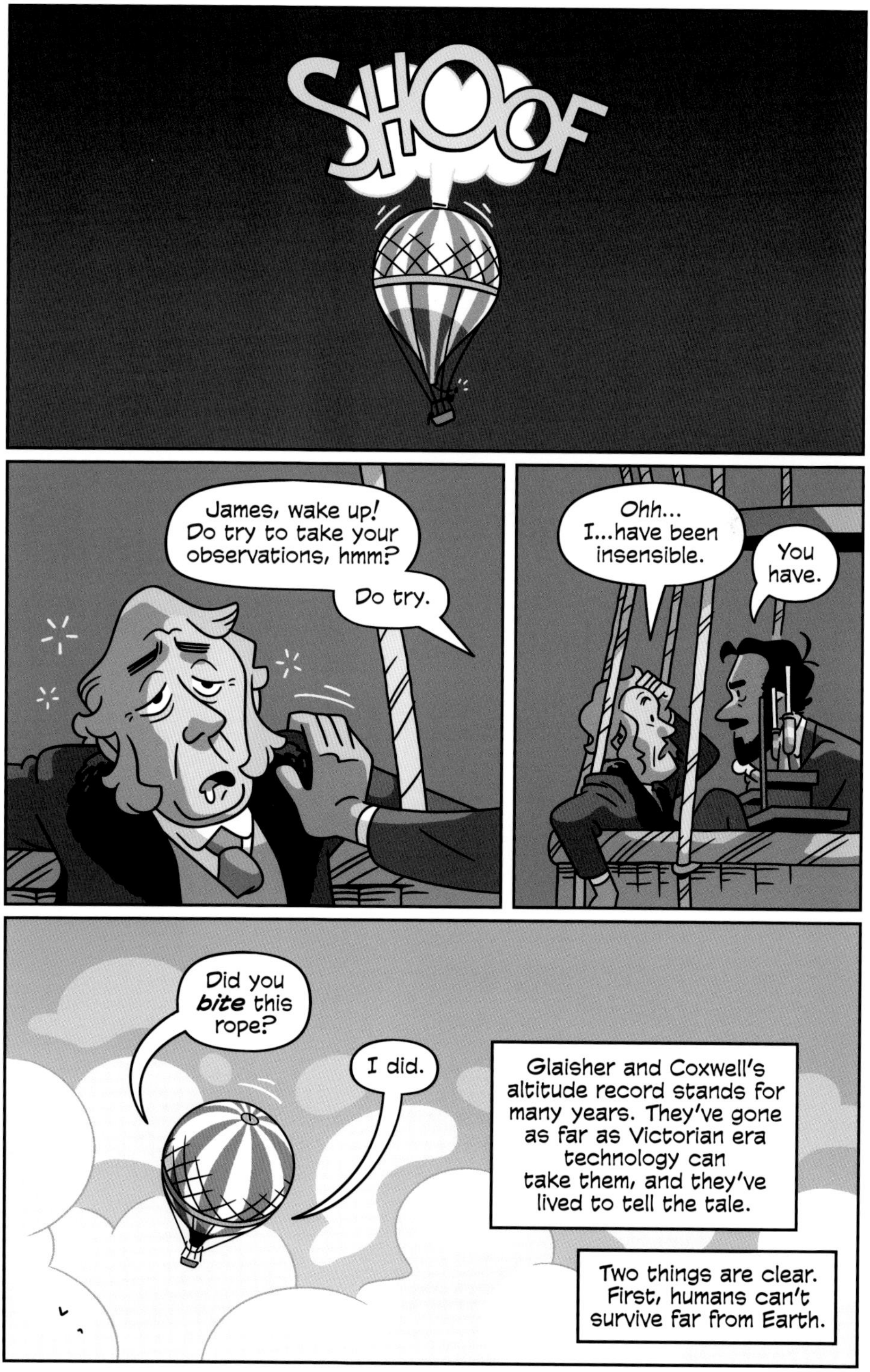

SHOOF
James, wake up! Do try to take your observations, hmm?
Do try.
Ohh... I...have been insensible.
You have.
Did you *bite* this rope?
I did.
Glaisher and Coxwell's altitude record stands for many years. They've gone as far as Victorian era technology can take them, and they've lived to tell the tale.
Two things are clear. First, humans can't survive far from Earth.

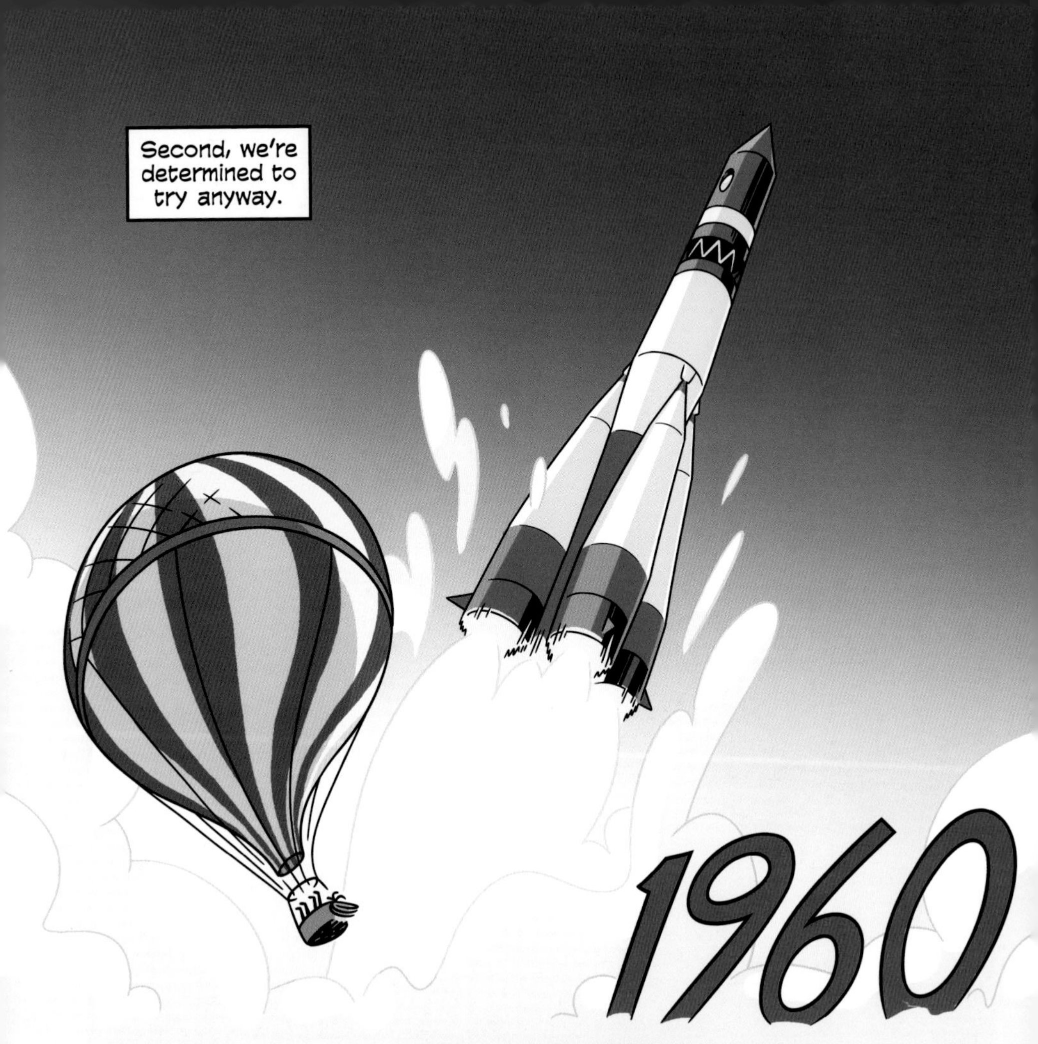
Second, we're determined to try anyway.
1960

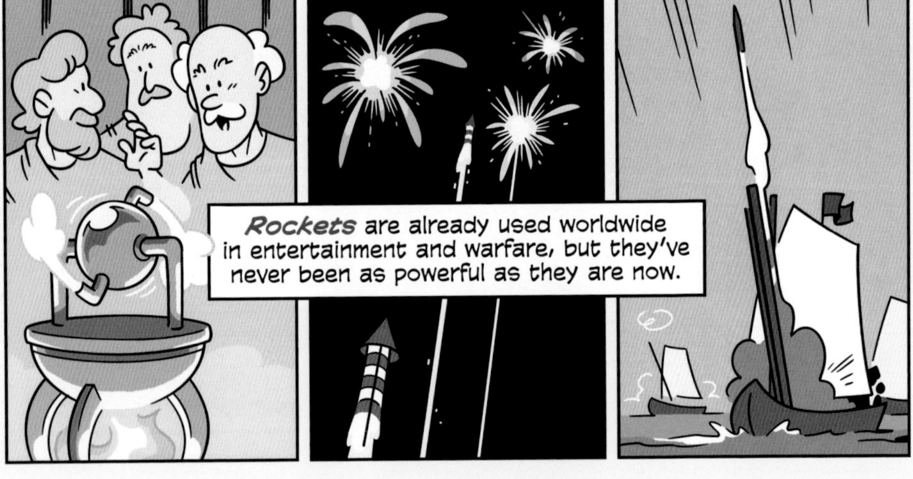
Rockets are already used worldwide in entertainment and warfare, but they've never been as powerful as they are now.

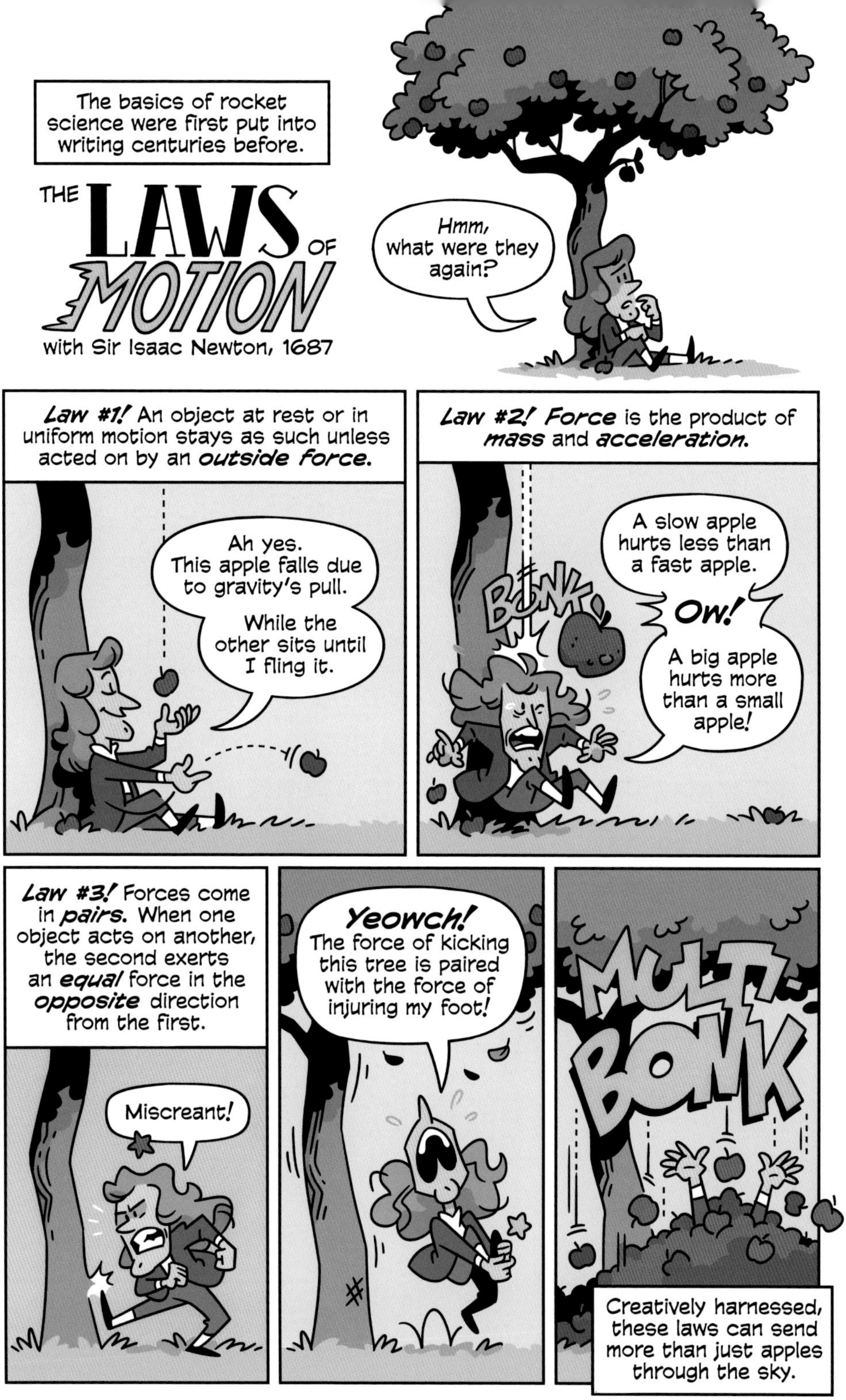
The basics of rocket science were first put into writing centuries before.
THE LAWS OF MOTION
with Sir Isaac Newton, 1687
Hmm, what were they again?
Law #1! An object at rest or in uniform motion stays as such unless acted on by an outside force.
Ah yes. This apple falls due to gravity's pull.
While the other sits until I fling it.
Law #2! Force is the product of mass and acceleration.
BONK!
A slow apple hurts less than a fast apple.
OW!
A big apple hurts more than a small apple!
Law #3! Forces come in pairs. When one object acts on another, the second exerts an equal force in the opposite direction from the first.
Miscreant!
Yeowch! The force of kicking this tree is paired with the force of injuring my foot!
MULTI-BONK
Creatively harnessed, these laws can send more than just apples through the sky.

A *rocket engine* holds a controlled, sustained *explosion*. Fuel ignites in a combustion chamber, becoming superhot gas that expands in every direction.

This gas is allowed to exit the chamber in just one direction as *exhaust*.

Newton's *third law* says every force is part of a pair, and the exhaust is paired with *thrust*.

The equal, opposite forces in other directions *cancel* each other out, but with exhaust leaving the engine, *thrust* is left alone to act!

The *first law* says the rocket will rise if that thrust force is greater than *gravity*.

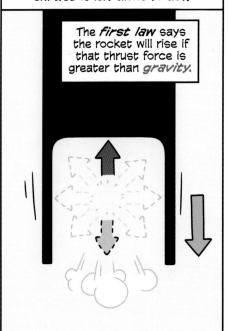

So the exhaust is made to *squeeze* through a smaller hole, causing it to move even faster. It's like a thumb on a hose's end!

The *second law* tells us that this greater acceleration results in greater force, just what we need to fly!

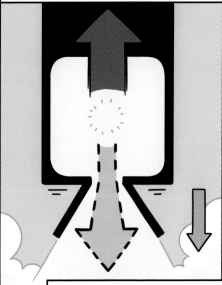

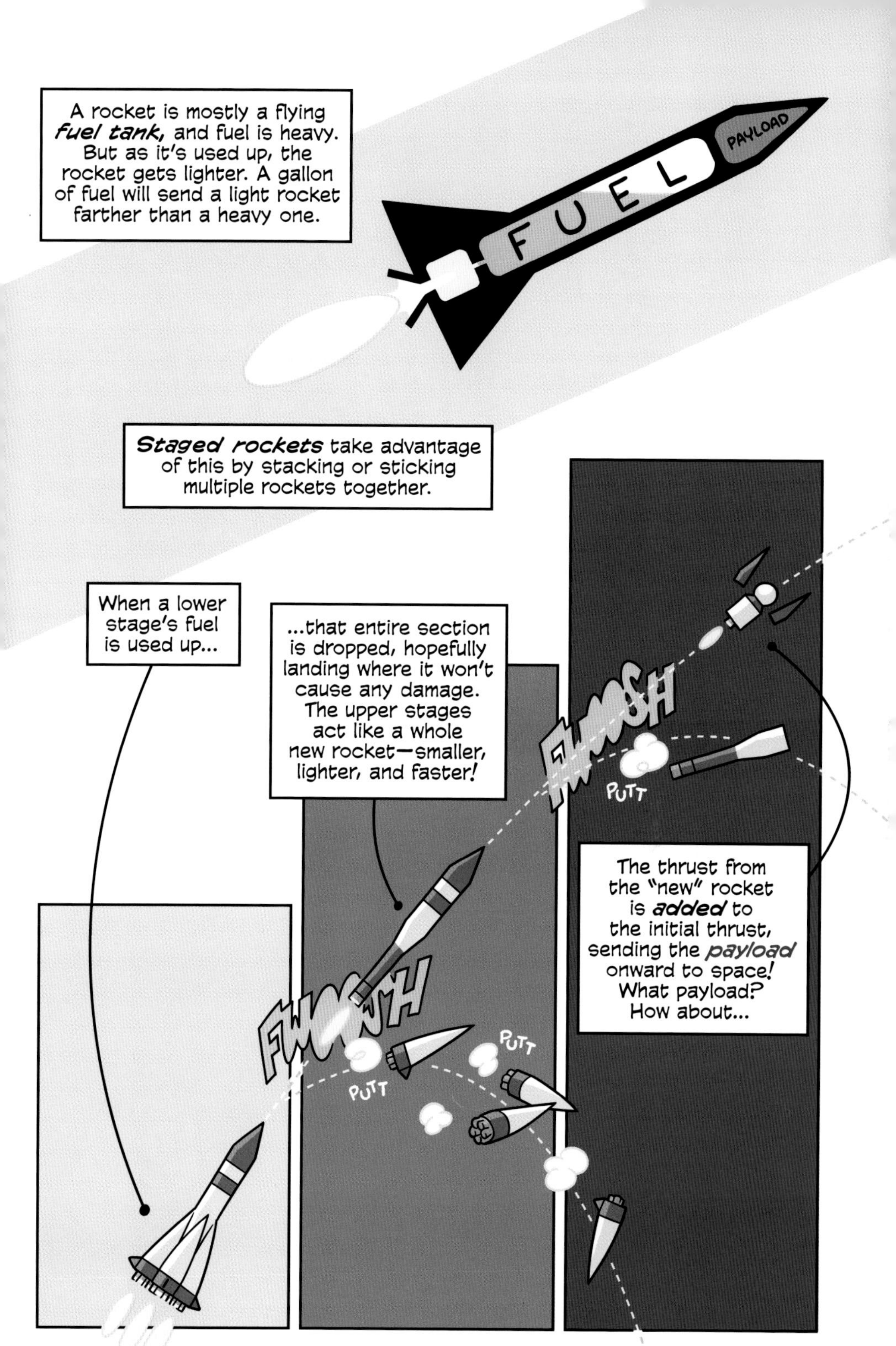
A rocket is mostly a flying *fuel tank,* and fuel is heavy. But as it's used up, the rocket gets lighter. A gallon of fuel will send a light rocket farther than a heavy one.
PAYLOAD
FUEL
Staged rockets take advantage of this by stacking or sticking multiple rockets together.
When a lower stage's fuel is used up...
...that entire section is dropped, hopefully landing where it won't cause any damage. The upper stages act like a whole new rocket—smaller, lighter, and faster!
FWOOSH
PUTT
PUTT
FWOOSH
PUTT
The thrust from the "new" rocket is *added* to the initial thrust, sending the *payload* onward to space! What payload? How about...

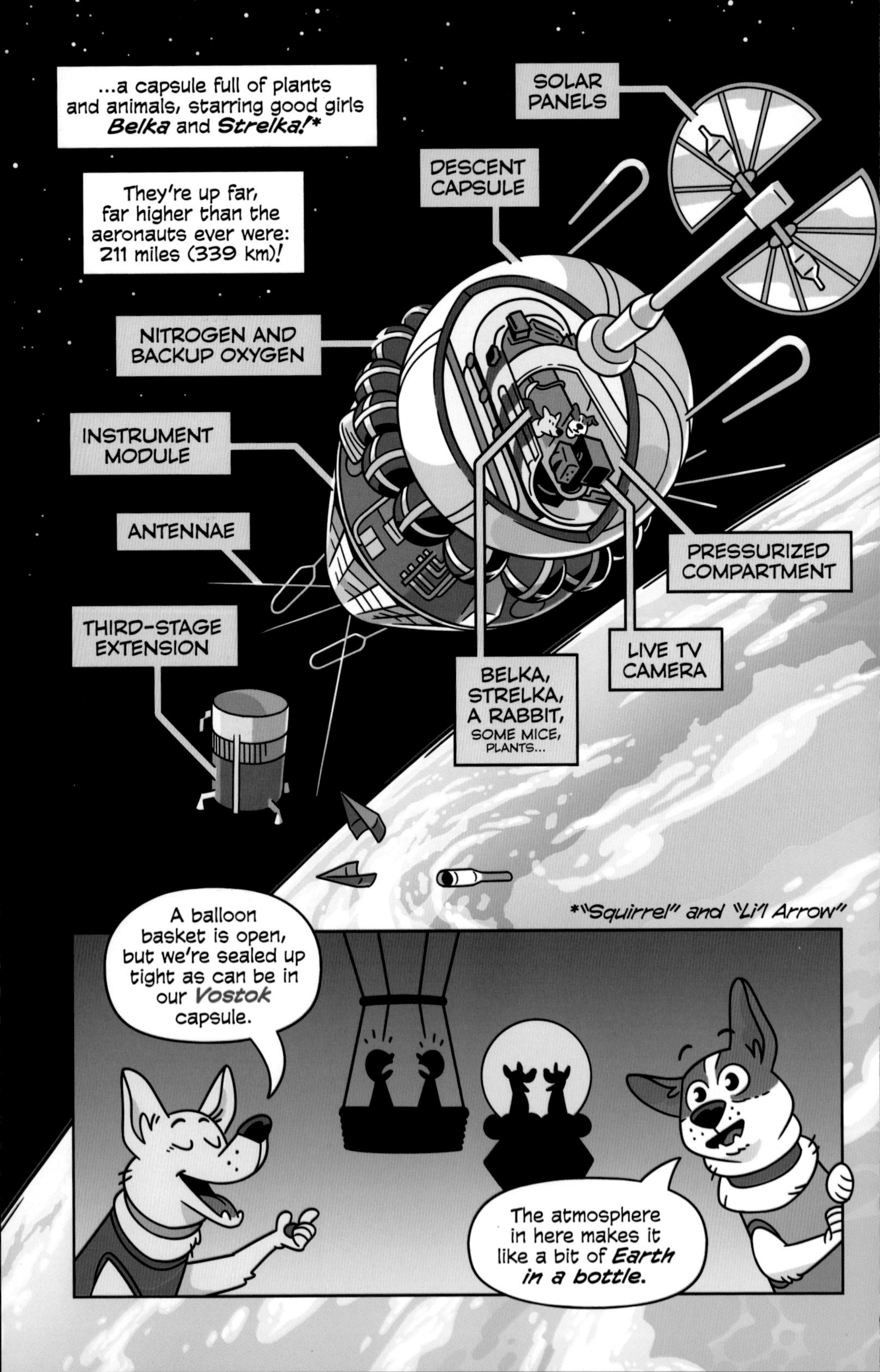
...a capsule full of plants and animals, starring good girls *Belka* and *Strelka!**
They're up far, far higher than the aeronauts ever were: 211 miles (339 km)!
SOLAR PANELS
DESCENT CAPSULE
NITROGEN AND BACKUP OXYGEN
INSTRUMENT MODULE
ANTENNAE
THIRD-STAGE EXTENSION
PRESSURIZED COMPARTMENT
LIVE TV CAMERA
BELKA, STRELKA, A RABBIT, SOME MICE, PLANTS...
*"Squirrel" and "Li'l Arrow"
A balloon basket is open, but we're sealed up tight as can be in our *Vostok* capsule.
The atmosphere in here makes it like a bit of *Earth in a bottle*.

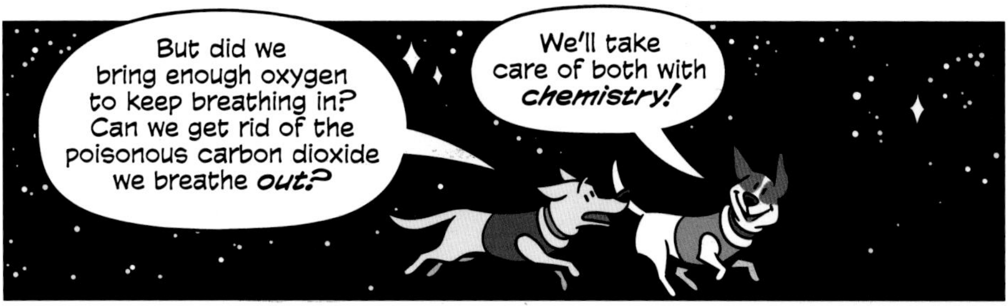
But did we bring enough oxygen to keep breathing in? Can we get rid of the poisonous carbon dioxide we breathe *out?*
We'll take care of both with ***chemistry!***

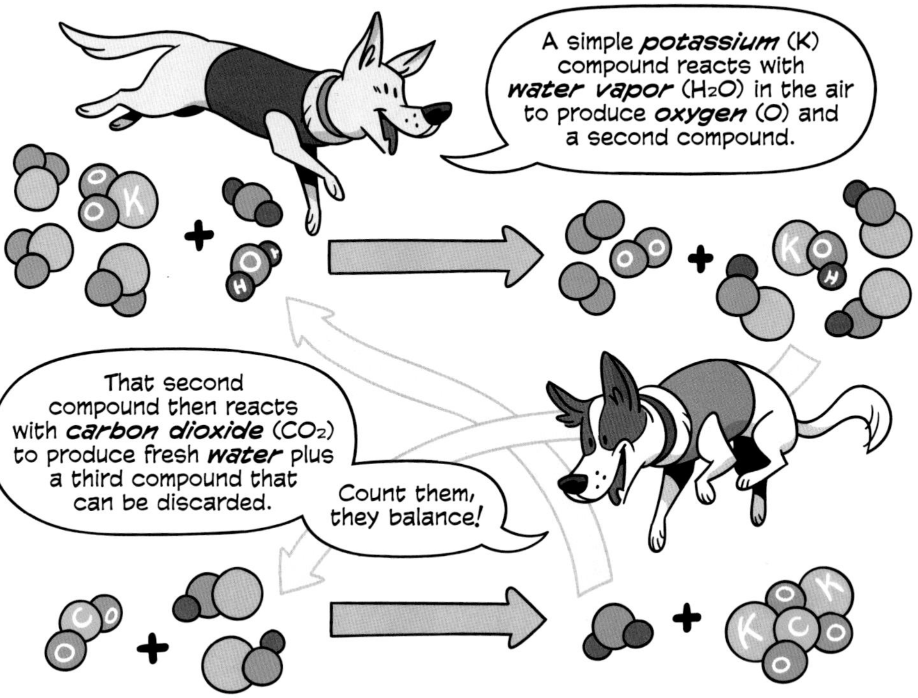
A simple ***potassium*** (K) compound reacts with ***water vapor*** (H_2O) in the air to produce ***oxygen*** (O) and a second compound.
That second compound then reacts with ***carbon dioxide*** (CO_2) to produce fresh ***water*** plus a third compound that can be discarded.
Count them, they balance!

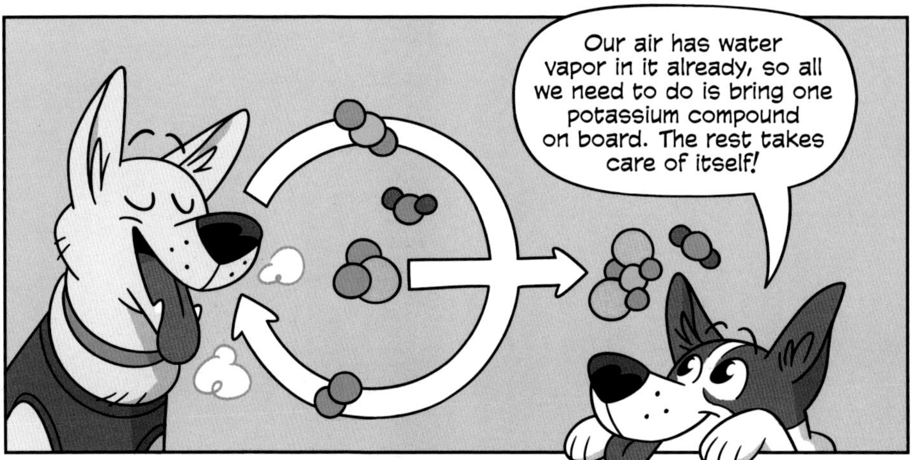
Our air has water vapor in it already, so all we need to do is bring one potassium compound on board. The rest takes care of itself!

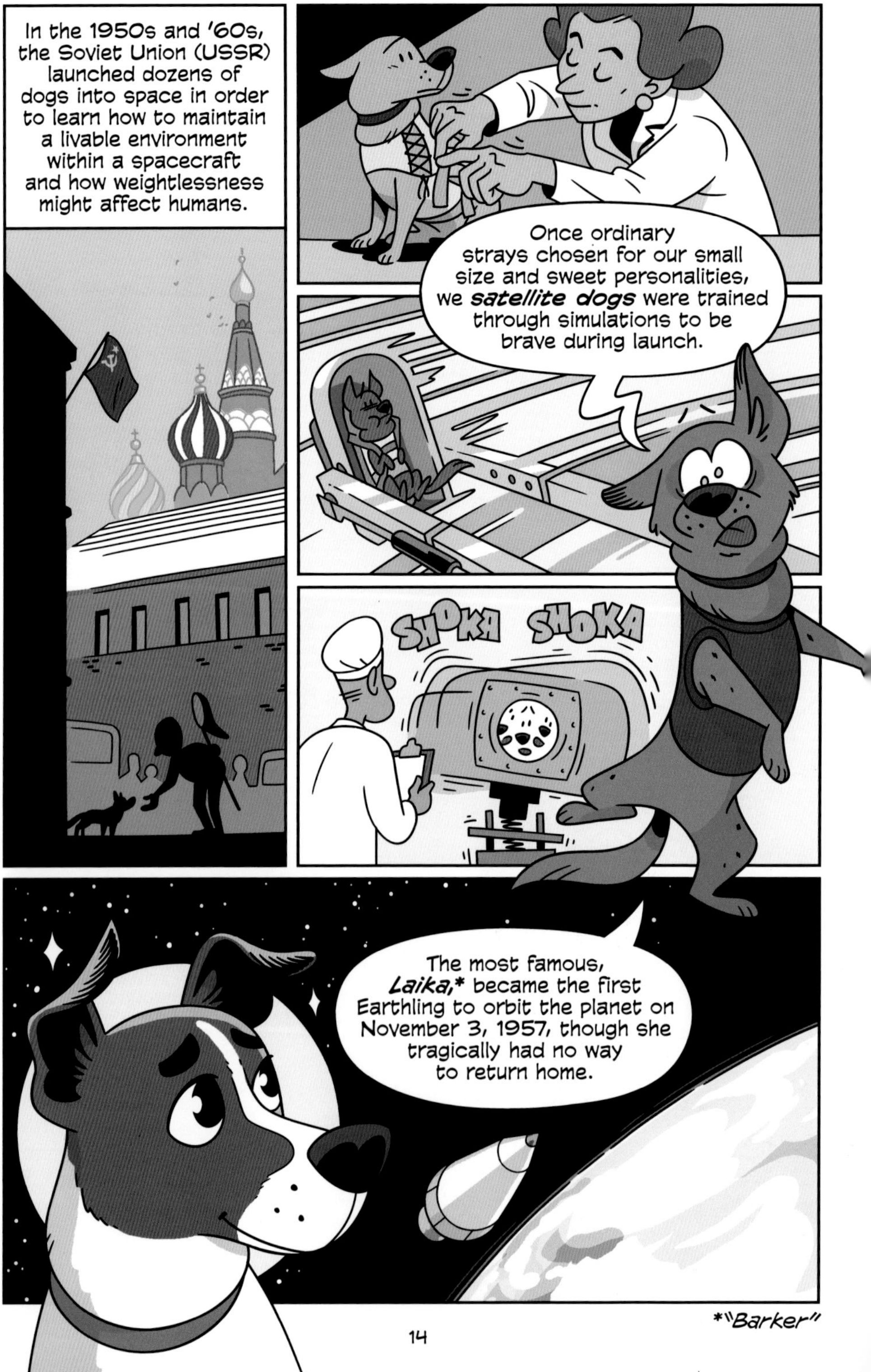
In the 1950s and '60s, the Soviet Union (USSR) launched dozens of dogs into space in order to learn how to maintain a livable environment within a spacecraft and how weightlessness might affect humans.
Once ordinary strays chosen for our small size and sweet personalities, we ***satellite dogs*** were trained through simulations to be brave during launch.
SHOKA SHOKA
The most famous, ***Laika,**** became the first Earthling to orbit the planet on November 3, 1957, though she tragically had no way to return home.

*"*Barker*"

Thankfully, this spacecraft has thrusters to send it back into Earth's atmosphere.

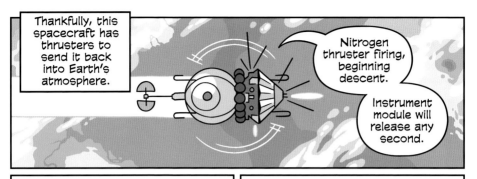

Nitrogen thruster firing, beginning descent.

Instrument module will release any second.

When one object, even a liquid or gas, moves along another, the two catch and snag, creating *heat* and a *friction* force that works opposite the object's motion.

In time, friction adds up to slow and eventually stop the moving object. These girls need to slow down from *17,500 mph* (28,164 km/h)!

The atmosphere gets denser as you approach the surface, meaning more friction and more heat. We're talking thousands of degrees!

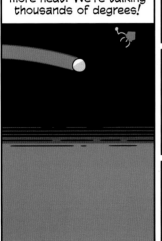

Neither the dogs nor their vehicle can handle a fast, steep dive.

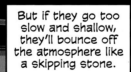

But if they go too slow and shallow, they'll bounce off the atmosphere like a skipping stone.

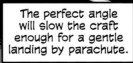

The perfect angle will slow the craft enough for a gentle landing by parachute.

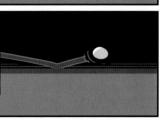

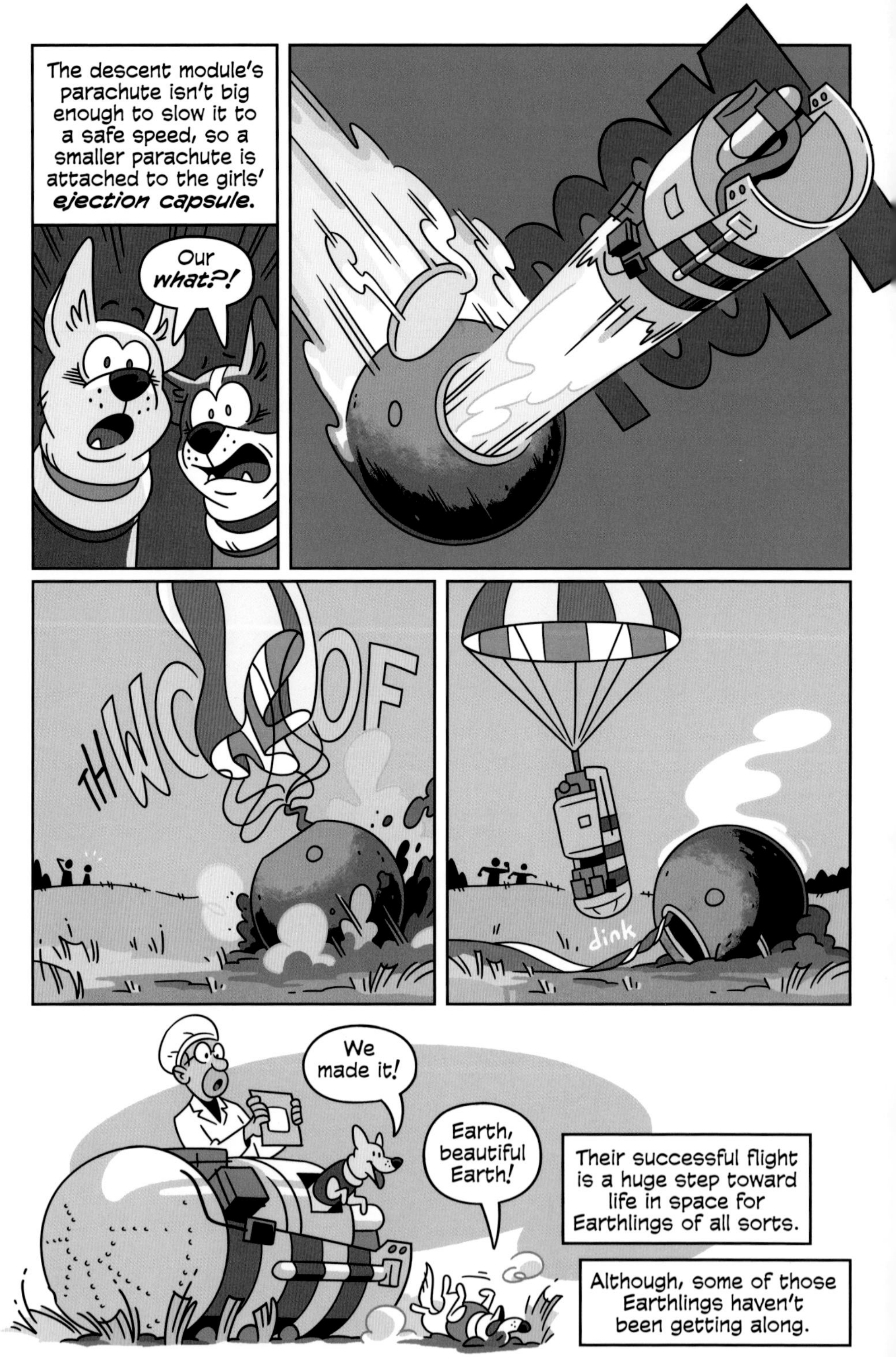
The descent module's parachute isn't big enough to slow it to a safe speed, so a smaller parachute is attached to the girls' *ejection capsule.*
Our *what?!*
THWOOF
dink
We made it!
Earth, beautiful Earth!
Their successful flight is a huge step toward life in space for Earthlings of all sorts.
Although, some of those Earthlings haven't been getting along.

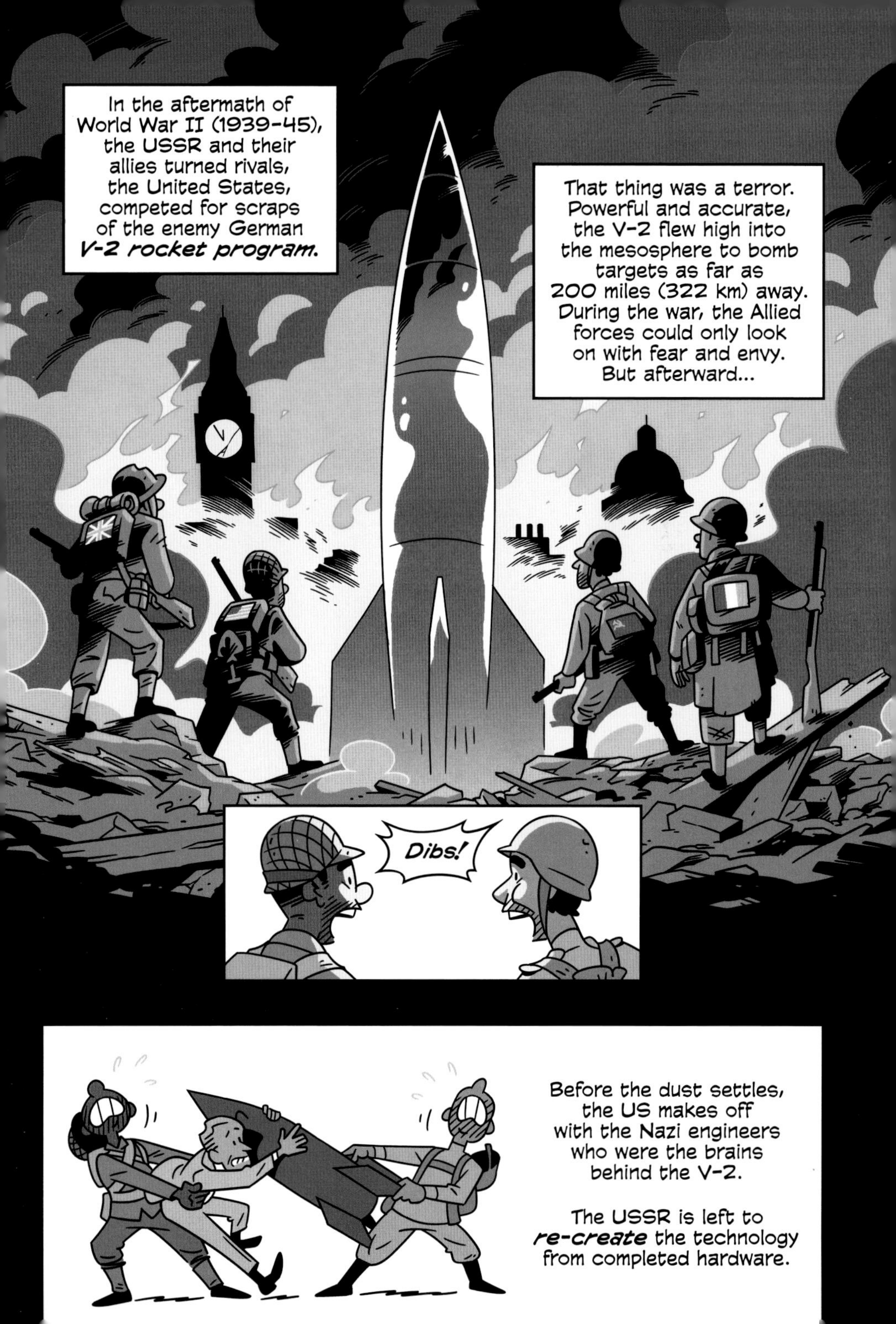
In the aftermath of World War II (1939–45), the USSR and their allies turned rivals, the United States, competed for scraps of the enemy German *V-2 rocket program.*
That thing was a terror. Powerful and accurate, the V-2 flew high into the mesosphere to bomb targets as far as 200 miles (322 km) away. During the war, the Allied forces could only look on with fear and envy. But afterward...
Dibs!
Before the dust settles, the US makes off with the Nazi engineers who were the brains behind the V-2.
The USSR is left to *re-create* the technology from completed hardware.

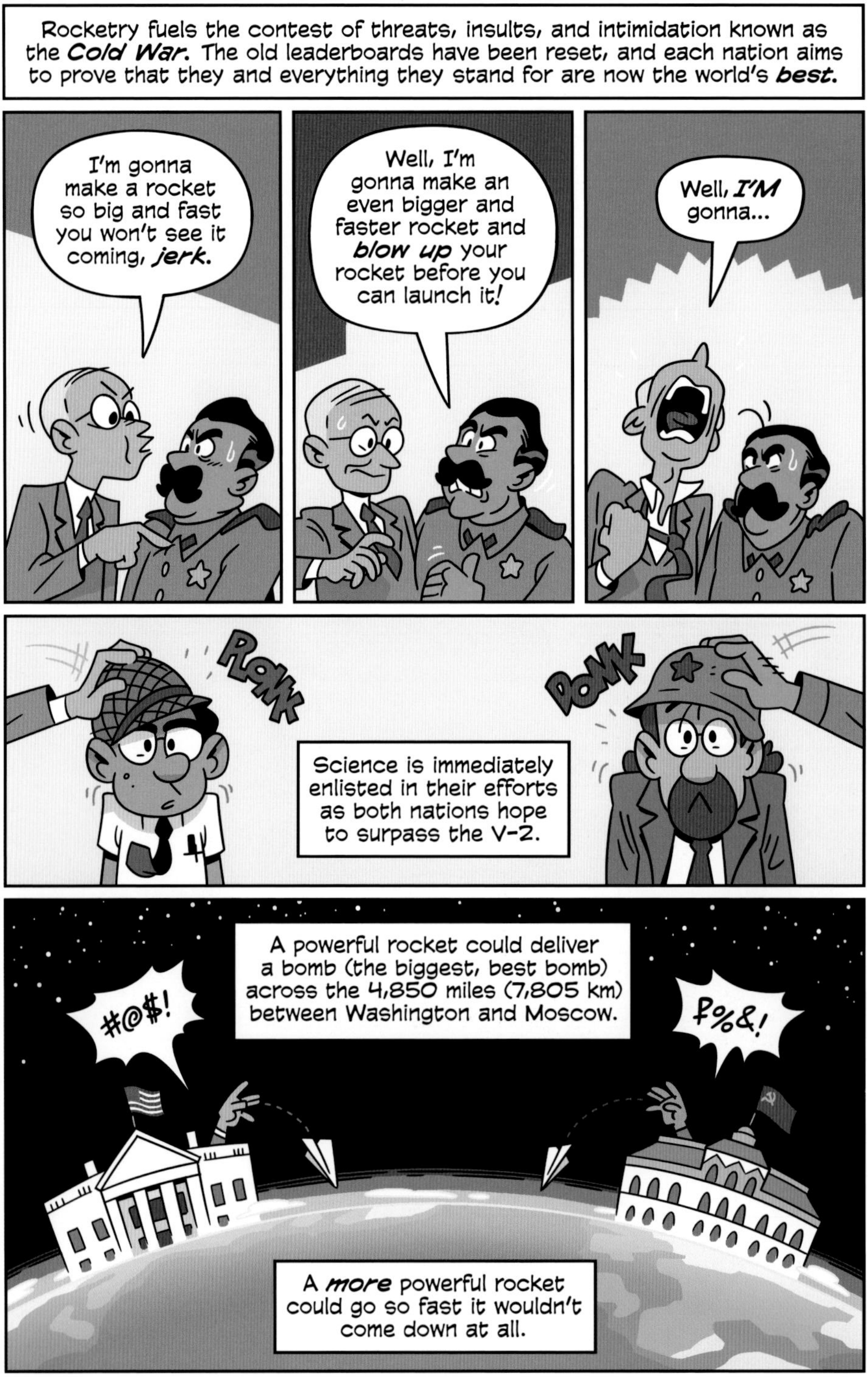
Rocketry fuels the contest of threats, insults, and intimidation known as the *Cold War.* The old leaderboards have been reset, and each nation aims to prove that they and everything they stand for are now the world's ***best.***
I'm gonna make a rocket so big and fast you won't see it coming, ***jerk.***
Well, I'm gonna make an even bigger and faster rocket and ***blow up*** your rocket before you can launch it!
Well, ***I'M*** gonna...
RONK
DONK
Science is immediately enlisted in their efforts as both nations hope to surpass the V-2.
#@$!
A powerful rocket could deliver a bomb (the biggest, best bomb) across the 4,850 miles (7,805 km) between Washington and Moscow.
£%&!
A ***more*** powerful rocket could go so fast it wouldn't come down at all.

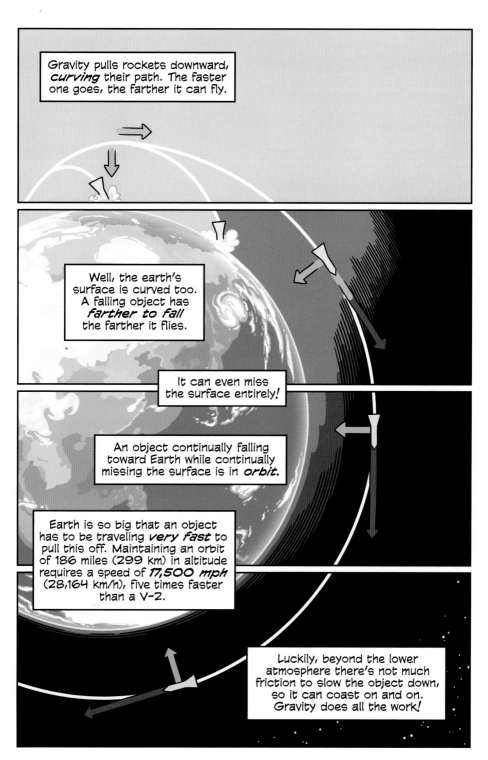

Gravity pulls rockets downward, *curving* their path. The faster one goes, the farther it can fly.

Well, the earth's surface is curved too. A falling object has *farther to fall* the farther it flies.

It can even miss the surface entirely!

An object continually falling toward Earth while continually missing the surface is in *orbit*.

Earth is so big that an object has to be traveling *very fast* to pull this off. Maintaining an orbit of 186 miles (299 km) in altitude requires a speed of *17,500 mph* (28,164 km/h), five times faster than a V-2.

Luckily, beyond the lower atmosphere there's not much friction to slow the object down, so it can coast on and on. Gravity does all the work!

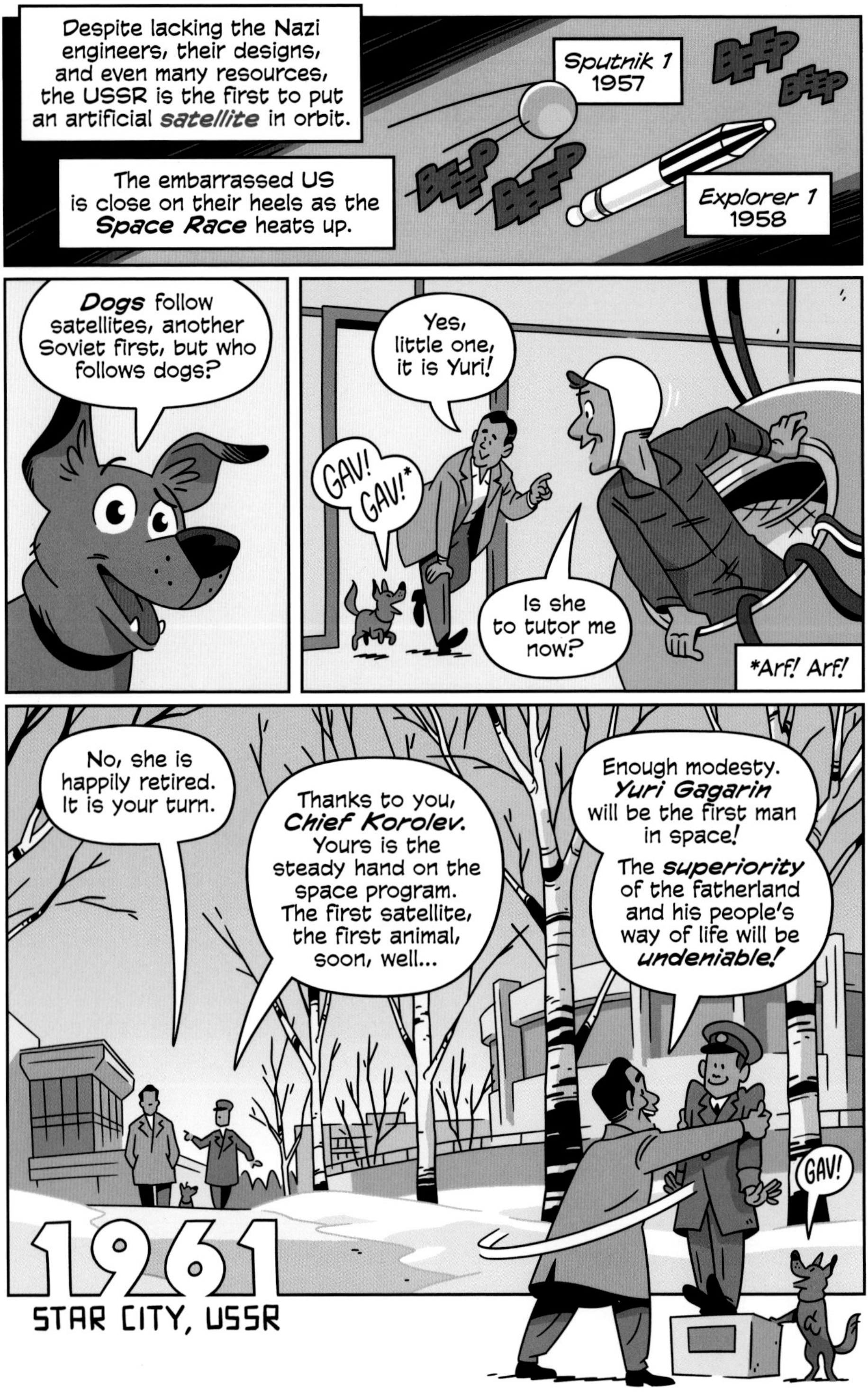

Despite lacking the Nazi engineers, their designs, and even many resources, the USSR is the first to put an artificial *satellite* in orbit.
Sputnik 1 1957
BEEP
BEEP
BEEP
BEEP
The embarrassed US is close on their heels as the *Space Race* heats up.
Explorer 1 1958
Dogs follow satellites, another Soviet first, but who follows dogs?
Yes, little one, it is Yuri!
GAV! GAV!*
Is she to tutor me now?
*Arf! Arf!
No, she is happily retired. It is your turn.
Thanks to you, *Chief Korolev.* Yours is the steady hand on the space program. The first satellite, the first animal, soon, well...
Enough modesty. *Yuri Gagarin* will be the first man in space!
The *superiority* of the fatherland and his people's way of life will be *undeniable!*
GAV!
1961
STAR CITY, USSR

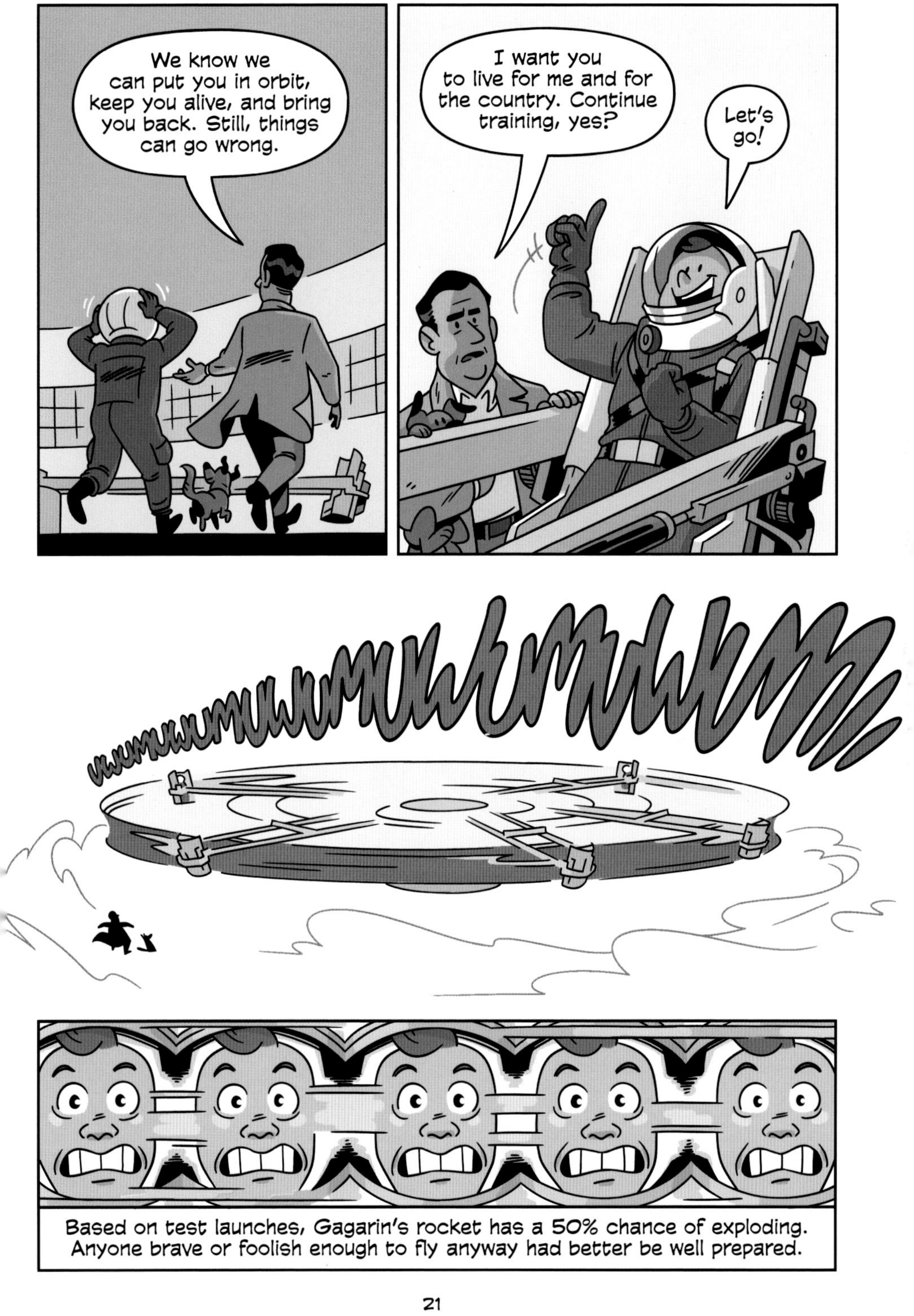
We know we can put you in orbit, keep you alive, and bring you back. Still, things can go wrong.
I want you to live for me and for the country. Continue training, yes?
Let's go!
VWUMVWUMVWUMVWUMVWUMVWUMVWUM
Based on test launches, Gagarin's rocket has a 50% chance of exploding. Anyone brave or foolish enough to fly anyway had better be well prepared.

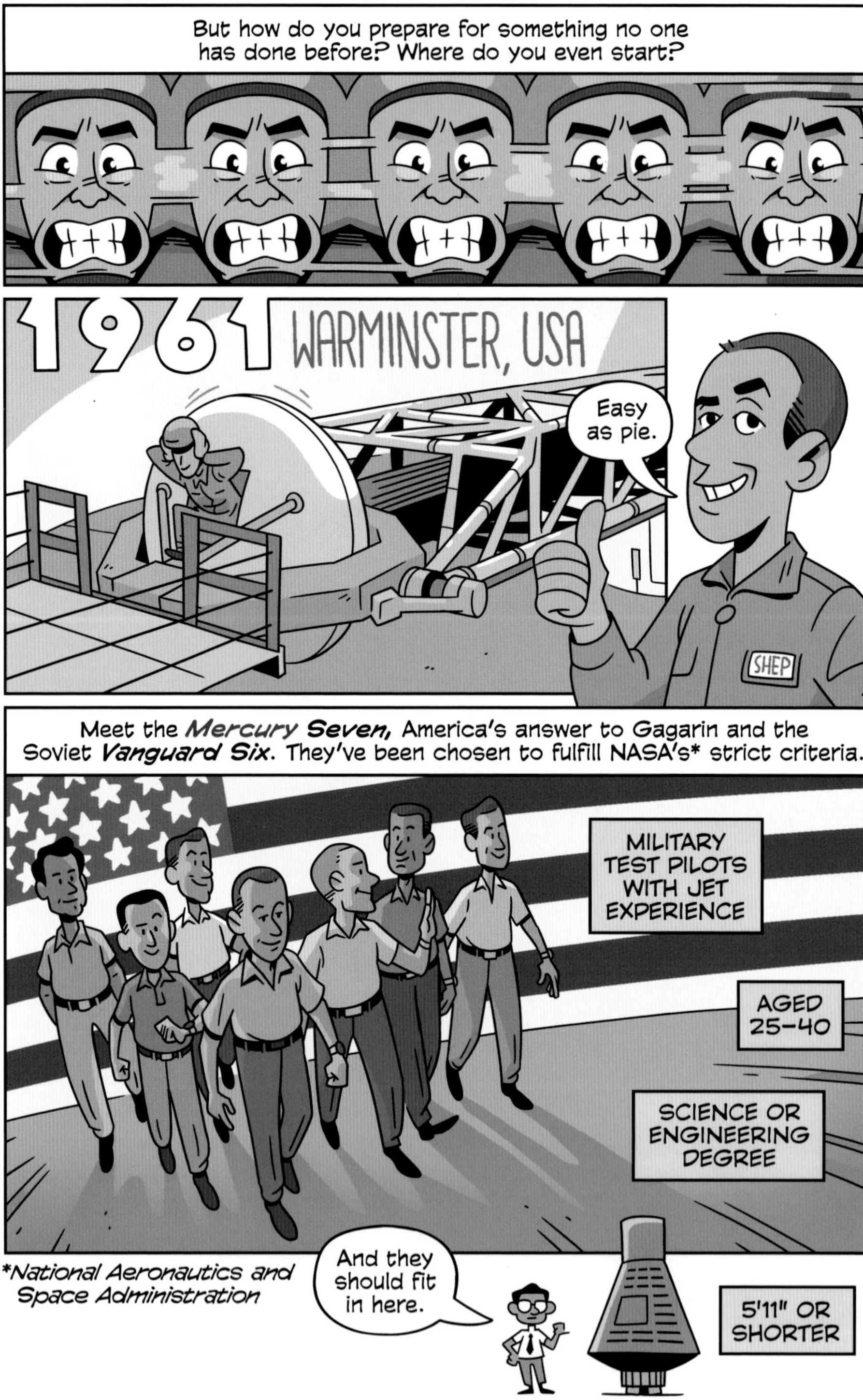
But how do you prepare for something no one has done before? Where do you even start?
1961
WARMINSTER, USA
Easy as pie.
SHEP
Meet the *Mercury Seven,* America's answer to Gagarin and the Soviet *Vanguard Six*. They've been chosen to fulfill NASA's* strict criteria.
MILITARY TEST PILOTS WITH JET EXPERIENCE
AGED 25–40
SCIENCE OR ENGINEERING DEGREE
*National Aeronautics and Space Administration
And they should fit in here.
5'11" OR SHORTER

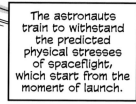

The astronauts train to withstand the predicted physical stresses of spaceflight, which start from the moment of launch.

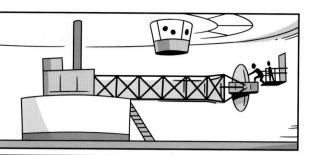

Gravity force, or simply *g-force*, creates the feeling of weight, the *pressing* sensation we all experience against the ground.

ding

1 G

It's measured in "g's," and you experience one g standing on the ground.

When an elevator starts upward, the paired force of your acceleration presses as well. You feel extra heavy!

G-FORCE   ACCELERATION

The faster your direction *changes*, the harder you're pressed the opposite way!

ACCELERATION   G-FORCE

LAW #1: FORCES CHANGE MOVEMENT
#3: FORCES COME IN OPPOSITE PAIRS

#2: GREATER ACCELERATION EQUALS GREATER FORCE

If you plan to ride a rocket from zero to 17,500 mph, you'd better prepare to feel a lot of g's!

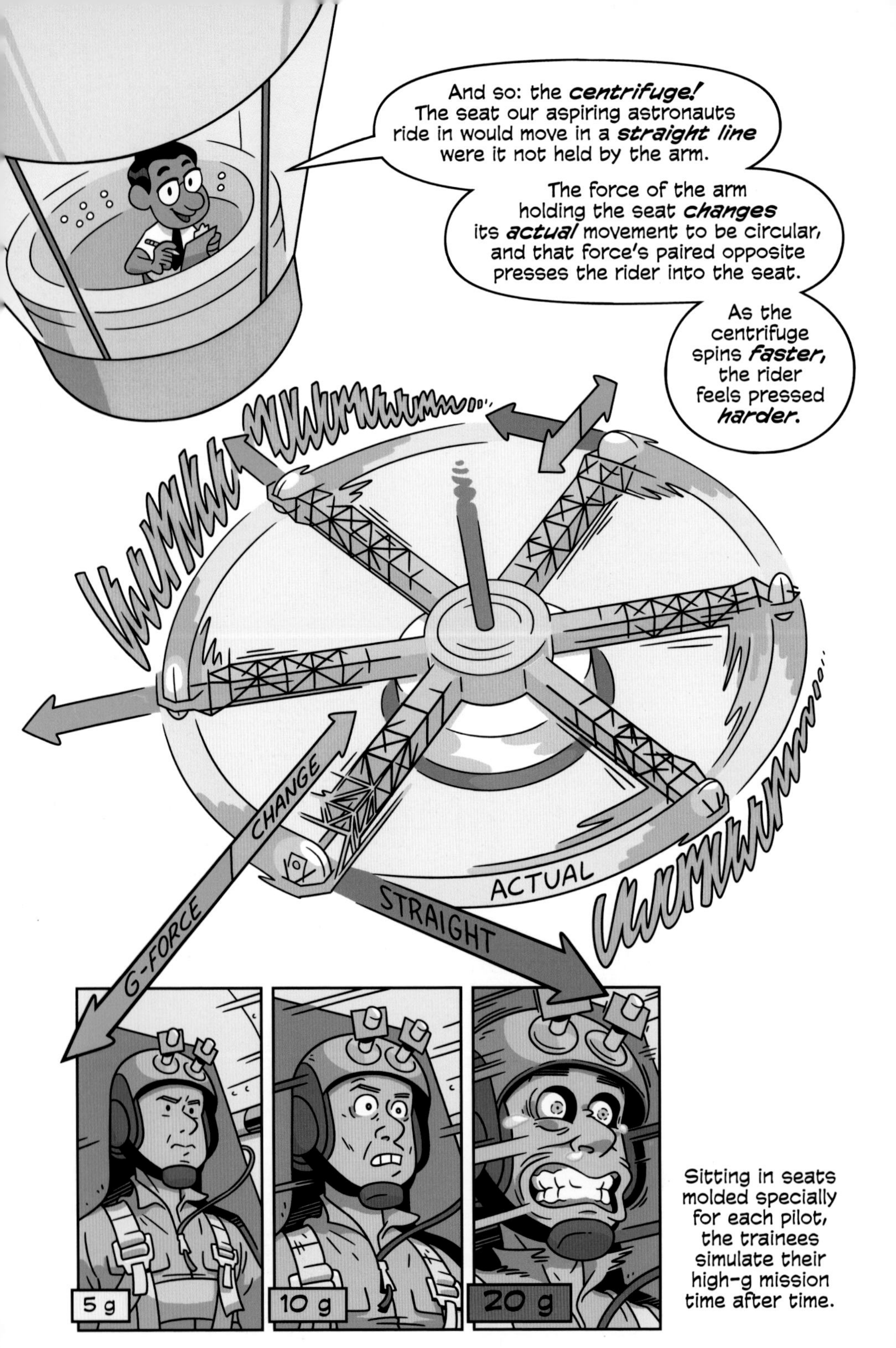
And so: the *centrifuge!* The seat our aspiring astronauts ride in would move in a *straight line* were it not held by the arm.
The force of the arm holding the seat *changes* its *actual* movement to be circular, and that force's paired opposite presses the rider into the seat.
As the centrifuge spins *faster,* the rider feels pressed *harder.*
VWUMMMWUMWUMMWUMMMM
VWUMMWUMMWUMMM
CHANGE
G-FORCE
ACTUAL
STRAIGHT
5 g
10 g
20 g

Sitting in seats molded specially for each pilot, the trainees simulate their high-g mission time after time.

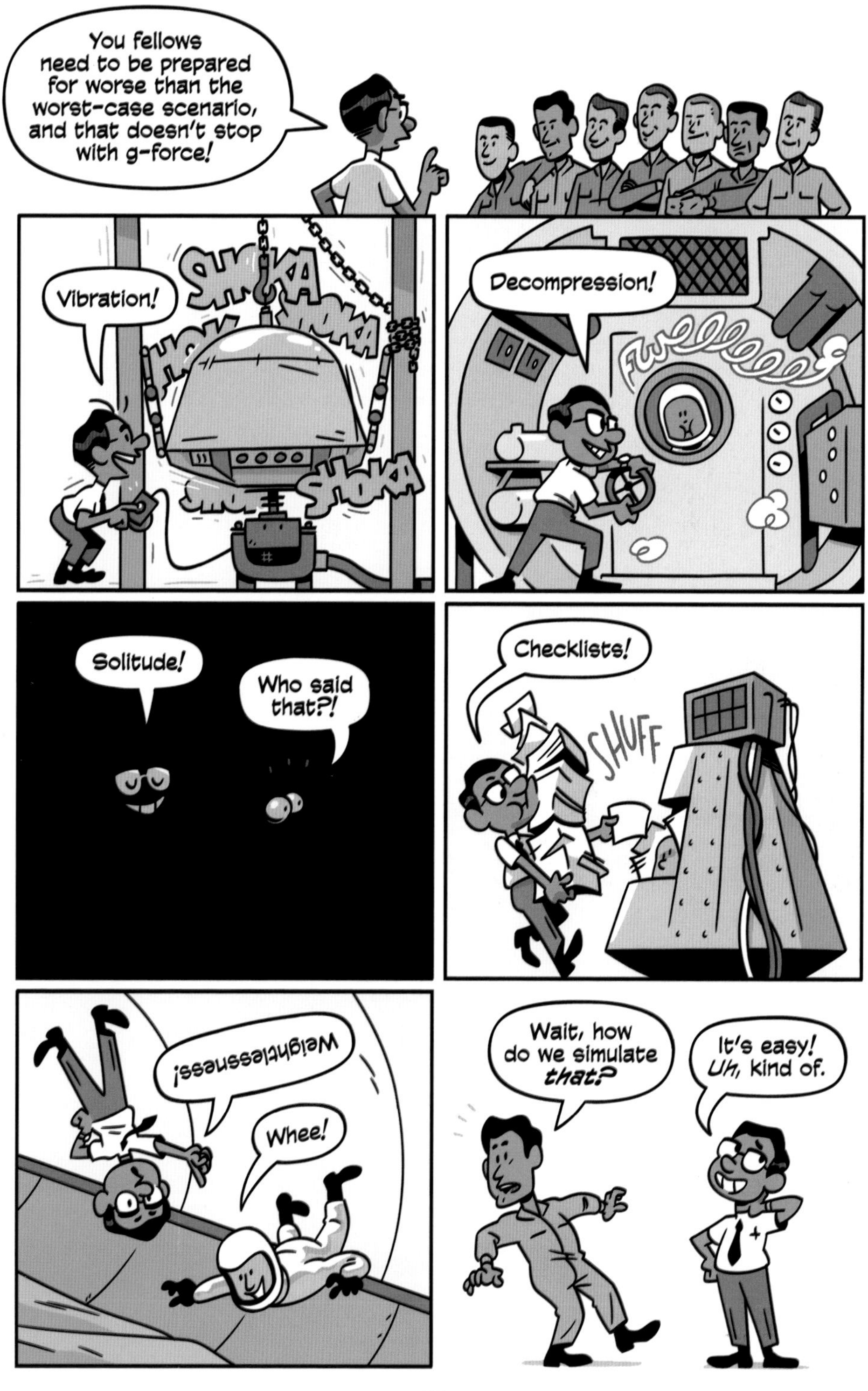

You fellows need to be prepared for worse than the worst-case scenario, and that doesn't stop with g-force!
Vibration!
SHOKA SHOKA SHOKA SHOKA
Decompression!
FWEEEEEEE
Solitude!
Who said that?!
Checklists!
SHUFF
Weightlessness!
Whee!
Wait, how do we simulate *that?*
It's easy! *Uh,* kind of.

The trick is to throw you into the air and then let you fall. On the way up, you and the reduced-gravity plane go the same speed in the same direction.

You have the same *velocity,* and with no seat belt, you keep moving up when the plane lowers its angle.

You and the plane are now flying *separately!* Gravity still affects you, but with nothing to press against, you feel *zero g.*

You're *weightless!* You fall like any object, and the plane flies along your path.

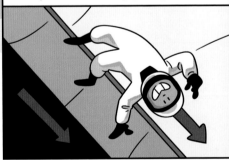

When the pilot pulls up (you don't want to crash, do you?) you feel almost two g as you once again press against the plane.

You feel zero g for less than a minute per dive, so training involves a lot of ups and downs. Eat a light breakfast—there's a reason they call this plane the "Vomit Comet."

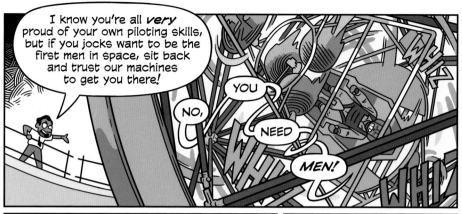

I know you're all *very* proud of your own piloting skills, but if you jocks want to be the first men in space, sit back and trust our machines to get you there!

NO,

YOU

NEED

MEN!

Yeah, we're more than "Spam in a can"!

Is that so?

You wouldn't!

This could have been one of us!

Let's talk this over...

Ook?

"HAM"

As if to prove the point, *"Ham"* launches on a suborbital flight in the same sort of capsule atop the same type of rocket that the astronauts will ride. He flips fake switches for banana pellets before landing safe and sound.

27

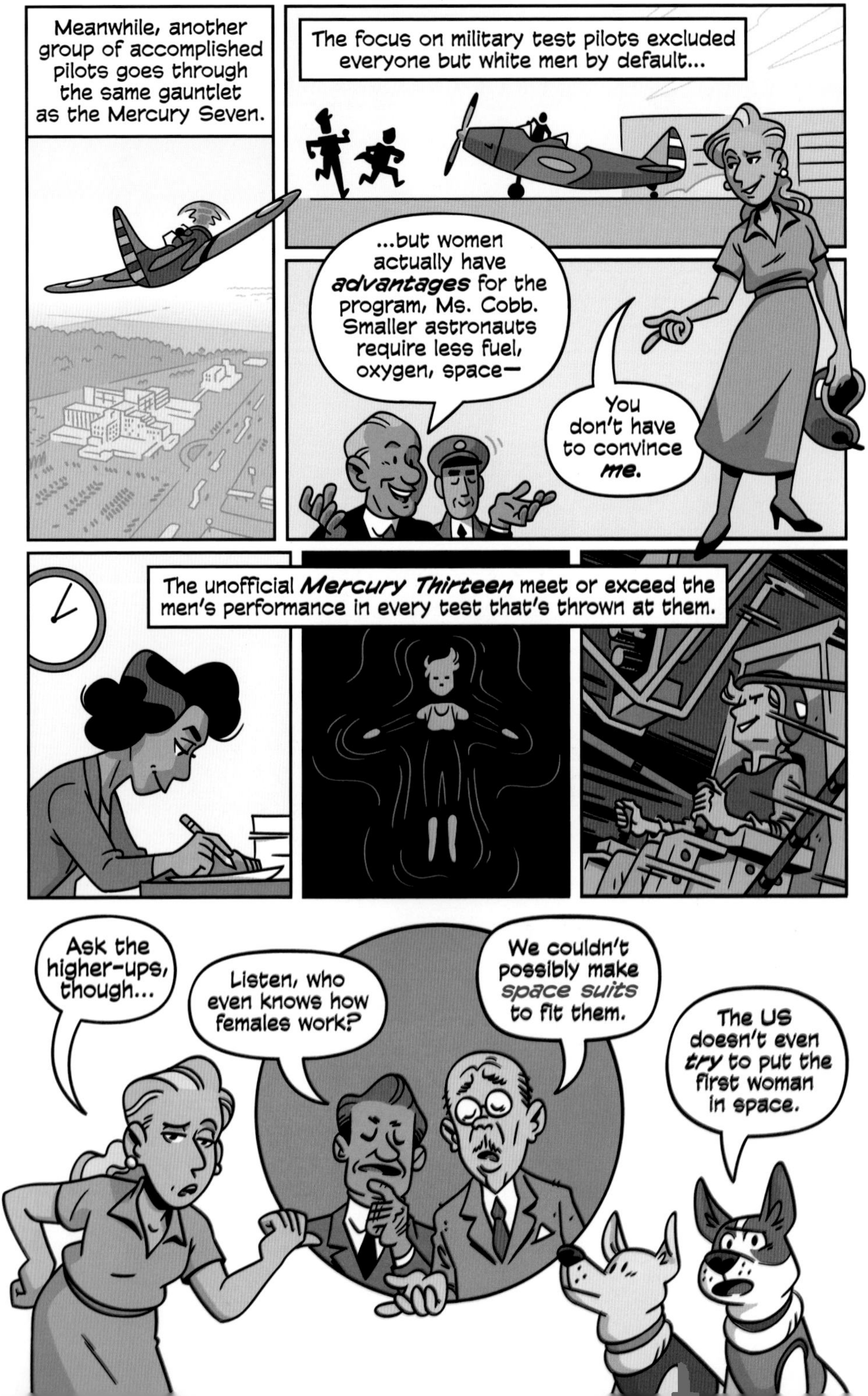
Meanwhile, another group of accomplished pilots goes through the same gauntlet as the Mercury Seven.
The focus on military test pilots excluded everyone but white men by default...
...but women actually have *advantages* for the program, Ms. Cobb. Smaller astronauts require less fuel, oxygen, space—
You don't have to convince *me*.
The unofficial *Mercury Thirteen* meet or exceed the men's performance in every test that's thrown at them.
Ask the higher-ups, though...
Listen, who even knows how females work?
We couldn't possibly make *space suits* to fit them.
The US doesn't even *try* to put the first woman in space.

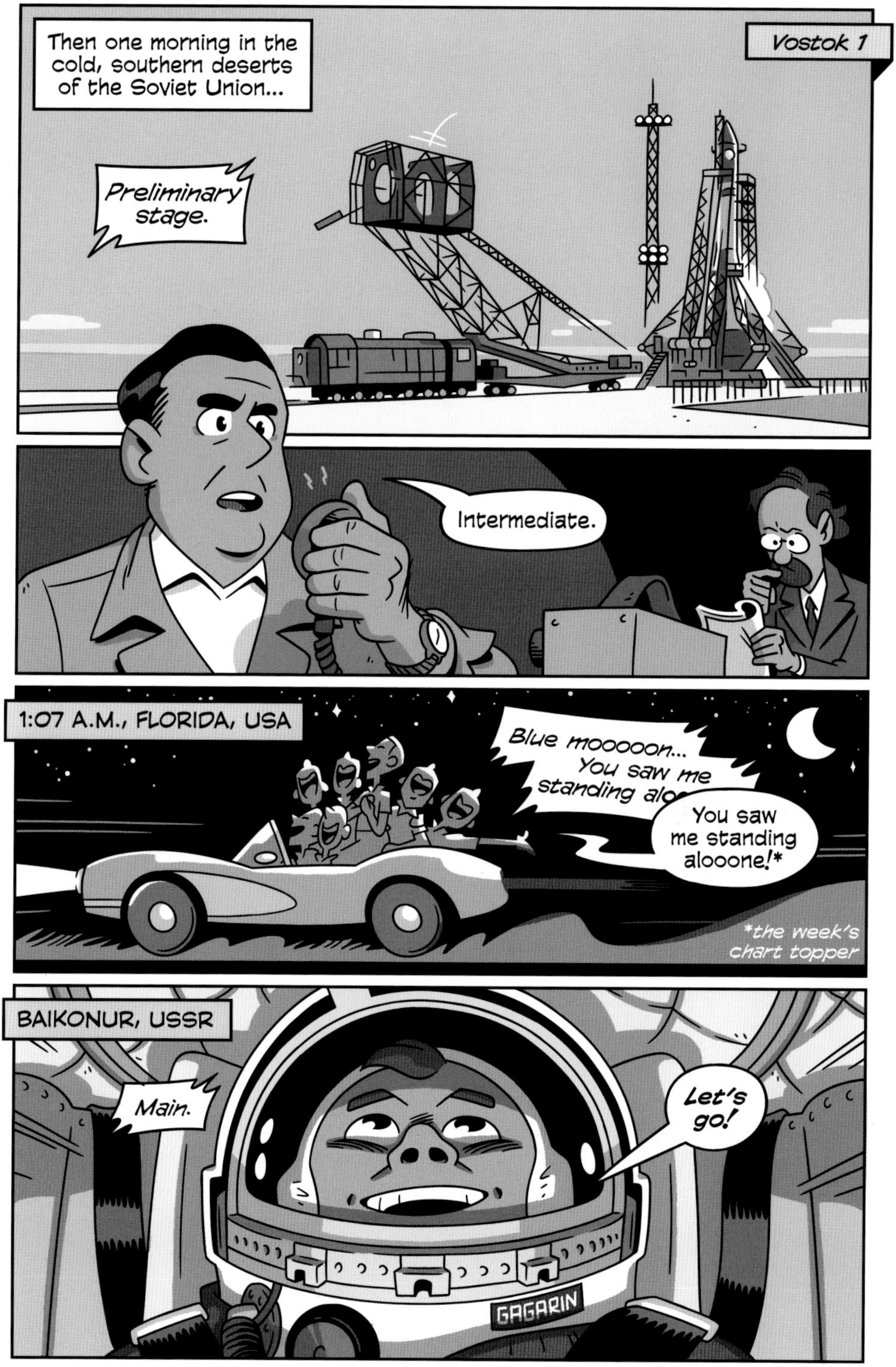
Then one morning in the cold, southern deserts of the Soviet Union...
Vostok 1
Preliminary stage.
Intermediate.
1:07 A.M., FLORIDA, USA
Blue moooooon... You saw me standing alo
You saw me standing alooone!*
*the week's chart topper
BAIKONUR, USSR
Main.
Let's go!
GAGARIN

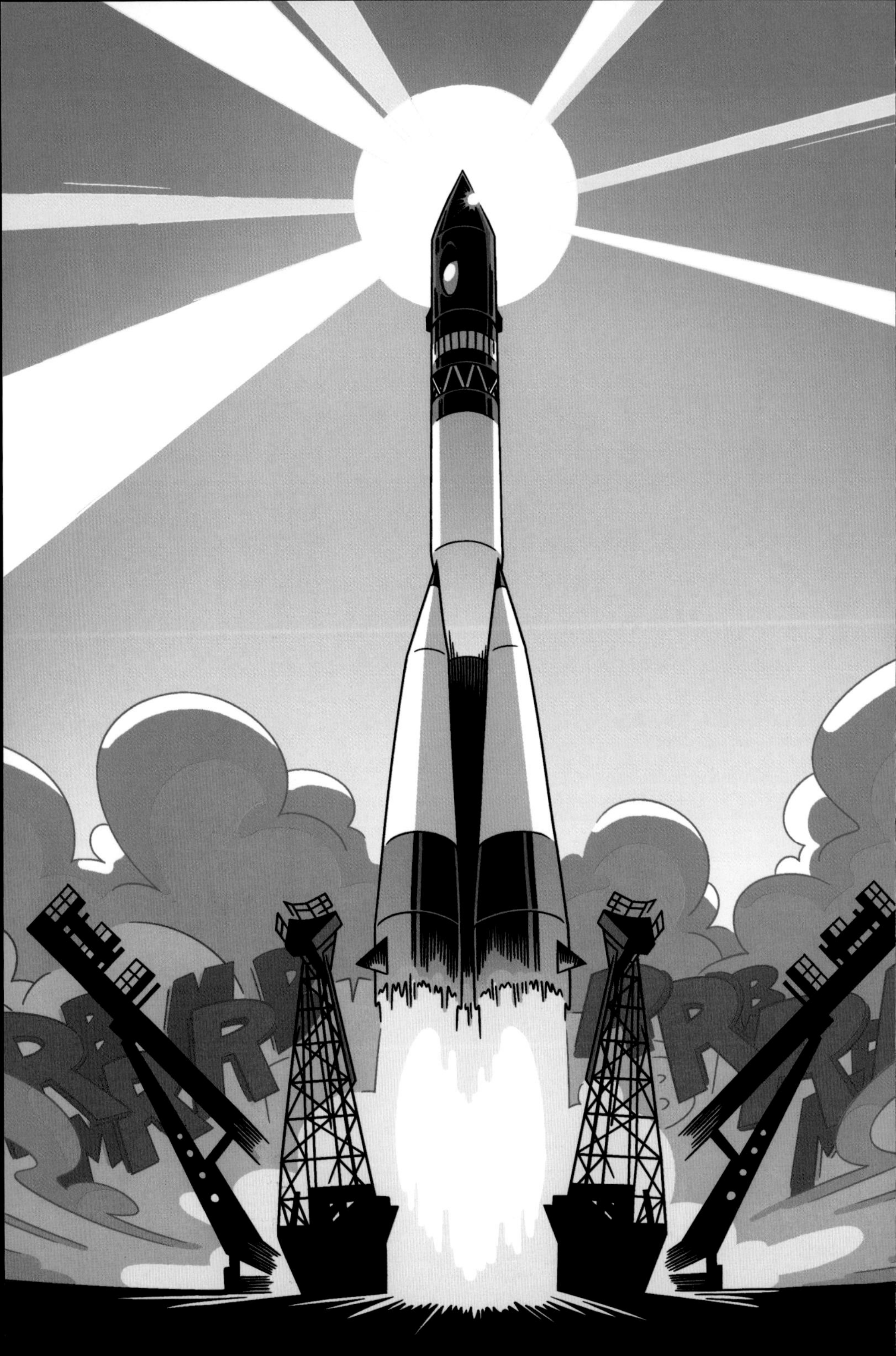

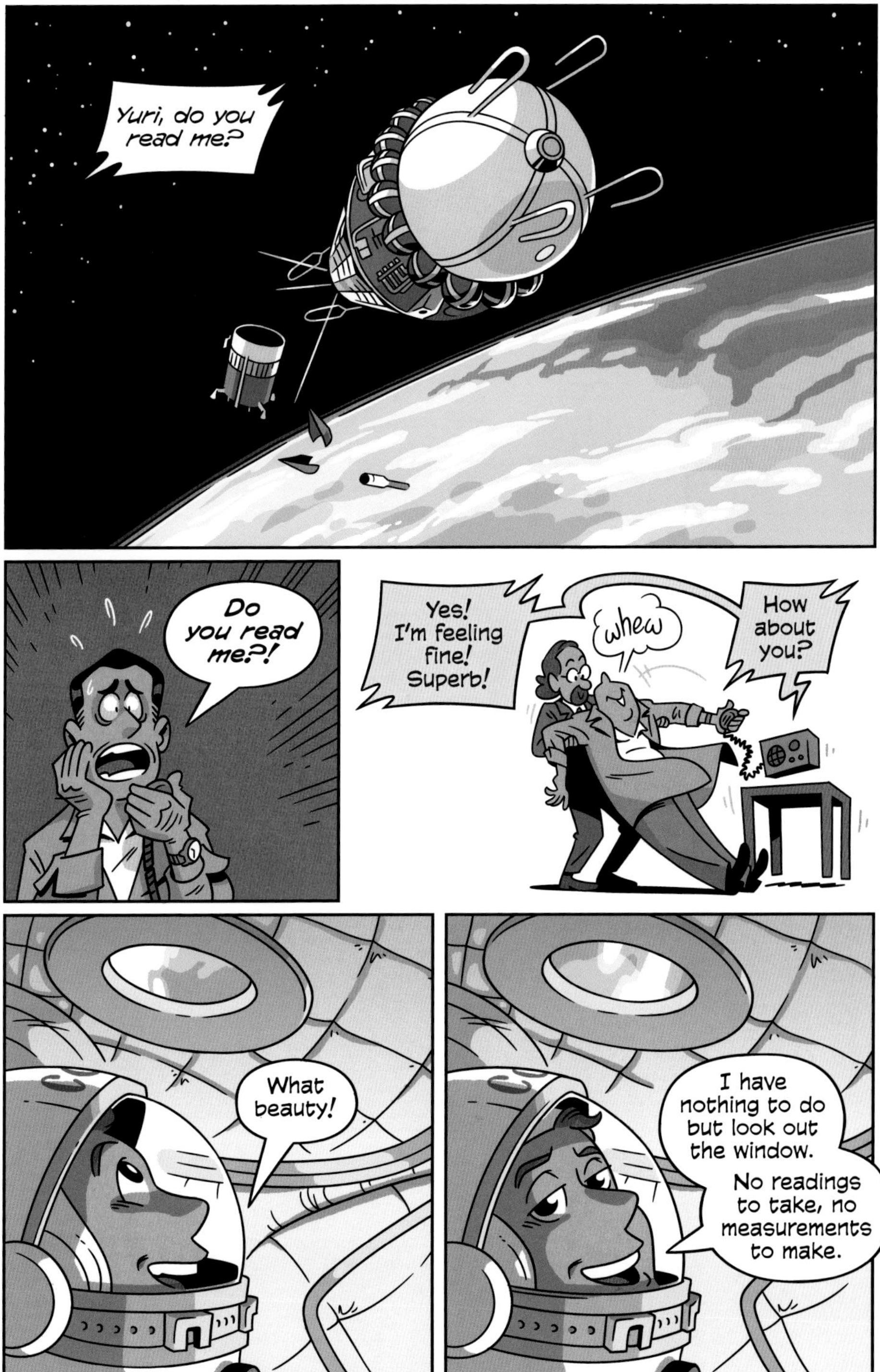
Yuri, do you read me?
Do you read me?!
Yes! I'm feeling fine! Superb!
whew
How about you?
What beauty!
I have nothing to do but look out the window.
No readings to take, no measurements to make.

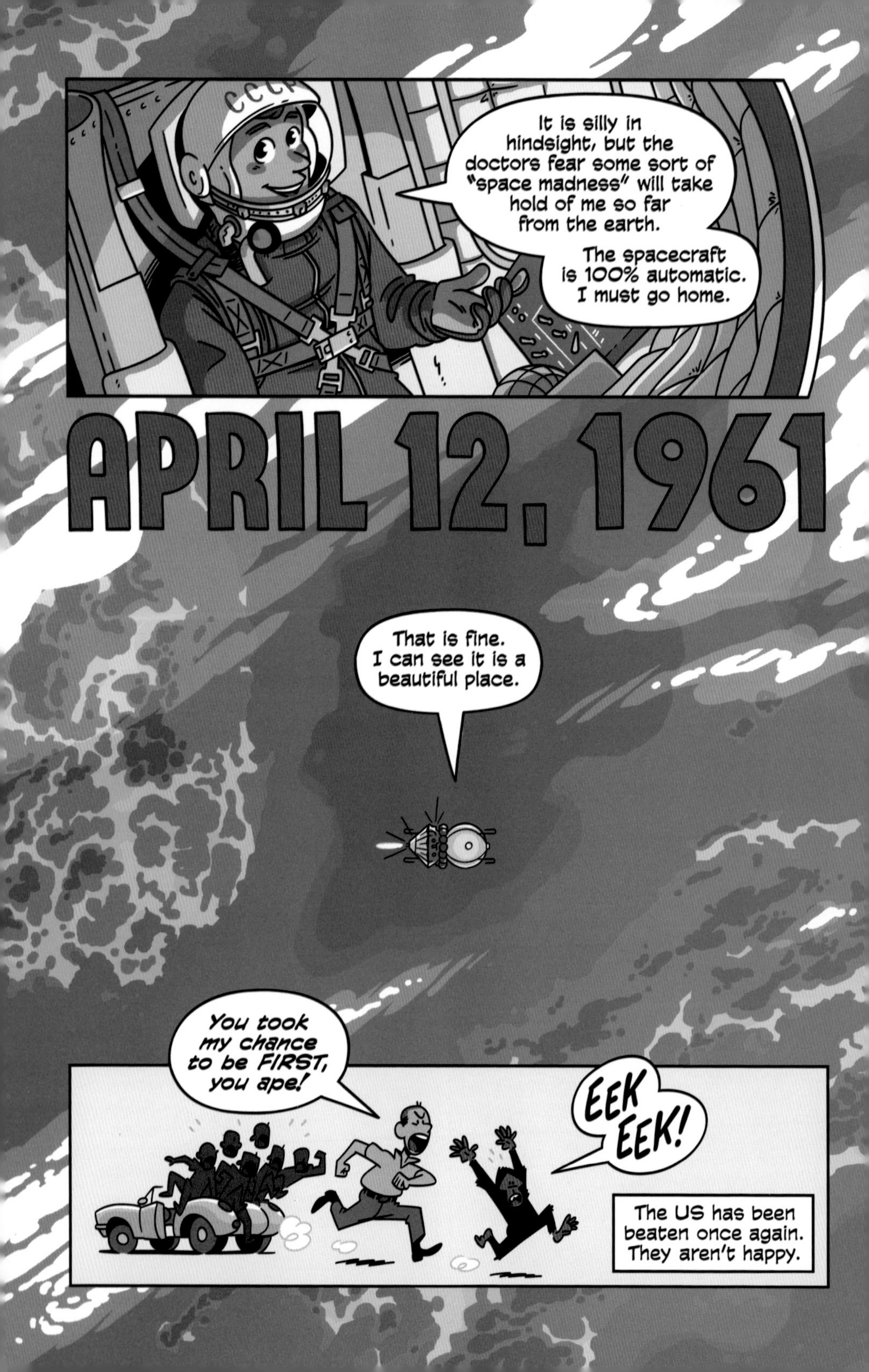
It is silly in hindsight, but the doctors fear some sort of "space madness" will take hold of me so far from the earth.
The spacecraft is 100% automatic. I must go home.
APRIL 12, 1961
That is fine. I can see it is a beautiful place.
You took my chance to be FIRST, you ape!
EEK EEK!
The US has been beaten once again. They aren't happy.

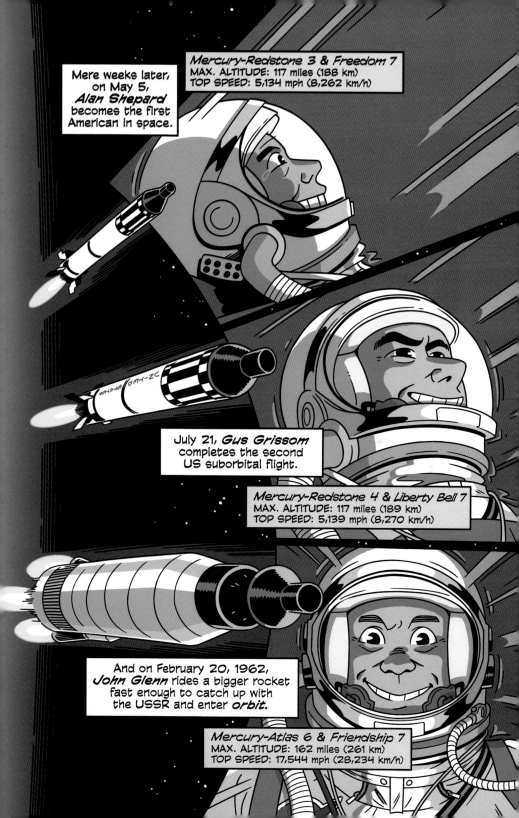

Mere weeks later, on May 5, *Alan Shepard* becomes the first American in space.

Mercury-Redstone 3 & Freedom 7
MAX. ALTITUDE: 117 miles (188 km)
TOP SPEED: 5,134 mph (8,262 km/h)

July 21, *Gus Grissom* completes the second US suborbital flight.

Mercury-Redstone 4 & Liberty Bell 7
MAX. ALTITUDE: 117 miles (189 km)
TOP SPEED: 5,139 mph (8,270 km/h)

And on February 20, 1962, *John Glenn* rides a bigger rocket fast enough to catch up with the USSR and enter *orbit*.

Mercury-Atlas 6 & Friendship 7
MAX. ALTITUDE: 162 miles (261 km)
TOP SPEED: 17,544 mph (28,234 km/h)

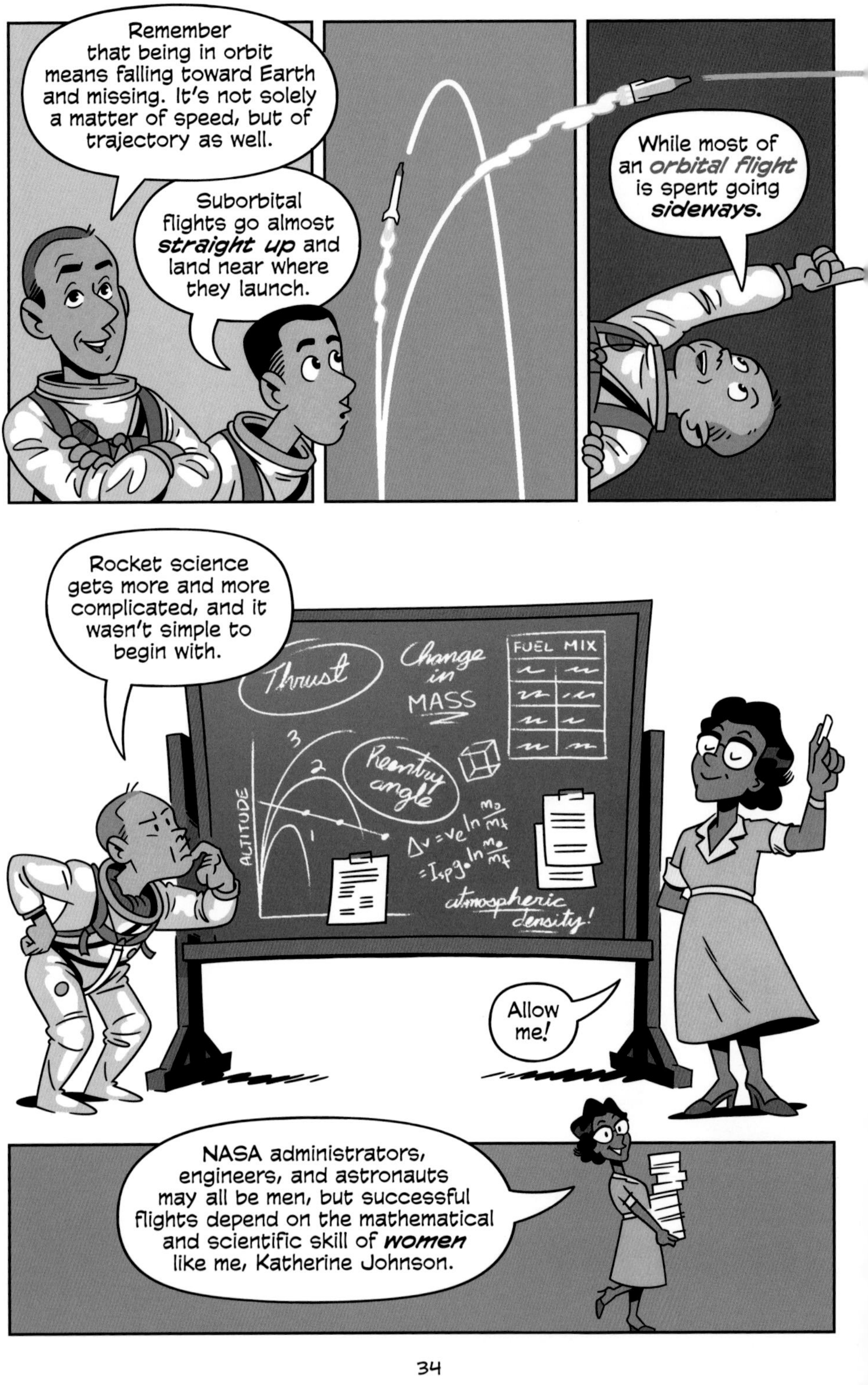

Remember that being in orbit means falling toward Earth and missing. It's not solely a matter of speed, but of trajectory as well.
Suborbital flights go almost ***straight up*** and land near where they launch.
While most of an ***orbital flight*** is spent going ***sideways.***
Rocket science gets more and more complicated, and it wasn't simple to begin with.
Thrust
Change in MASS
FUEL MIX
Reentry angle
ALTITUDE
3
2
1
$\Delta v = v_e \ln \frac{m_0}{m_f} = I_{sp} g_0 \ln \frac{m_0}{m_f}$
atmospheric density!
Allow me!
NASA administrators, engineers, and astronauts may all be men, but successful flights depend on the mathematical and scientific skill of ***women*** like me, Katherine Johnson.

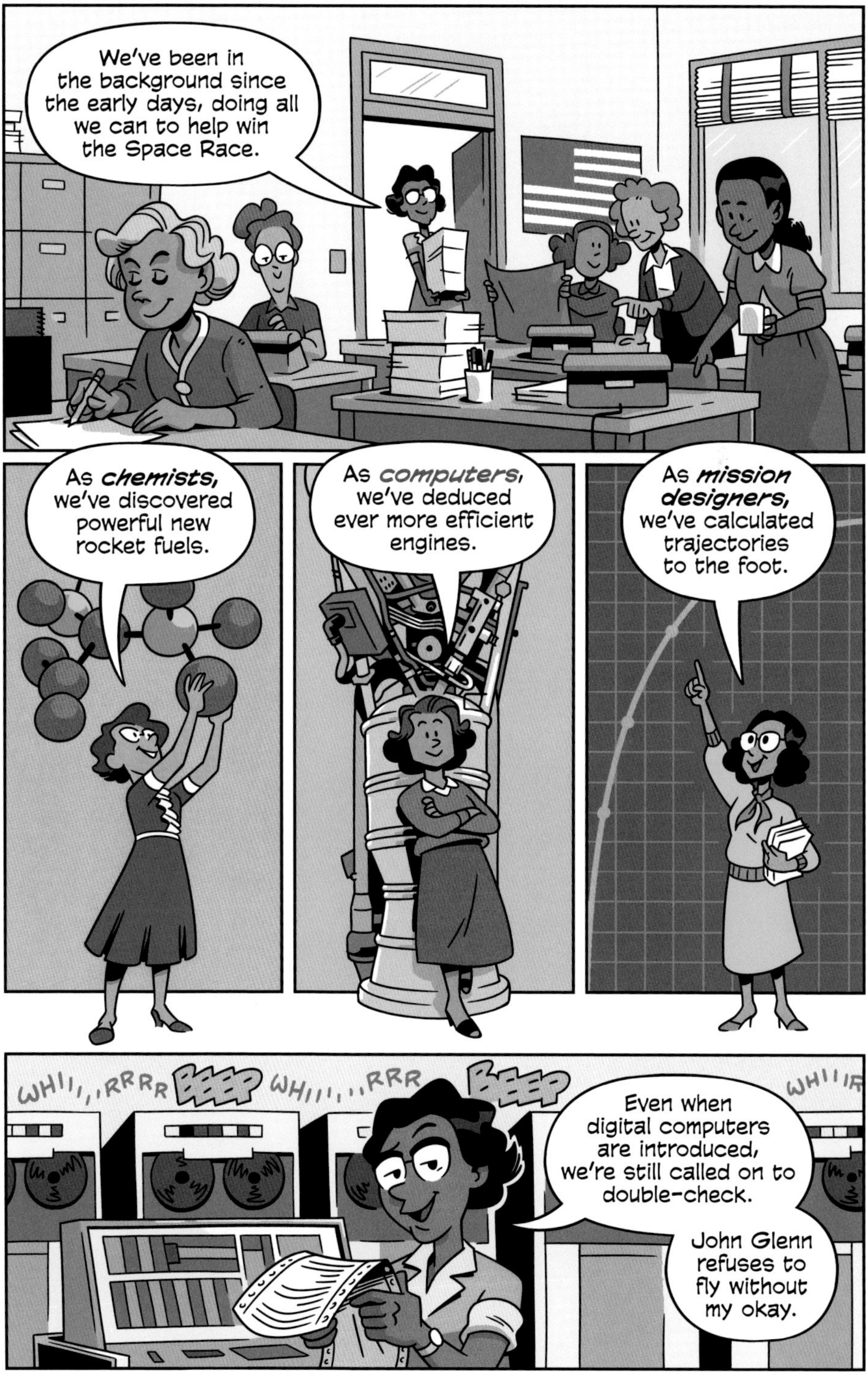

We've been in the background since the early days, doing all we can to help win the Space Race.
As chemists, we've discovered powerful new rocket fuels.
As computers, we've deduced ever more efficient engines.
As mission designers, we've calculated trajectories to the foot.
WHIII,,,RRRR
BEEP
WHIII,,,RRR
BEEP
Even when digital computers are introduced, we're still called on to double-check.
John Glenn refuses to fly without my okay.

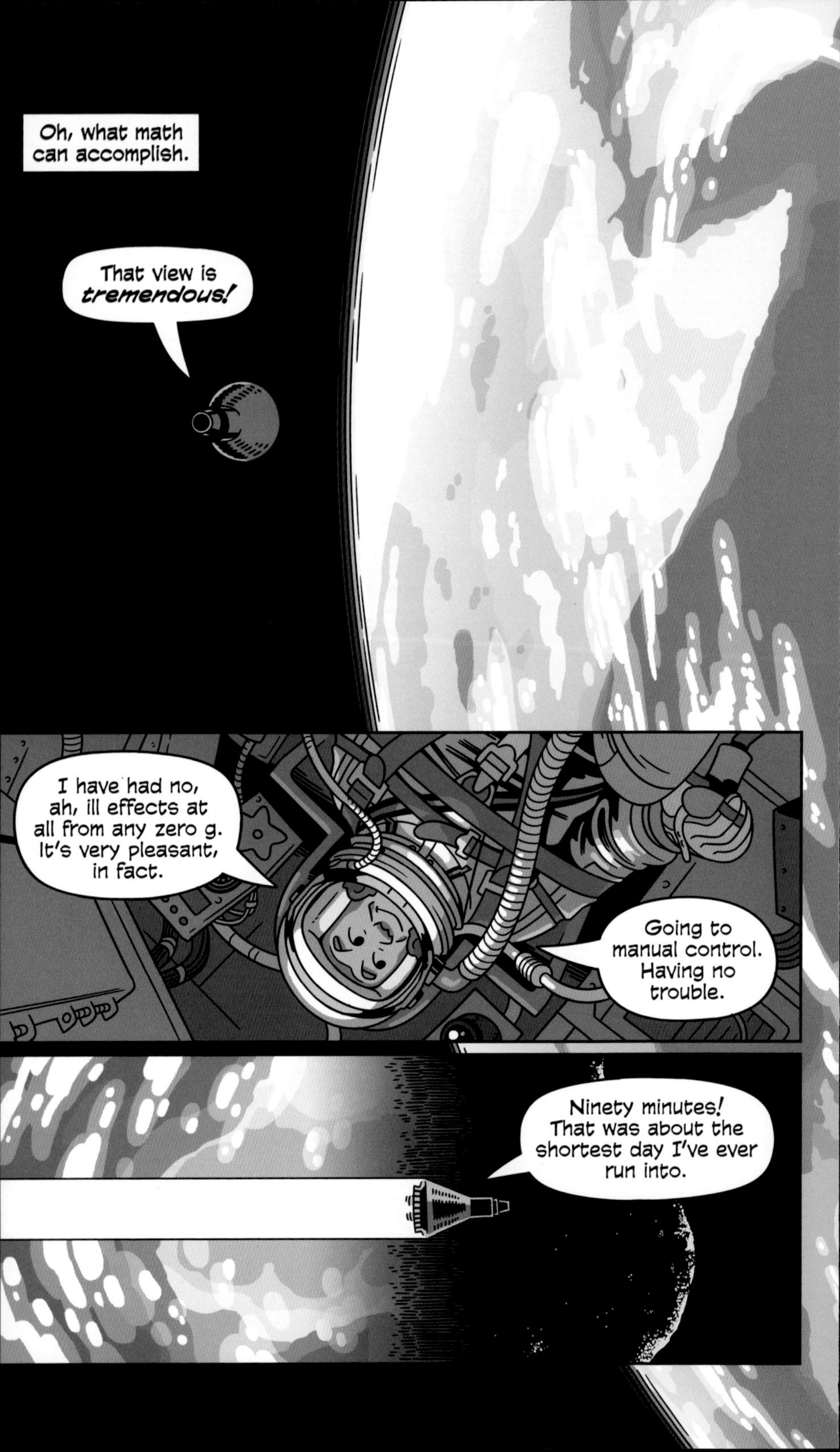
Oh, what math can accomplish.
That view is *tremendous!*
I have had no, ah, ill effects at all from any zero g. It's very pleasant, in fact.
Going to manual control. Having no trouble.
Ninety minutes! That was about the shortest day I've ever run into.

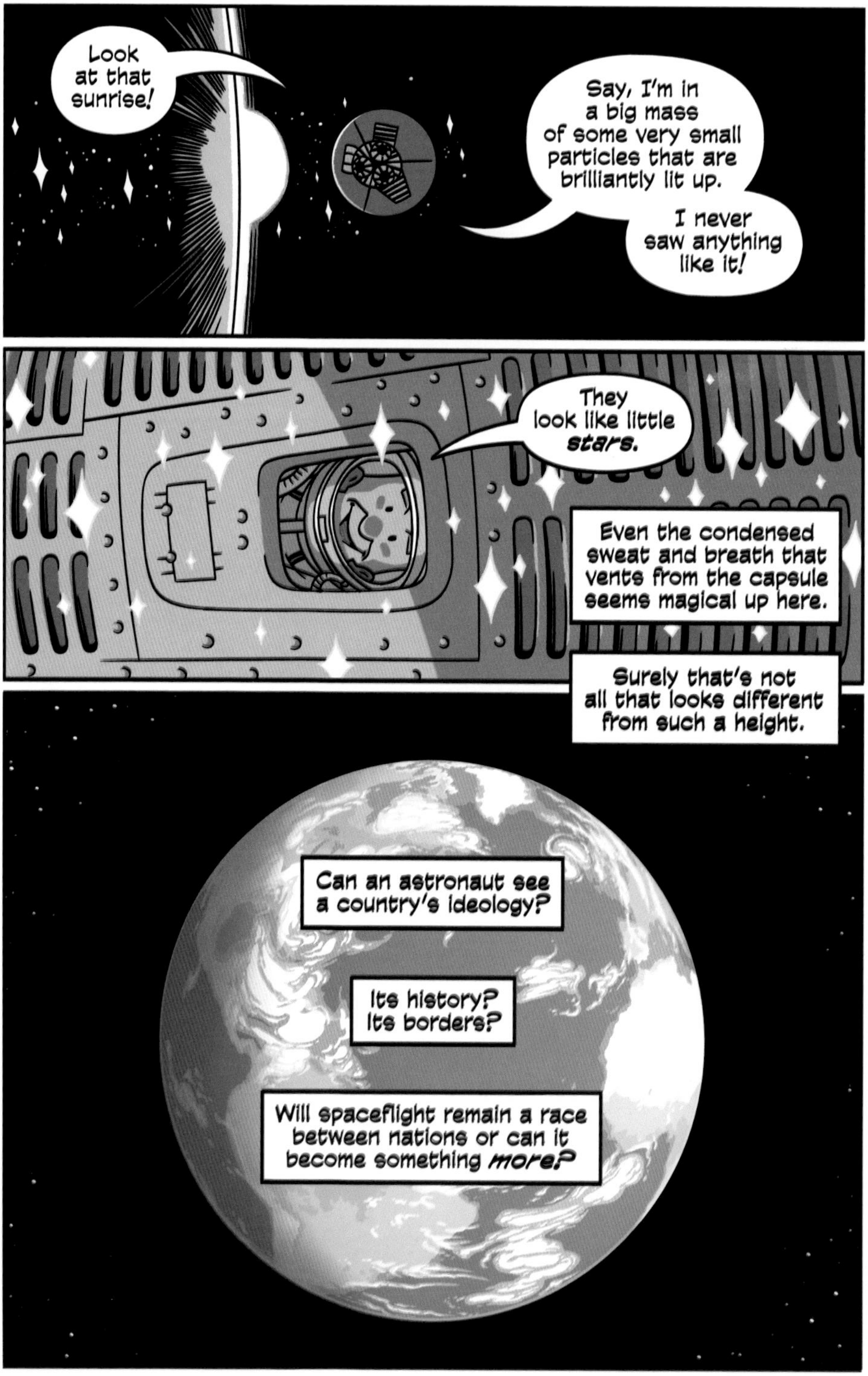
Look at that sunrise!
Say, I'm in a big mass of some very small particles that are brilliantly lit up.
I never saw anything like it!
They look like little *stars.*
Even the condensed sweat and breath that vents from the capsule seems magical up here.
Surely that's not all that looks different from such a height.
Can an astronaut see a country's ideology?
Its history? Its borders?
Will spaceflight remain a race between nations or can it become something *more?*

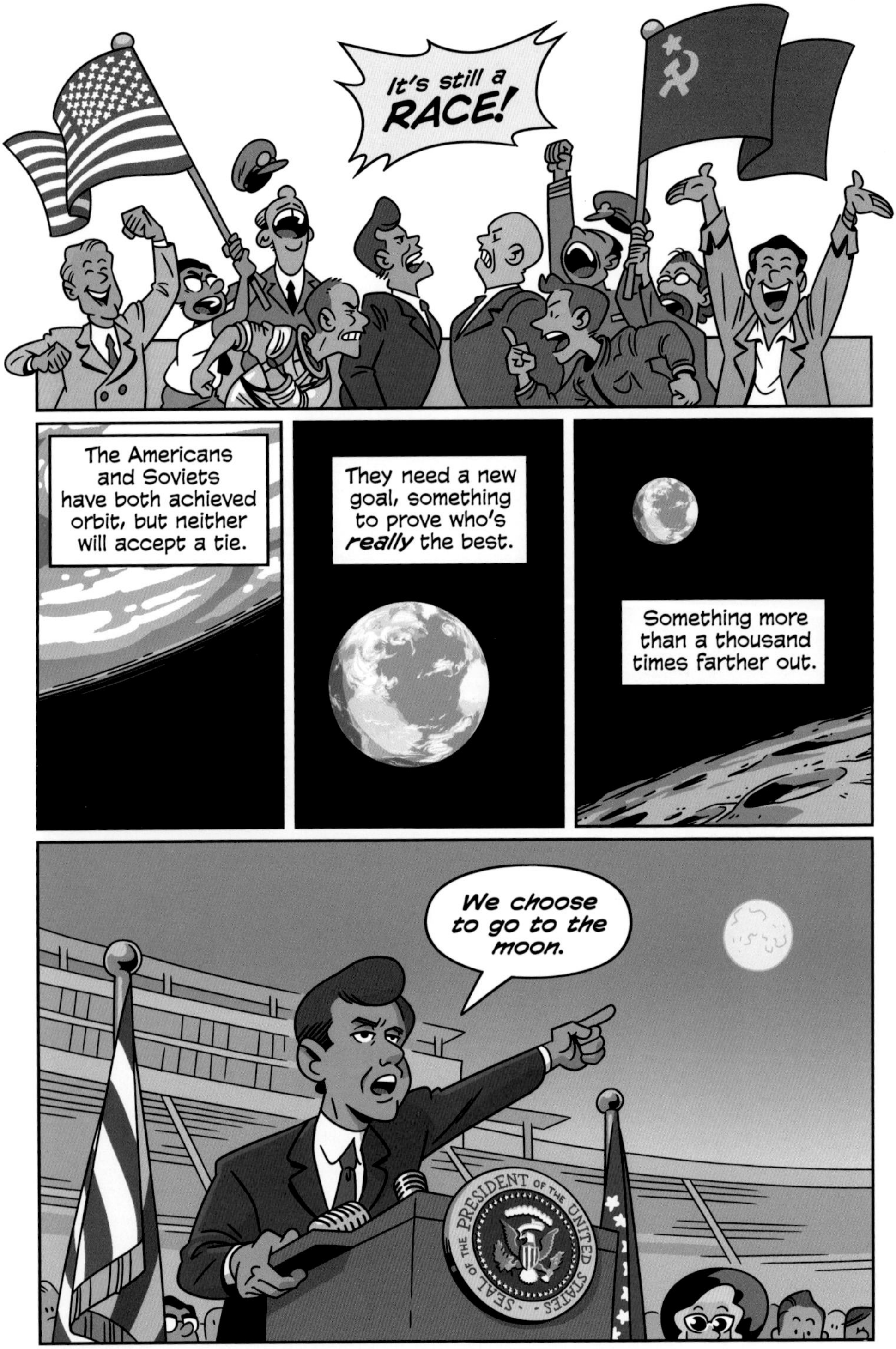
It's still a RACE!
The Americans and Soviets have both achieved orbit, but neither will accept a tie.
They need a new goal, something to prove who's *really* the best.
Something more than a thousand times farther out.
We choose to go to the moon.
SEAL OF THE PRESIDENT OF THE UNITED STATES

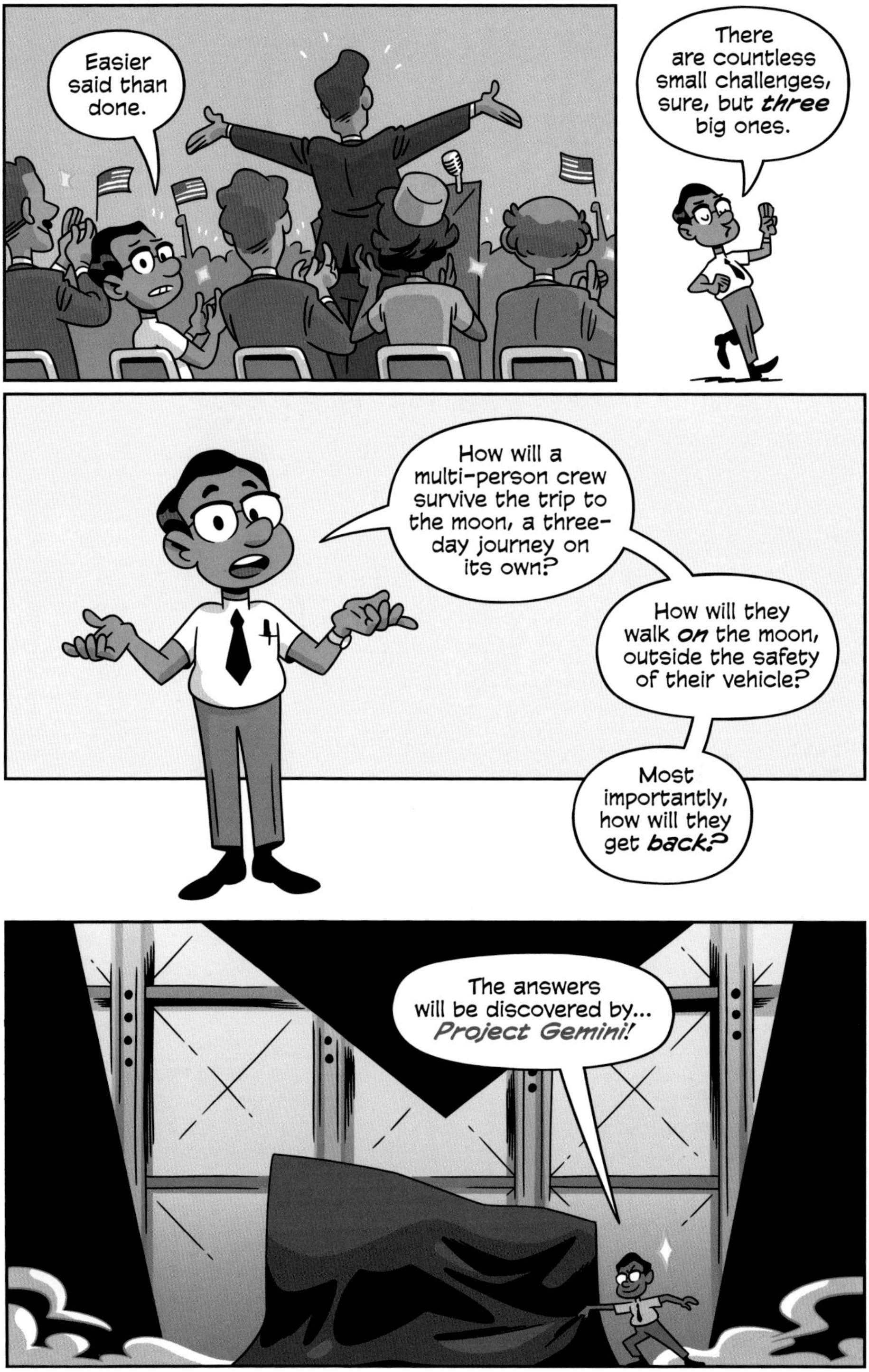
Easier said than done.
There are countless small challenges, sure, but *three* big ones.
How will a multi-person crew survive the trip to the moon, a three-day journey on its own?
How will they walk *on* the moon, outside the safety of their vehicle?
Most importantly, how will they get *back?*
The answers will be discovered by... *Project Gemini!*

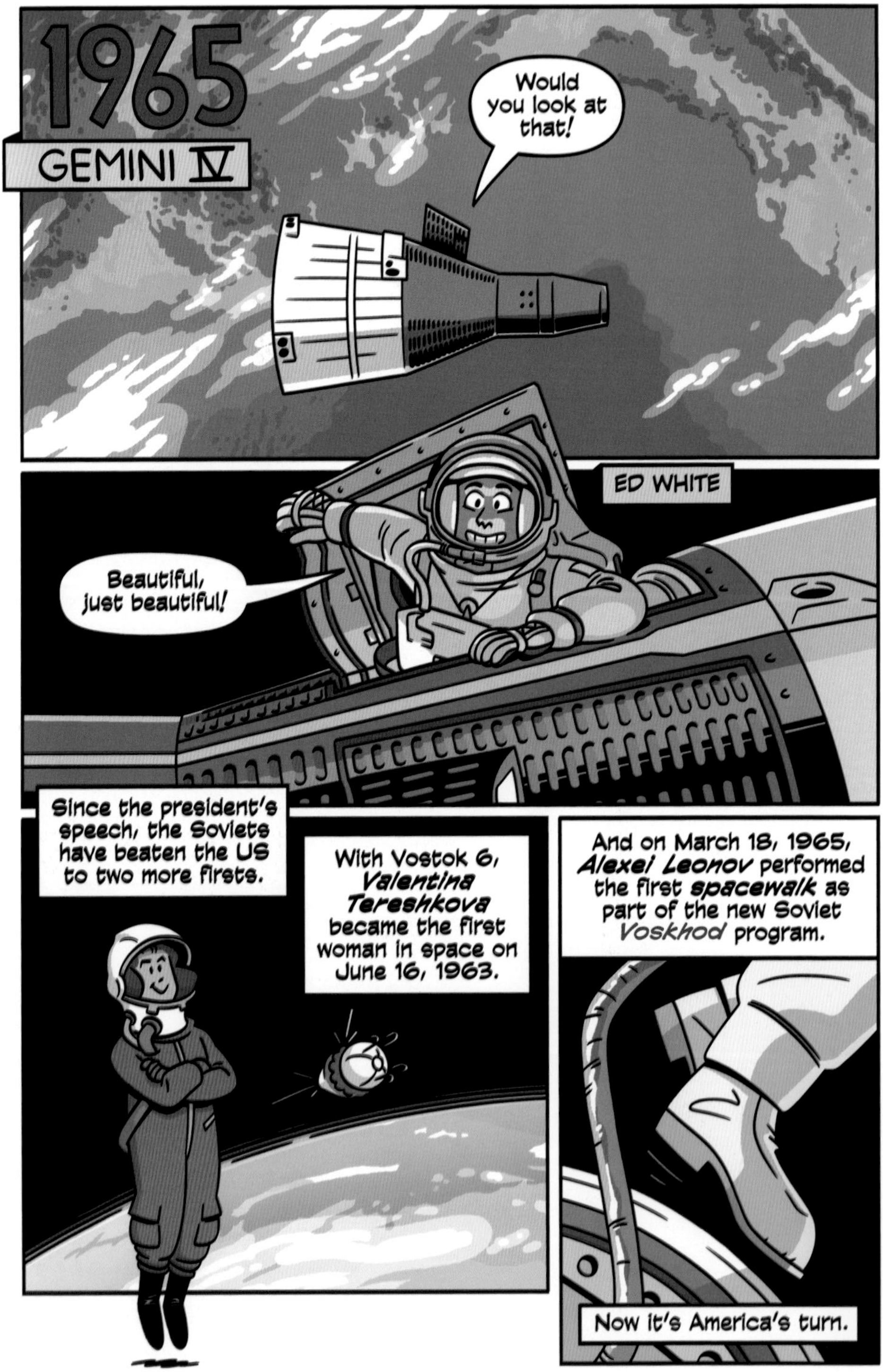
1965
GEMINI IV
Would you look at that!
ED WHITE
Beautiful, just beautiful!
Since the president's speech, the Soviets have beaten the US to two more firsts.
With Vostok 6, *Valentina Tereshkova* became the first woman in space on June 16, 1963.
And on March 18, 1965, *Alexei Leonov* performed the first *spacewalk* as part of the new Soviet *Voskhod* program.
Now it's America's turn.

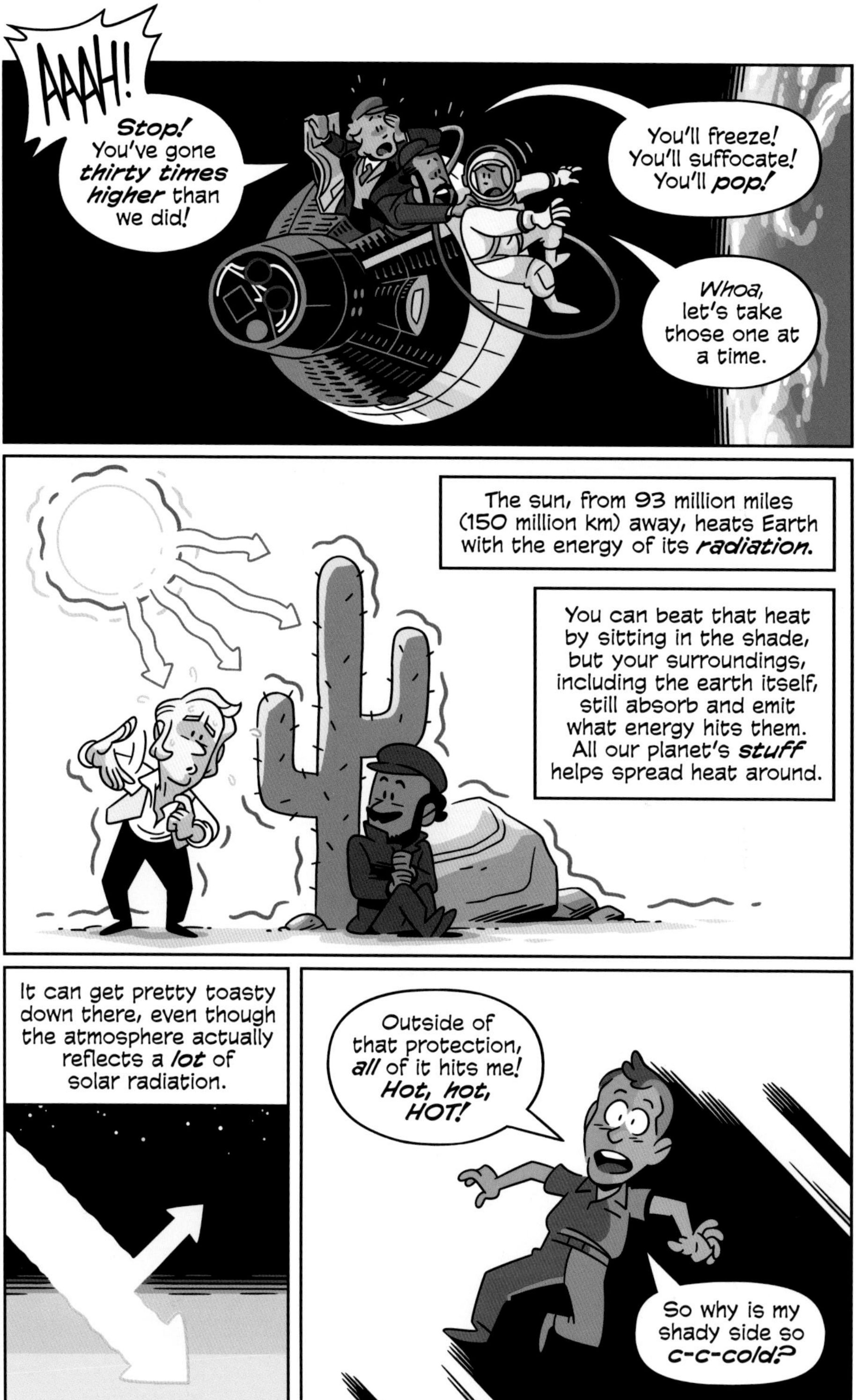
AAAH!
Stop! You've gone thirty times higher than we did!
You'll freeze! You'll suffocate! You'll pop!
Whoa, let's take those one at a time.
The sun, from 93 million miles (150 million km) away, heats Earth with the energy of its radiation.
You can beat that heat by sitting in the shade, but your surroundings, including the earth itself, still absorb and emit what energy hits them. All our planet's stuff helps spread heat around.
It can get pretty toasty down there, even though the atmosphere actually reflects a lot of solar radiation.
Outside of that protection, all of it hits me! Hot, hot, HOT!
So why is my shady side so c-c-cold?

Temperature, when you look really closely, measures how energetically atoms vibrate.

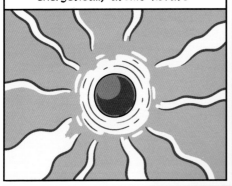

Empty space doesn't have *any* temperature because it's, well, empty!

Without any heat coming *in* from around you, heat only goes *out* until you've got nothing left.

So a *space suit* has to account for a huge range of hot *and* cold. Layer over layer of high-tech materials combine to *reflect* radiant heat from the sun and *retain* it from the wearer.

But this solution causes a new problem: now the wearer gets hotter and hotter from their own trapped body heat!

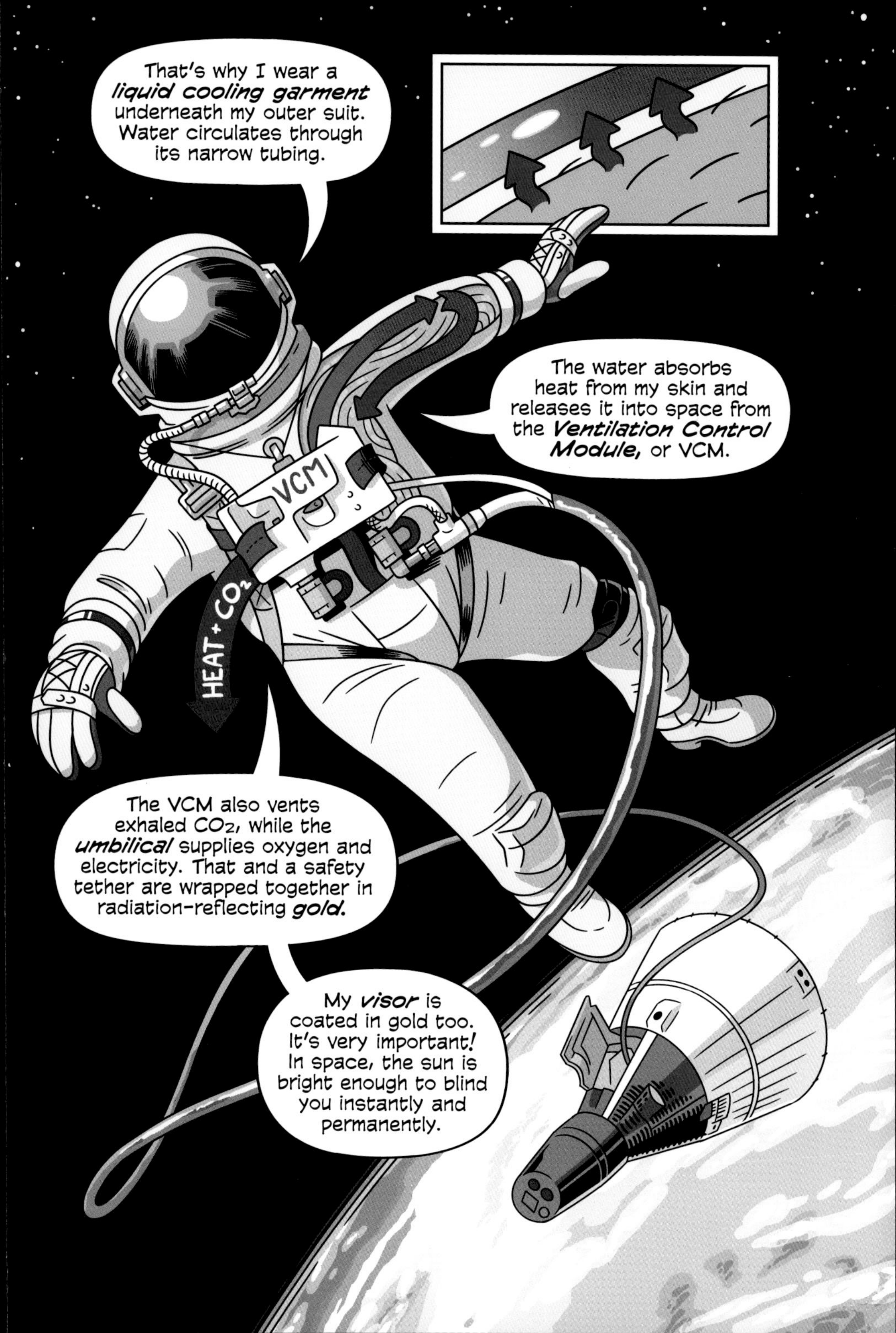
That's why I wear a *liquid cooling garment* underneath my outer suit. Water circulates through its narrow tubing.
The water absorbs heat from my skin and releases it into space from the *Ventilation Control Module,* or VCM.
VCM
HEAT + CO_2
The VCM also vents exhaled CO_2, while the *umbilical* supplies oxygen and electricity. That and a safety tether are wrapped together in radiation-reflecting *gold.*
My *visor* is coated in gold too. It's very important! In space, the sun is bright enough to blind you instantly and permanently.

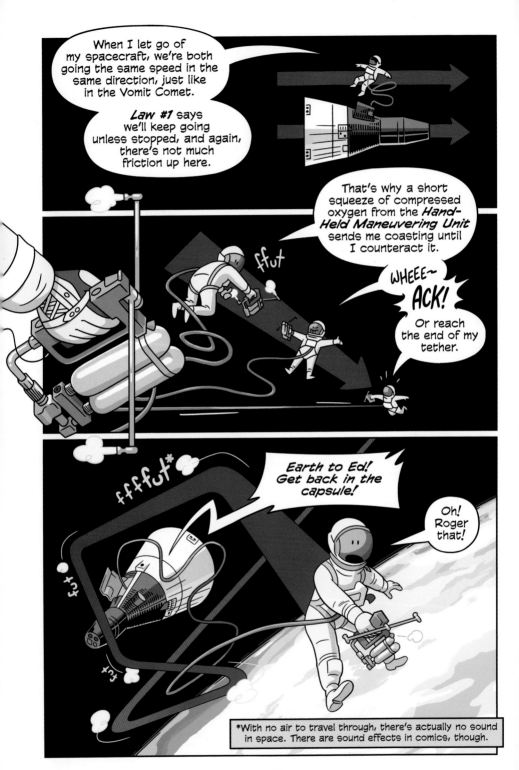

When I let go of my spacecraft, we're both going the same speed in the same direction, just like in the Vomit Comet.

Law #1 says we'll keep going unless stopped, and again, there's not much friction up here.

That's why a short squeeze of compressed oxygen from the *Hand-Held Maneuvering Unit* sends me coasting until I counteract it.

ffut

WHEEE~ **ACK!**

Or reach the end of my tether.

fffut*

Earth to Ed! Get back in the capsule!

Oh! Roger that!

*With no air to travel through, there's actually no sound in space. There are sound effects in comics, though.

44

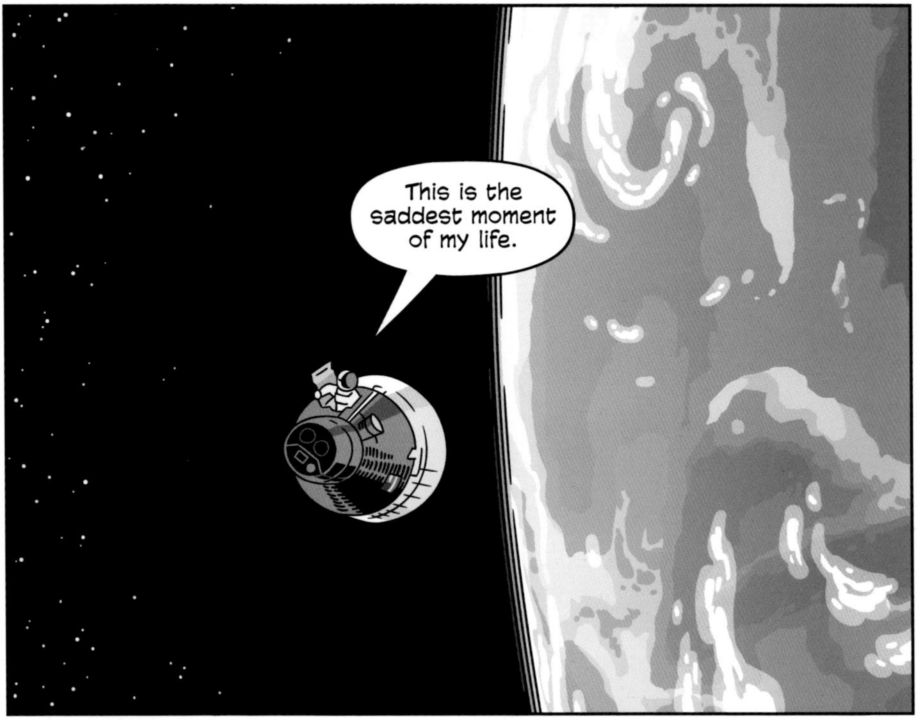
This is the saddest moment of my life.

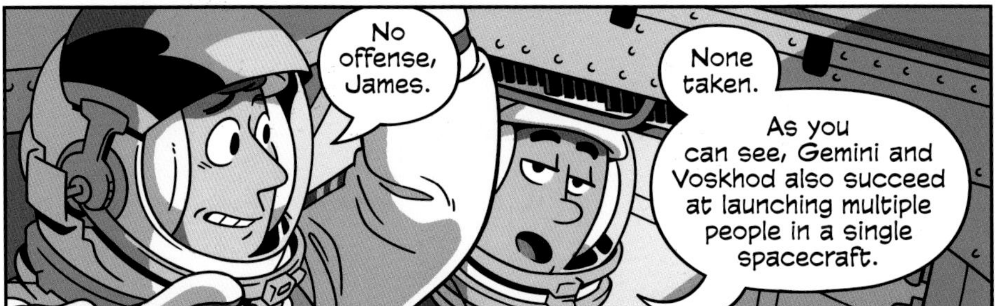
No offense, James.
None taken.
As you can see, Gemini and Voskhod also succeed at launching multiple people in a single spacecraft.
JAMES McDIVITT

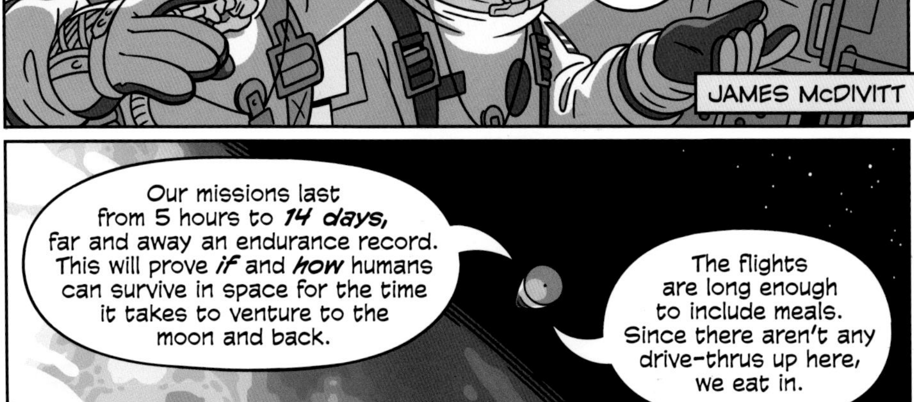
Our missions last from 5 hours to *14 days,* far and away an endurance record. This will prove *if* and *how* humans can survive in space for the time it takes to venture to the moon and back.
The flights are long enough to include meals. Since there aren't any drive-thrus up here, we eat in.

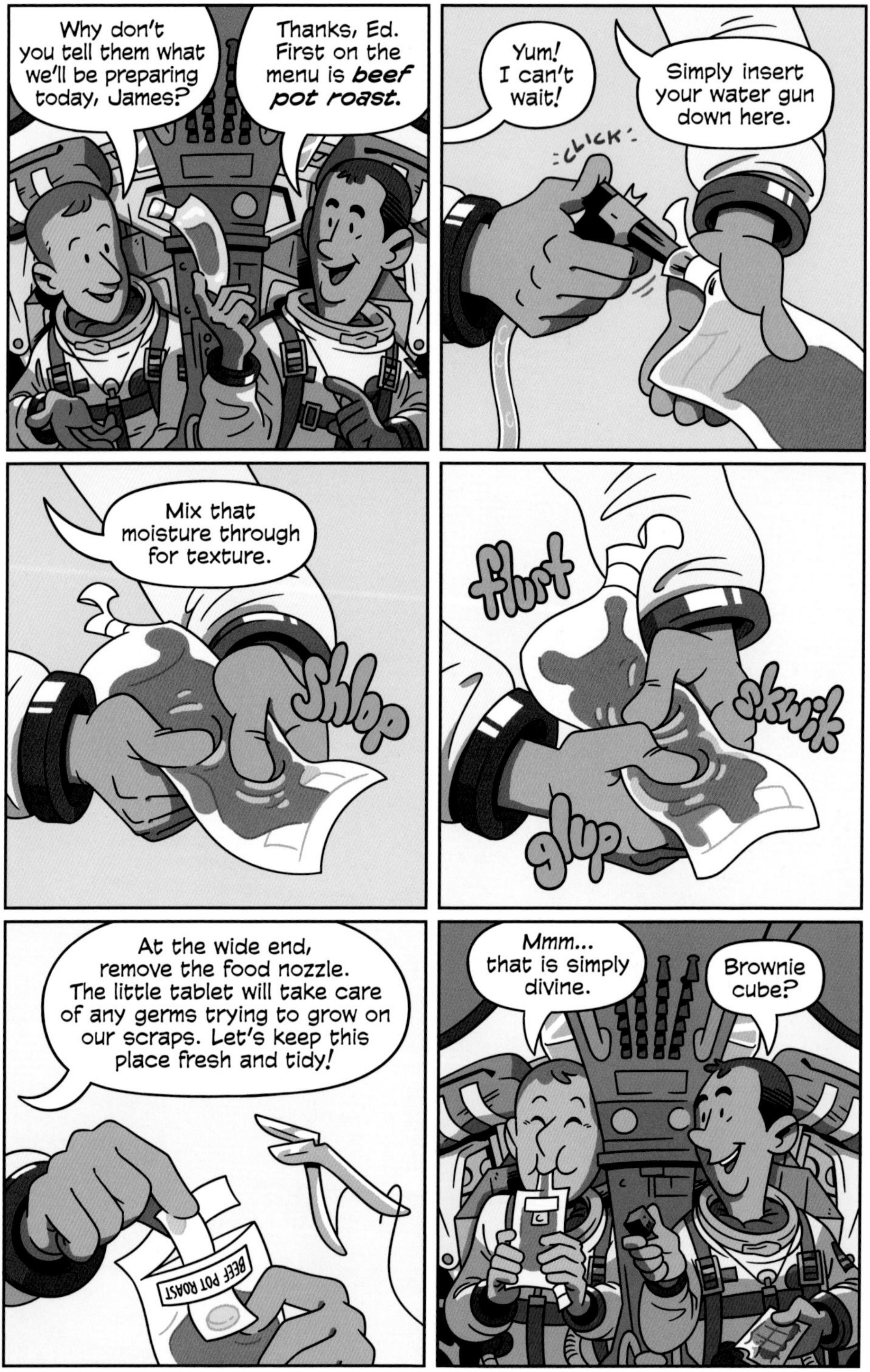
Why don't you tell them what we'll be preparing today, James?
Thanks, Ed. First on the menu is ***beef pot roast.***
Yum! I can't wait!
Simply insert your water gun down here.
CLICK
Mix that moisture through for texture.
shlop
flurt
skwik
glup
At the wide end, remove the food nozzle. The little tablet will take care of any germs trying to grow on our scraps. Let's keep this place fresh and tidy!
BEEF POT ROAST
Mmm... that is simply divine.
Brownie cube?

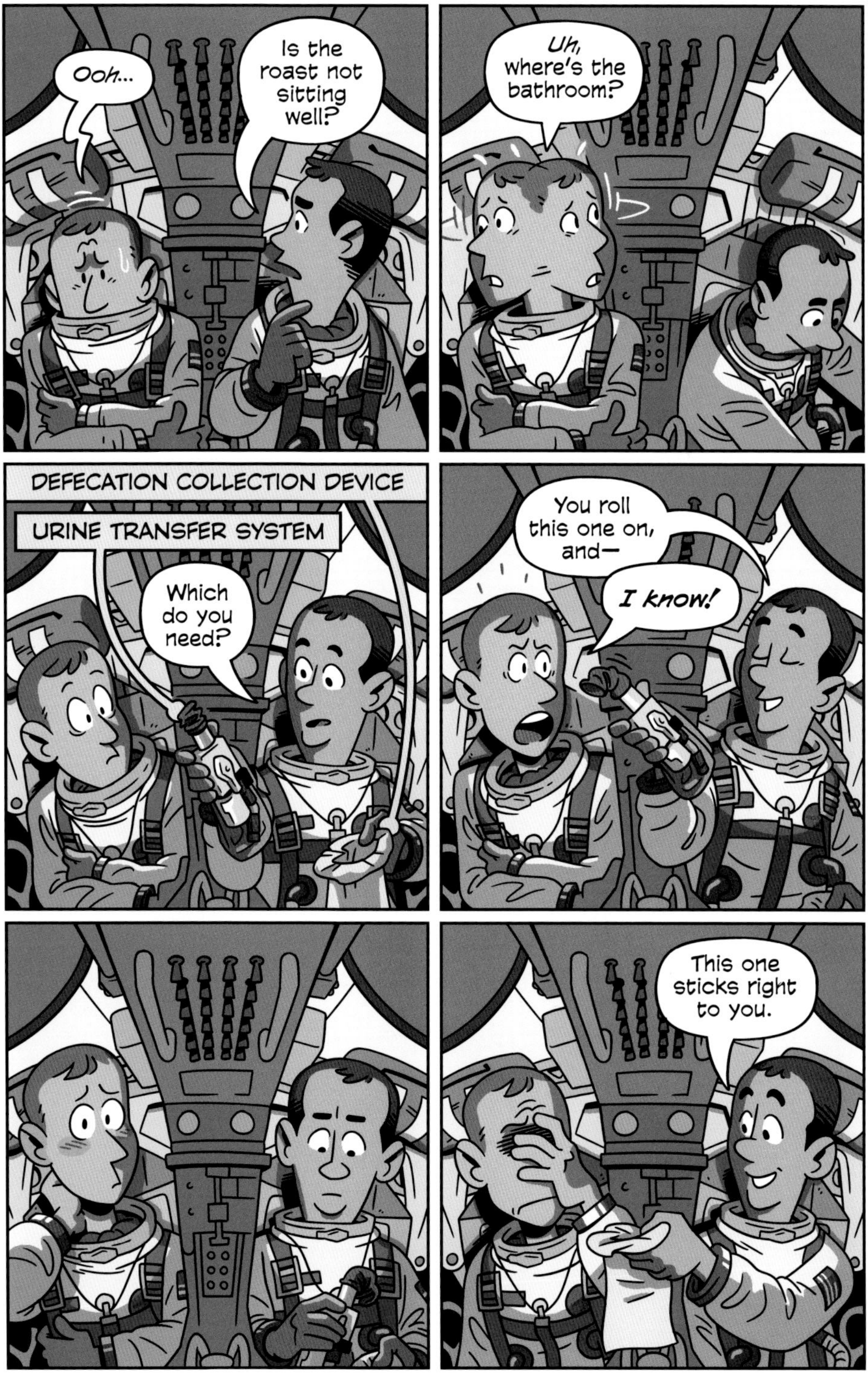
Ooh...
Is the roast not sitting well?
Uh, where's the bathroom?
DEFECATION COLLECTION DEVICE
URINE TRANSFER SYSTEM
Which do you need?
You roll this one on, and—
I know!
This one sticks right to you.

The lunar crew will have more privacy because they'll ***split up.*** The plan is to take a small lander down to the surface while the return capsule orbits above. That's why Gemini's final goal is to ***dock*** two spacecraft in orbit. It's the only way the lunar crew will be able to reunite and return home.

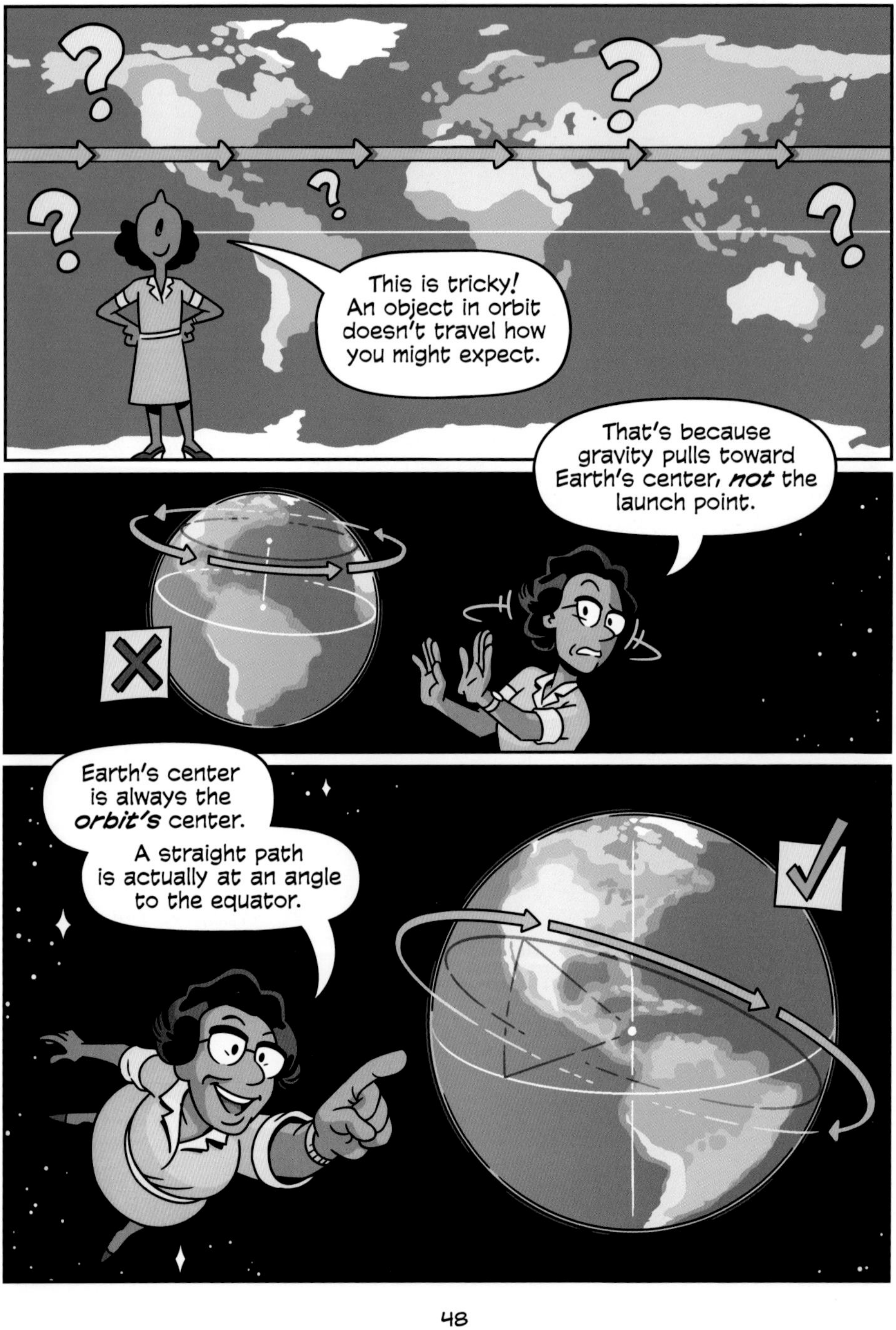

This is tricky! An object in orbit doesn't travel how you might expect.
That's because gravity pulls toward Earth's center, ***not*** the launch point.
Earth's center is always the ***orbit's*** center.
A straight path is actually at an angle to the equator.

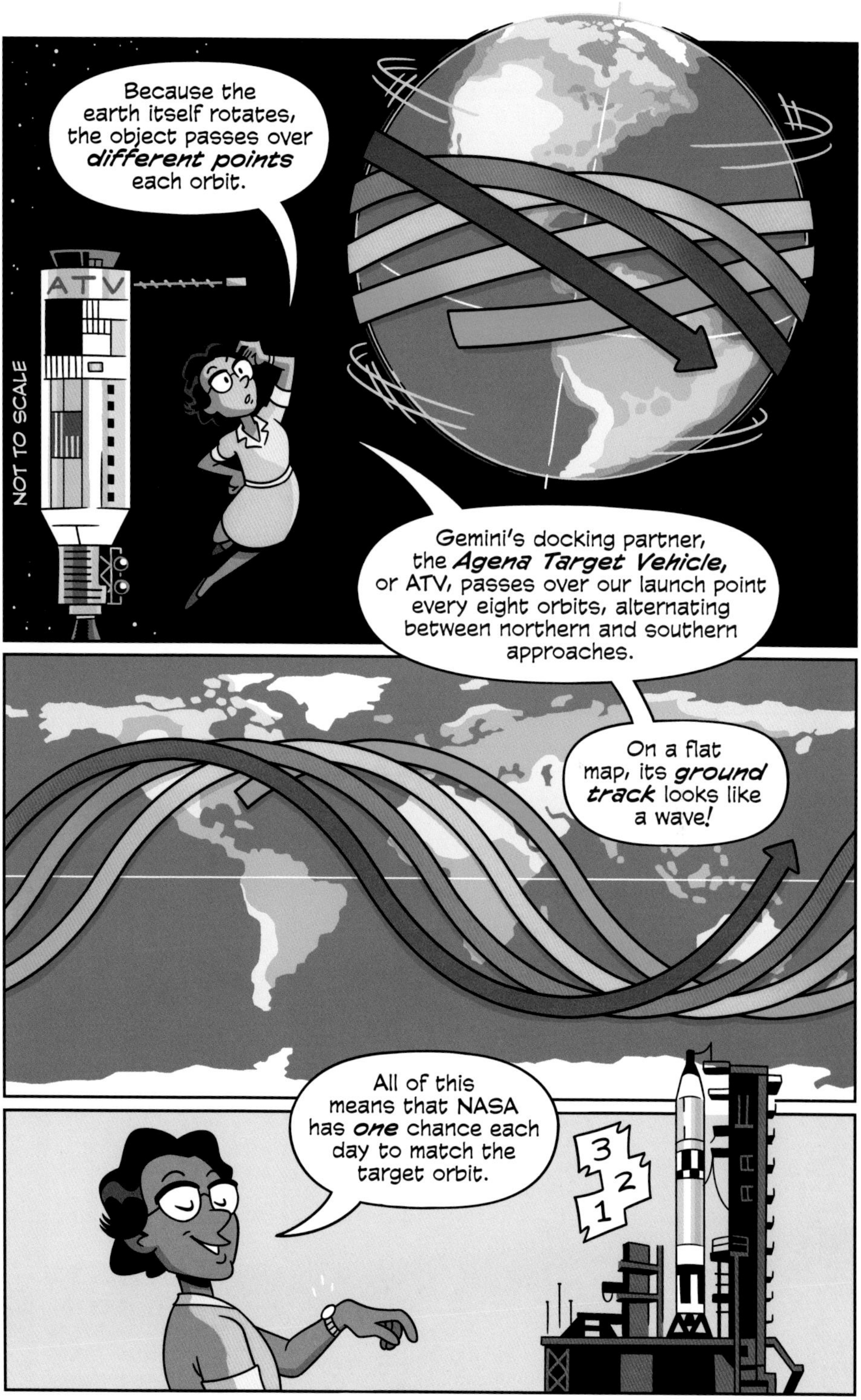
Because the earth itself rotates, the object passes over ***different points*** each orbit.
ATV
NOT TO SCALE
Gemini's docking partner, the ***Agena Target Vehicle,*** or ATV, passes over our launch point every eight orbits, alternating between northern and southern approaches.
On a flat map, its ***ground track*** looks like a wave!
All of this means that NASA has ***one*** chance each day to match the target orbit.
3
2
1

GEMINI VIII, 1966

Liftoff!

SKWOORMBRRRPRW

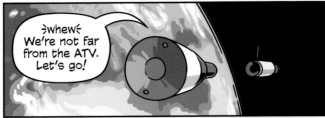

≥whew≤ We're not far from the ATV. Let's go!

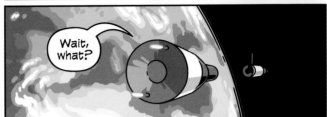

Wait, what?

Hey!

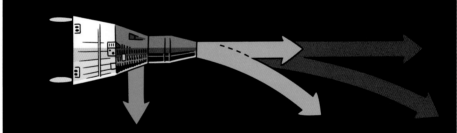

Surprise! In orbit, speeding up *increases altitude.* Your "forward" velocity changes, but gravity's pull doesn't.

And since an object in a higher orbit has to travel farther to circle the planet, it *orbits* more slowly even though it *moves* faster.

You need to *slow down* to *catch up!*

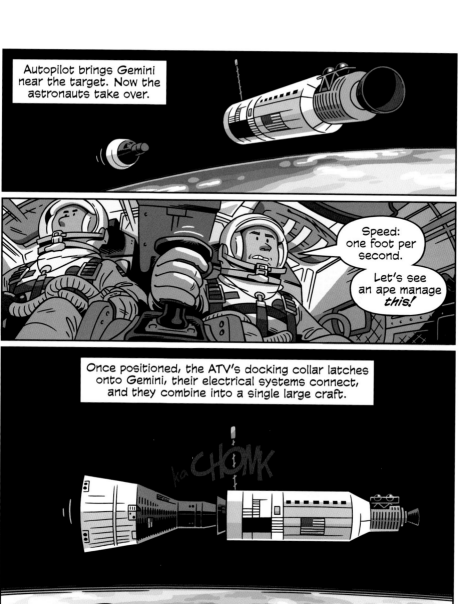

Autopilot brings Gemini near the target. Now the astronauts take over.

Speed: one foot per second.

Let's see an ape manage *this!*

Once positioned, the ATV's docking collar latches onto Gemini, their electrical systems connect, and they combine into a single large craft.

ka CHOMK

Houston, we are docked. It was a real smoothie.

NEIL ARMSTRONG

With that—multiple crew members, extravehicular space suits, longer durations, and docking capabilities— all of the pieces are in place for the *Apollo* program and a trip to the *moon.*

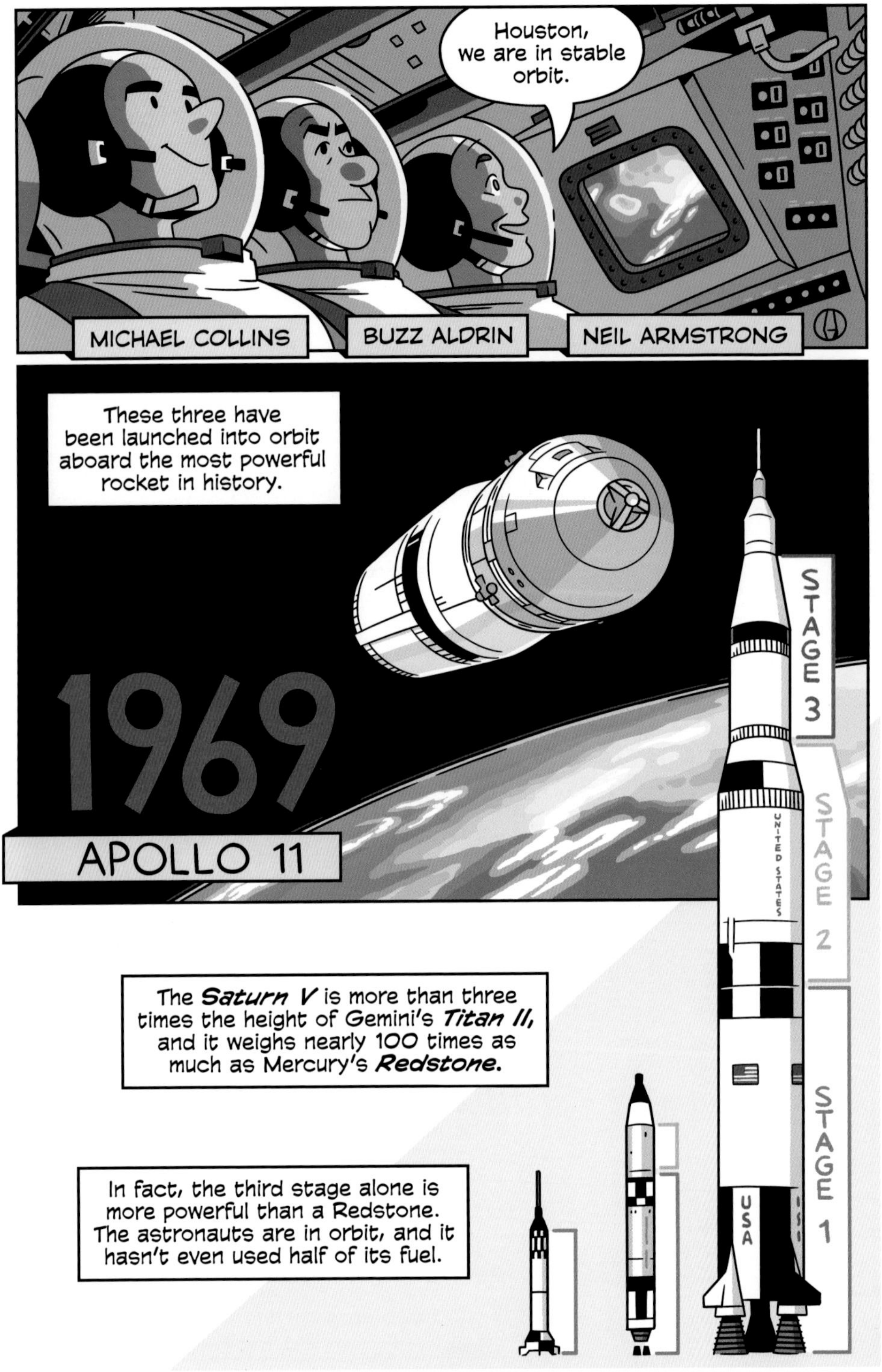
Houston, we are in stable orbit.
MICHAEL COLLINS
BUZZ ALDRIN
NEIL ARMSTRONG
These three have been launched into orbit aboard the most powerful rocket in history.
1969
APOLLO 11
STAGE 3
STAGE 2
STAGE 1
UNITED STATES
USA
The *Saturn V* is more than three times the height of Gemini's *Titan II*, and it weighs nearly 100 times as much as Mercury's ***Redstone***.
In fact, the third stage alone is more powerful than a Redstone. The astronauts are in orbit, and it hasn't even used half of its fuel.

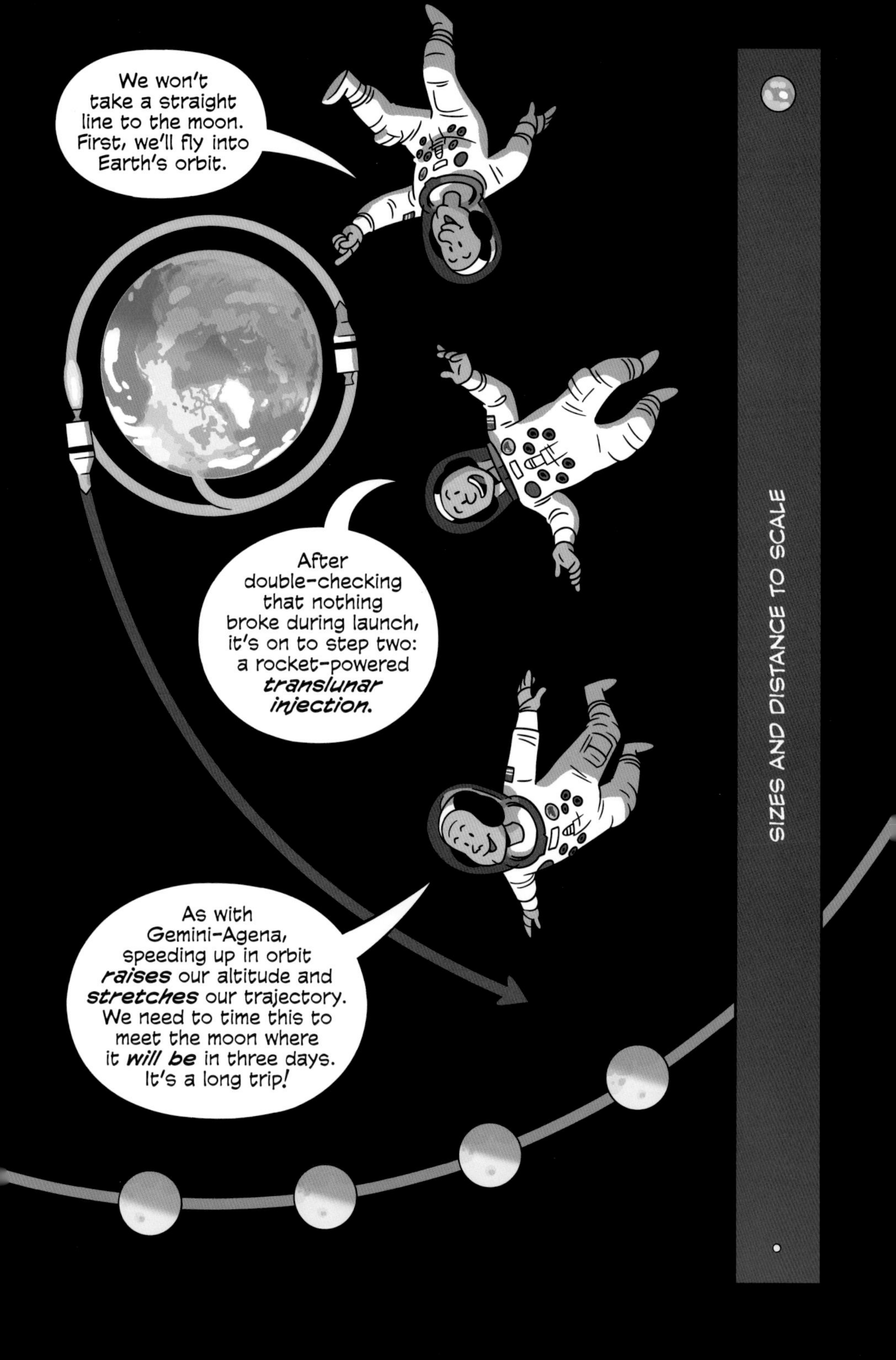
We won't take a straight line to the moon. First, we'll fly into Earth's orbit.
After double-checking that nothing broke during launch, it's on to step two: a rocket-powered ***translunar injection.***
As with Gemini-Agena, speeding up in orbit ***raises*** our altitude and ***stretches*** our trajectory. We need to time this to meet the moon where it ***will be*** in three days. It's a long trip!
SIZES AND DISTANCE TO SCALE

With its fuel spent on the injection, the third stage is mostly useless mass.
In order to land on the moon, though, we still need to retrieve the *lunar module* stowed behind us.
USA
Hmm, there seems to be a rocket engine in the way.
USA
To reach the lander, we'll release the ***command module***...
USA
...turn it around to line up the hatches...
USA
...and inch back in.
We'll spend the rest of our trip sitting backward!

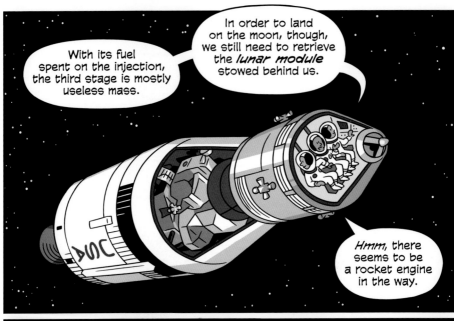

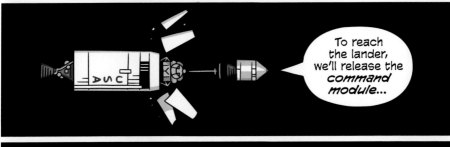

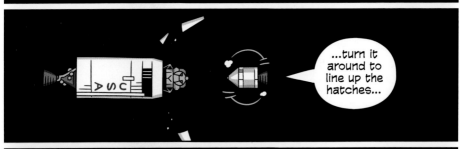

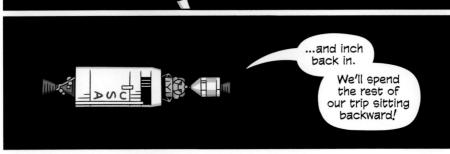

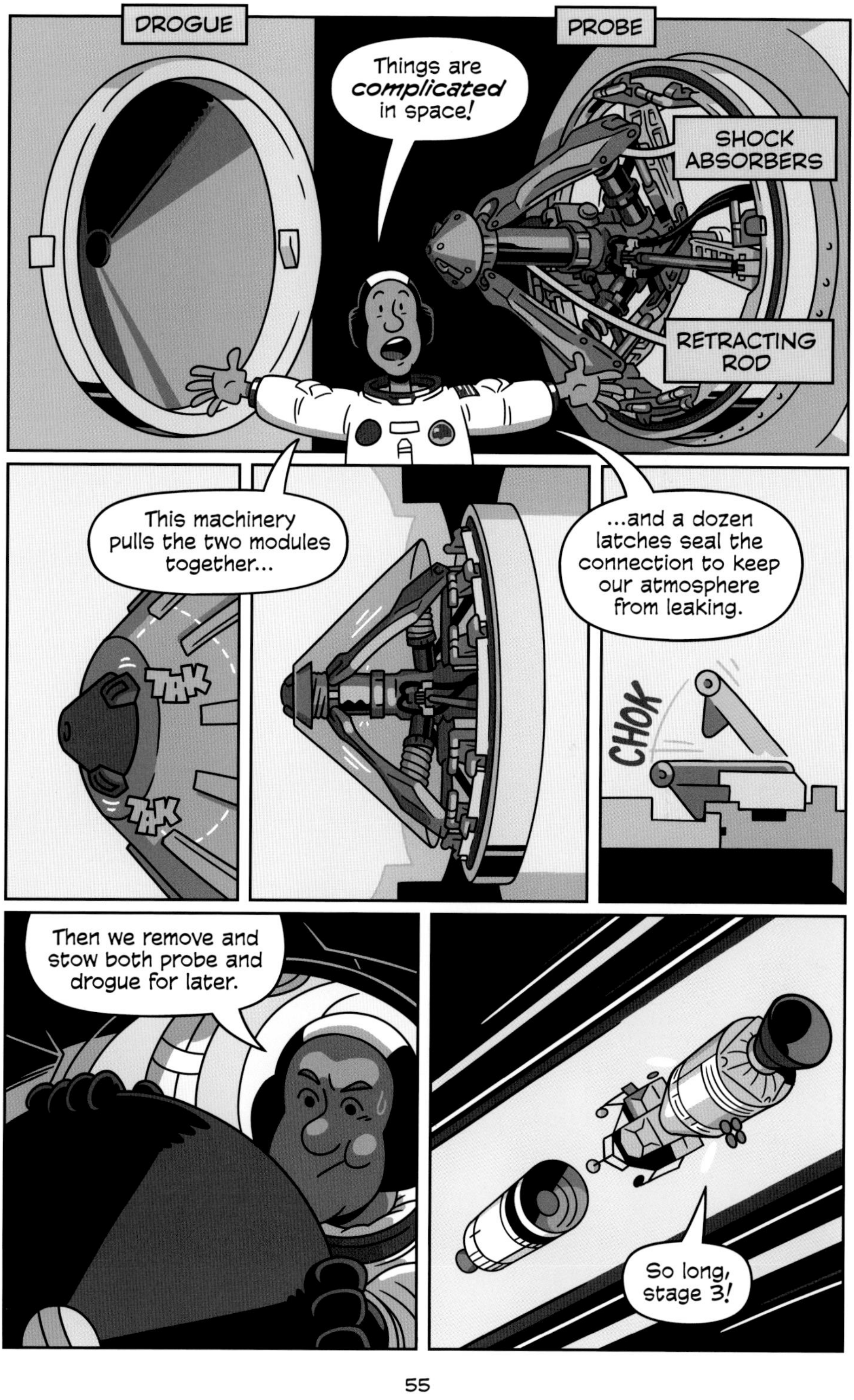
DROGUE
PROBE
Things are *complicated* in space!
SHOCK ABSORBERS
RETRACTING ROD
This machinery pulls the two modules together...
...and a dozen latches seal the connection to keep our atmosphere from leaking.
TAK
TAK
CHOK
Then we remove and stow both probe and drogue for later.
So long, stage 3!

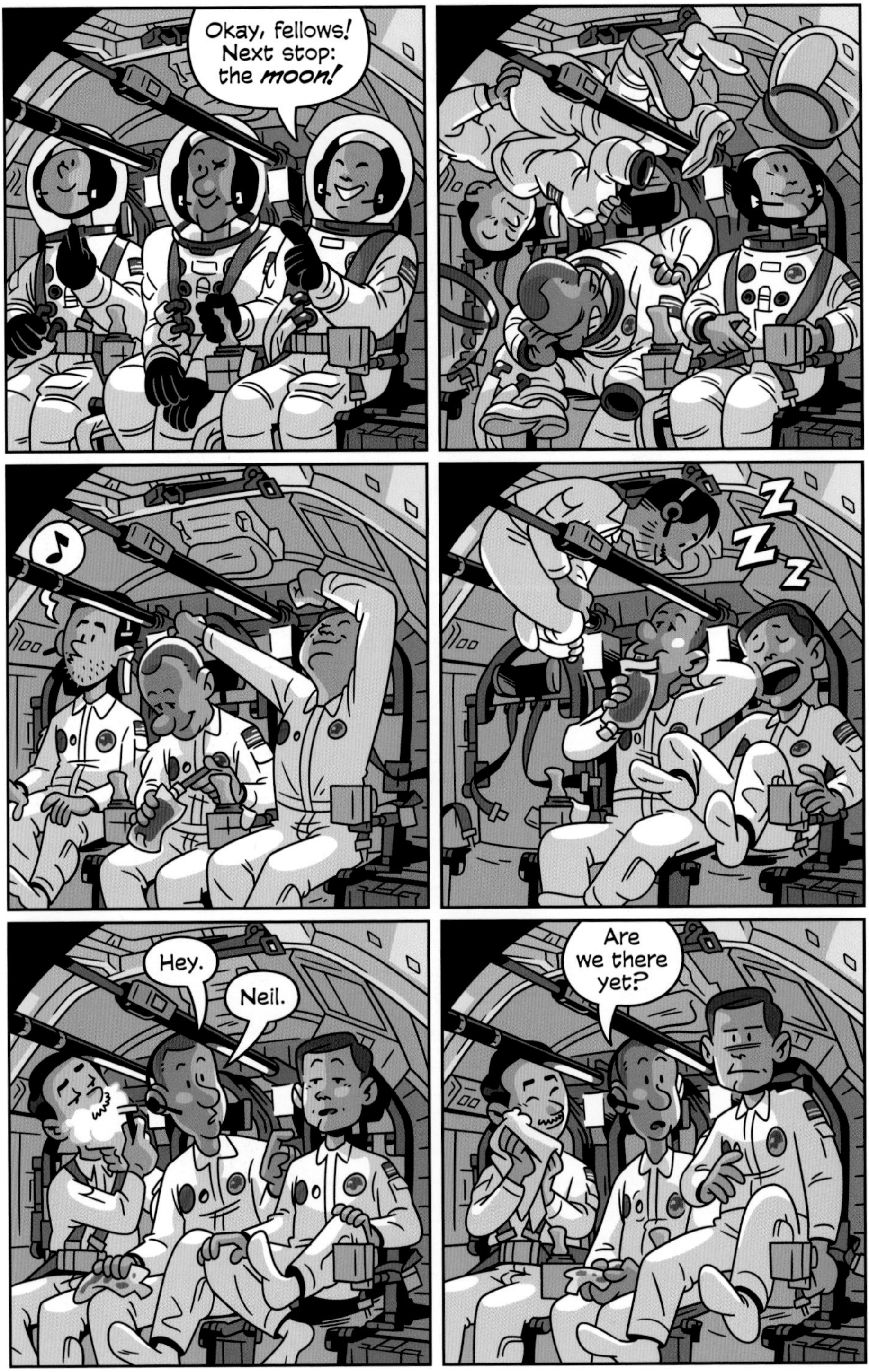
Okay, fellows! Next stop: the *moon!*
♪
ZZZ
Hey.
Neil.
Are we there yet?

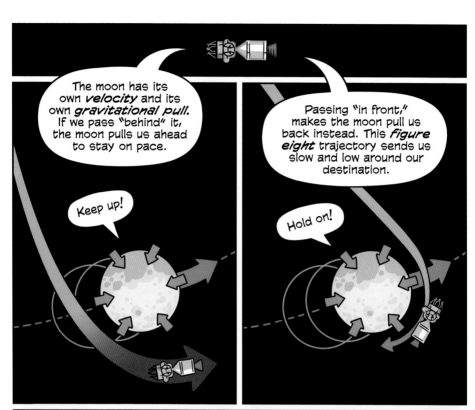

The moon has its own *velocity* and its own *gravitational pull.* If we pass "behind" it, the moon pulls us ahead to stay on pace.

Keep up!

Passing "in front," makes the moon pull us back instead. This *figure eight* trajectory sends us slow and low around our destination.

Hold on!

The craft is *still* going too fast for the moon to hang on to, though.

Last year, the Soviet *Zond 5* mission used this nonstop loop to carry the first Earthlings around the moon and back.

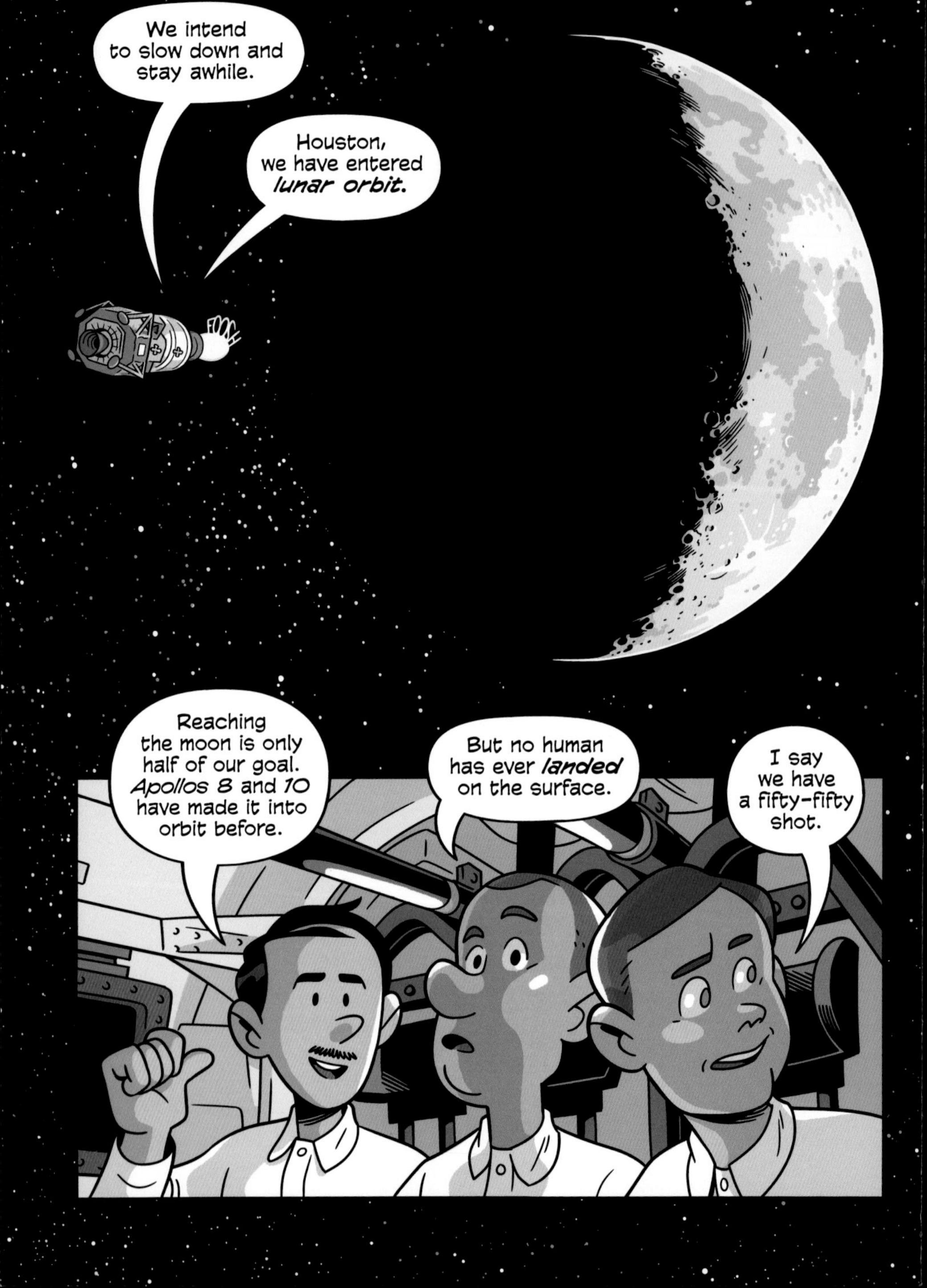

We intend to slow down and stay awhile.
Houston, we have entered *lunar orbit.*
Reaching the moon is only half of our goal. *Apollos* 8 and 10 have made it into orbit before.
But no human has ever *landed* on the surface.
I say we have a fifty-fifty shot.

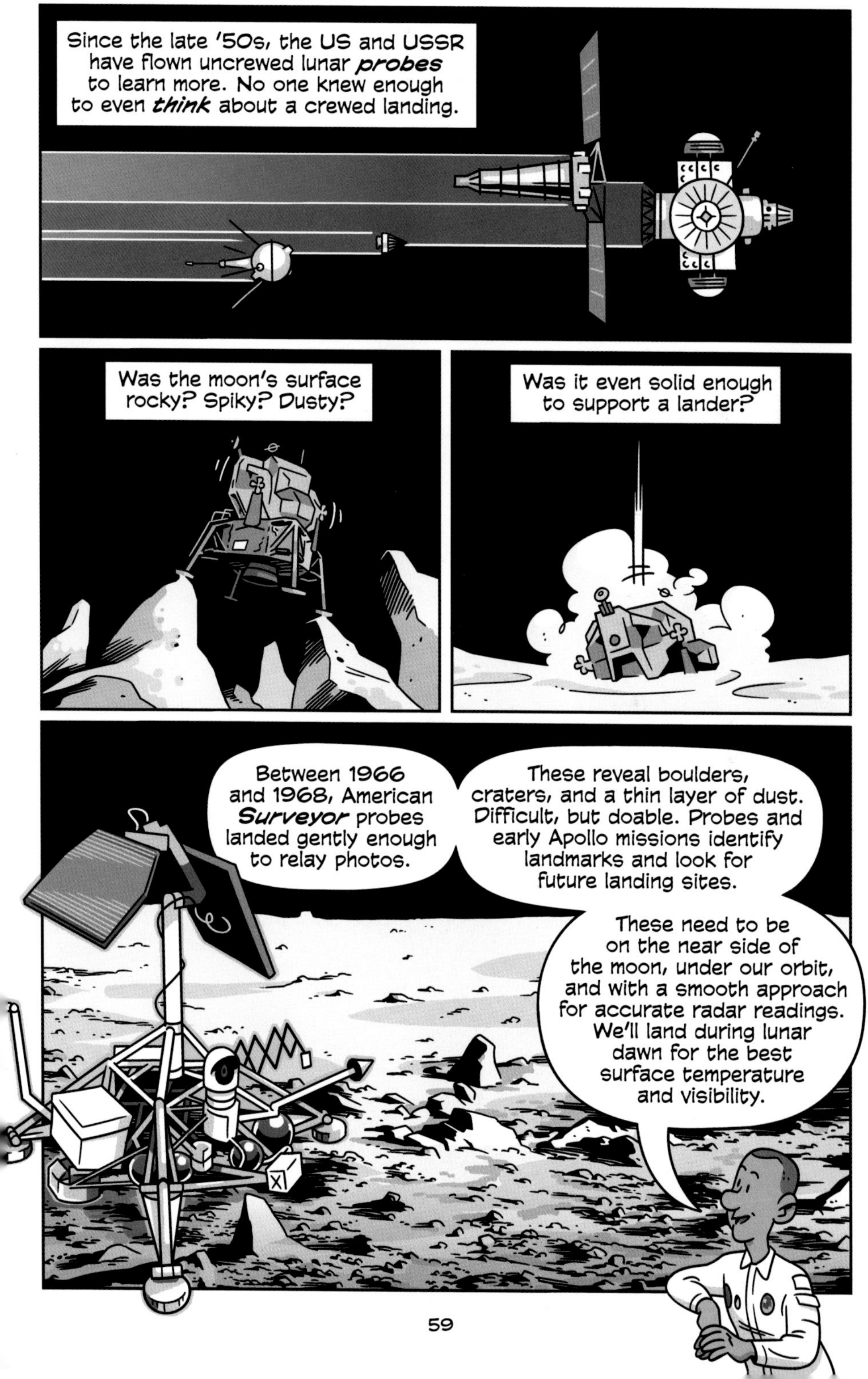
Since the late '50s, the US and USSR have flown uncrewed lunar *probes* to learn more. No one knew enough to even *think* about a crewed landing.
Was the moon's surface rocky? Spiky? Dusty?
Was it even solid enough to support a lander?
Between 1966 and 1968, American *Surveyor* probes landed gently enough to relay photos.
These reveal boulders, craters, and a thin layer of dust. Difficult, but doable. Probes and early Apollo missions identify landmarks and look for future landing sites.
These need to be on the near side of the moon, under our orbit, and with a smooth approach for accurate radar readings. We'll land during lunar dawn for the best surface temperature and visibility.

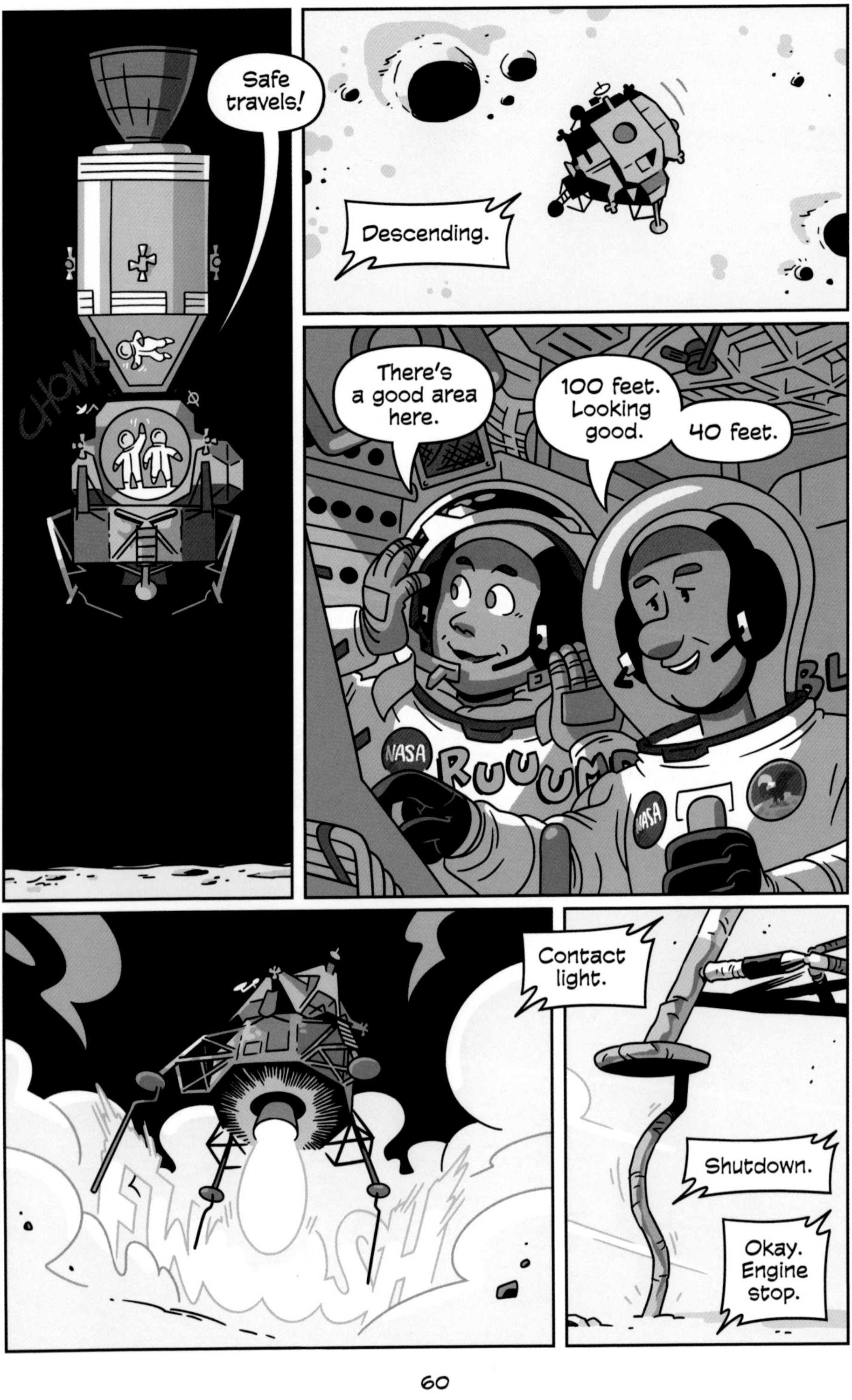
Safe travels!
CHOMK
Descending.
There's a good area here.
100 feet. Looking good.
40 feet.
RUUUMB
Contact light.
FWOOSH
Shutdown.
Okay. Engine stop.

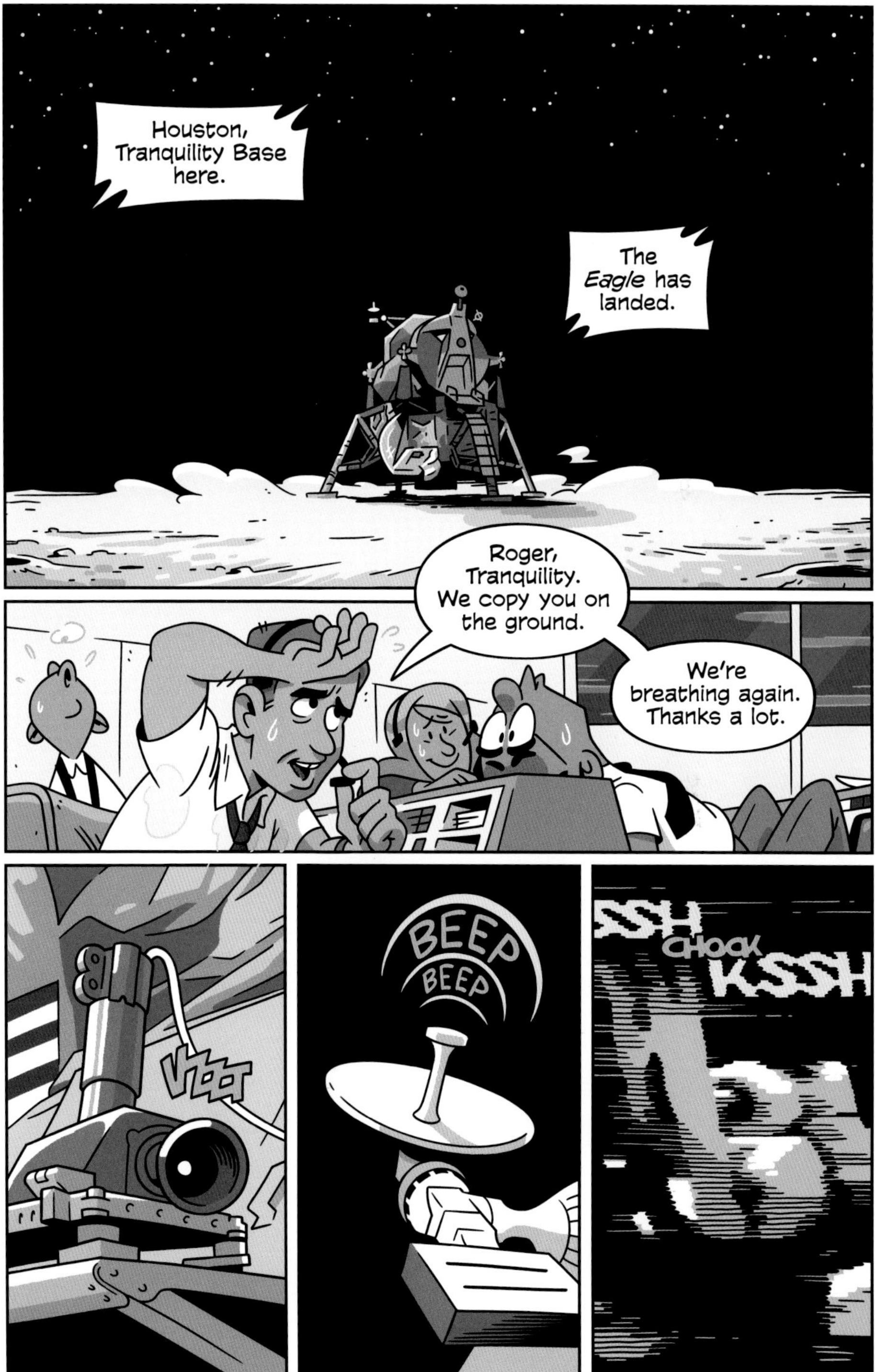
Houston, Tranquility Base here.
The *Eagle* has landed.
Roger, Tranquility. We copy you on the ground.
We're breathing again. Thanks a lot.
VZZT
BEEP
BEEP
KSSH
CHOCK
KSSH

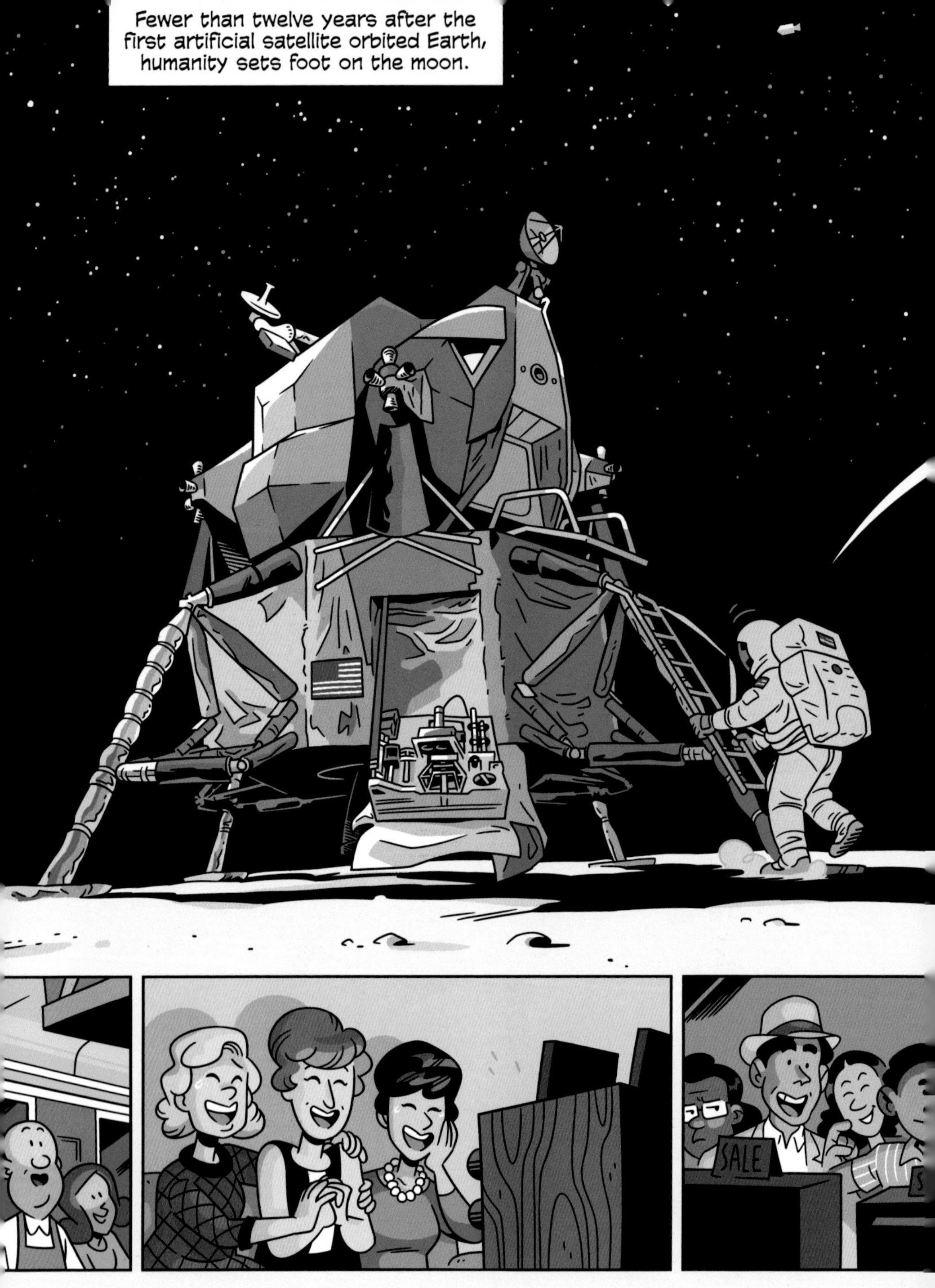
Fewer than twelve years after the first artificial satellite orbited Earth, humanity sets foot on the moon.
SALE

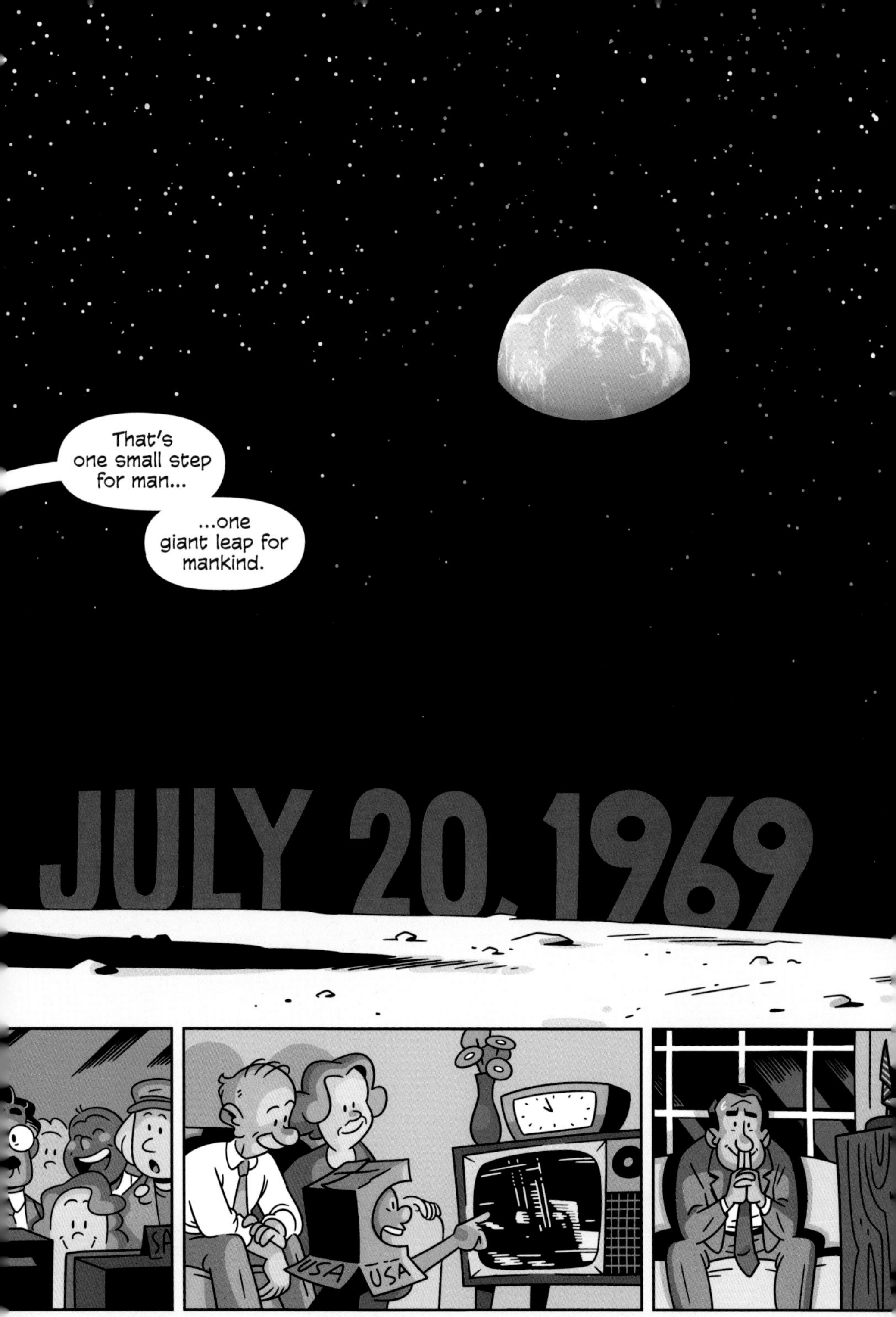
That's one small step for man...
...one giant leap for mankind.
JULY 20, 1969
USA
USA

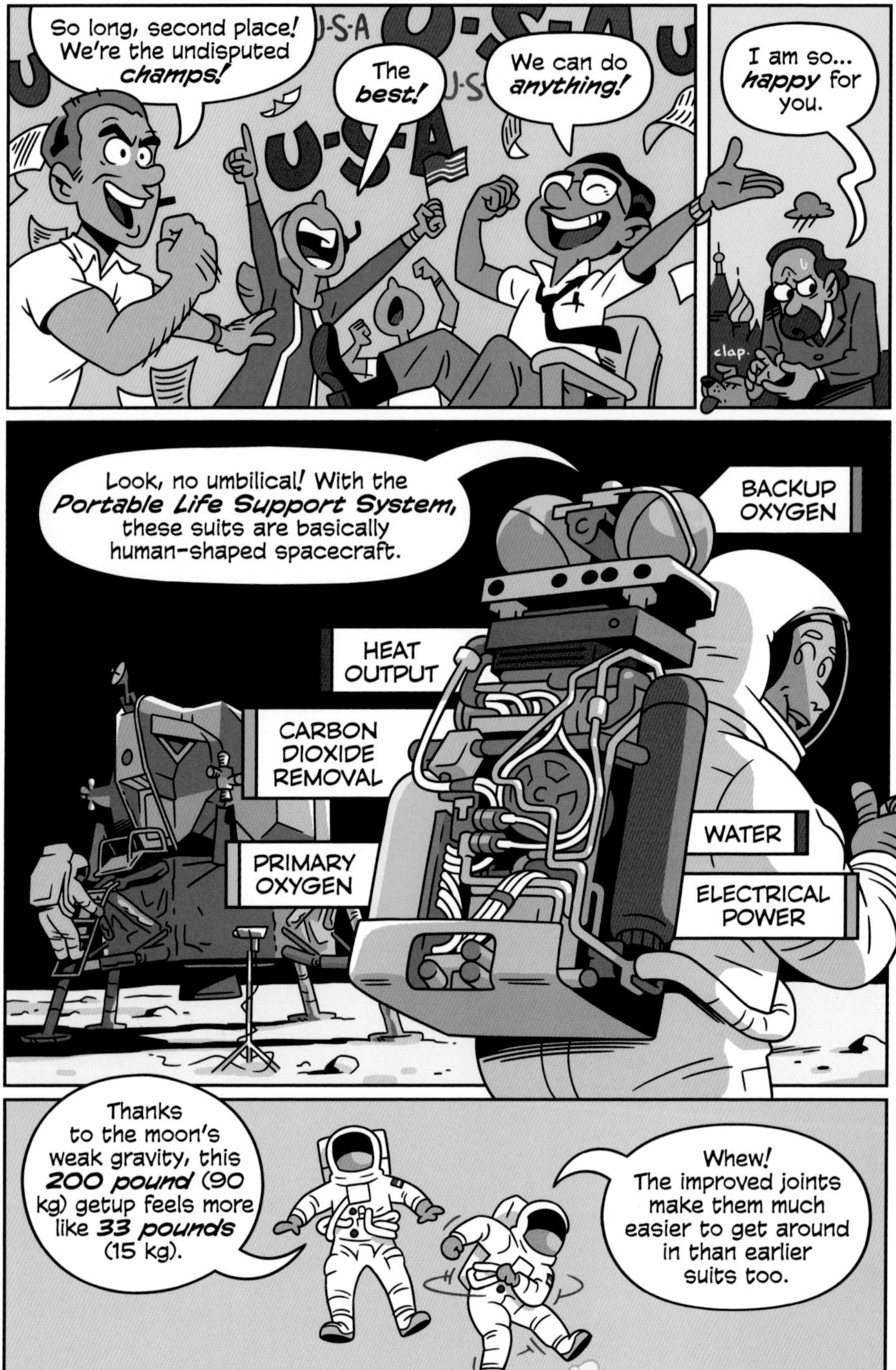
So long, second place! We're the undisputed ***champs!***
U-S-A
The ***best!***
We can do ***anything!***
I am so... ***happy*** for you.
clap.
Look, no umbilical! With the ***Portable Life Support System,*** these suits are basically human-shaped spacecraft.
BACKUP OXYGEN
HEAT OUTPUT
CARBON DIOXIDE REMOVAL
WATER
PRIMARY OXYGEN
ELECTRICAL POWER
Thanks to the moon's weak gravity, this ***200 pound*** (90 kg) getup feels more like ***33 pounds*** (15 kg).
Whew! The improved joints make them much easier to get around in than earlier suits too.

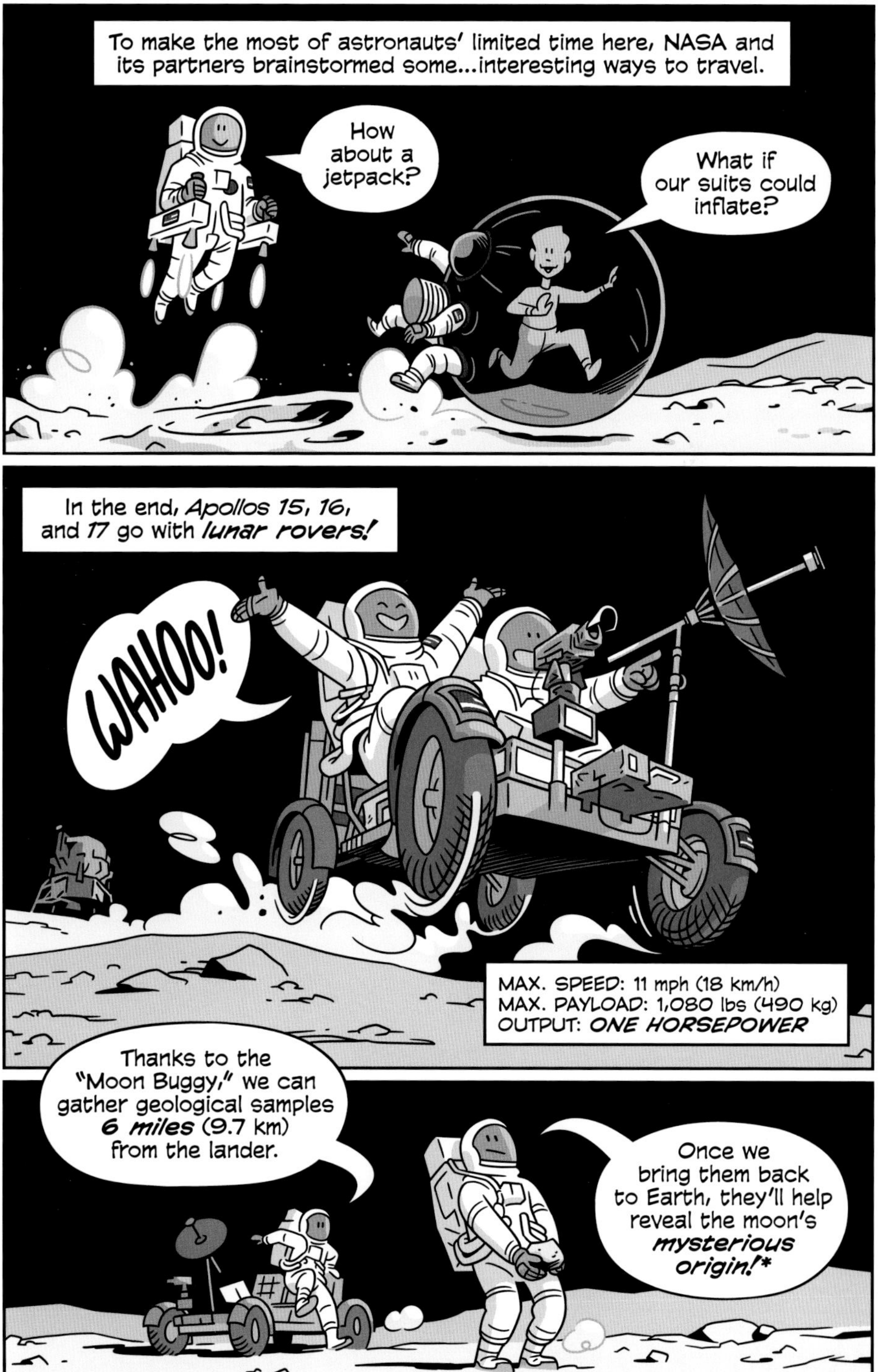
To make the most of astronauts' limited time here, NASA and its partners brainstormed some...interesting ways to travel.
How about a jetpack?
What if our suits could inflate?
In the end, *Apollos 15, 16,* and *17* go with ***lunar rovers!***
WAHOO!
MAX. SPEED: 11 mph (18 km/h)
MAX. PAYLOAD: 1,080 lbs (490 kg)
OUTPUT: ***ONE HORSEPOWER***
Thanks to the "Moon Buggy," we can gather geological samples ***6 miles*** (9.7 km) from the lander.
Once we bring them back to Earth, they'll help reveal the moon's ***mysterious origin!****

**a massive collision with early Earth!*

In 1970, between *Apollos 13* and *14*, the USSR secures its *own* samples using the robotic probe *Luna 16*.

3.5 oz (101 g)

CLONK

SHUFF

WHOOSH

No cosmonauts required.

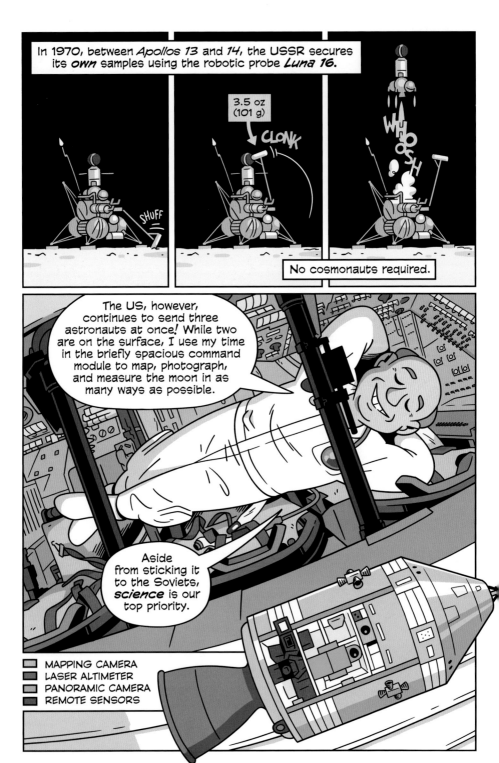

The US, however, continues to send three astronauts at once! While two are on the surface, I use my time in the briefly spacious command module to map, photograph, and measure the moon in as many ways as possible.

Aside from sticking it to the Soviets, *science* is our top priority.

☐ MAPPING CAMERA
■ LASER ALTIMETER
☐ PANORAMIC CAMERA
■ REMOTE SENSORS

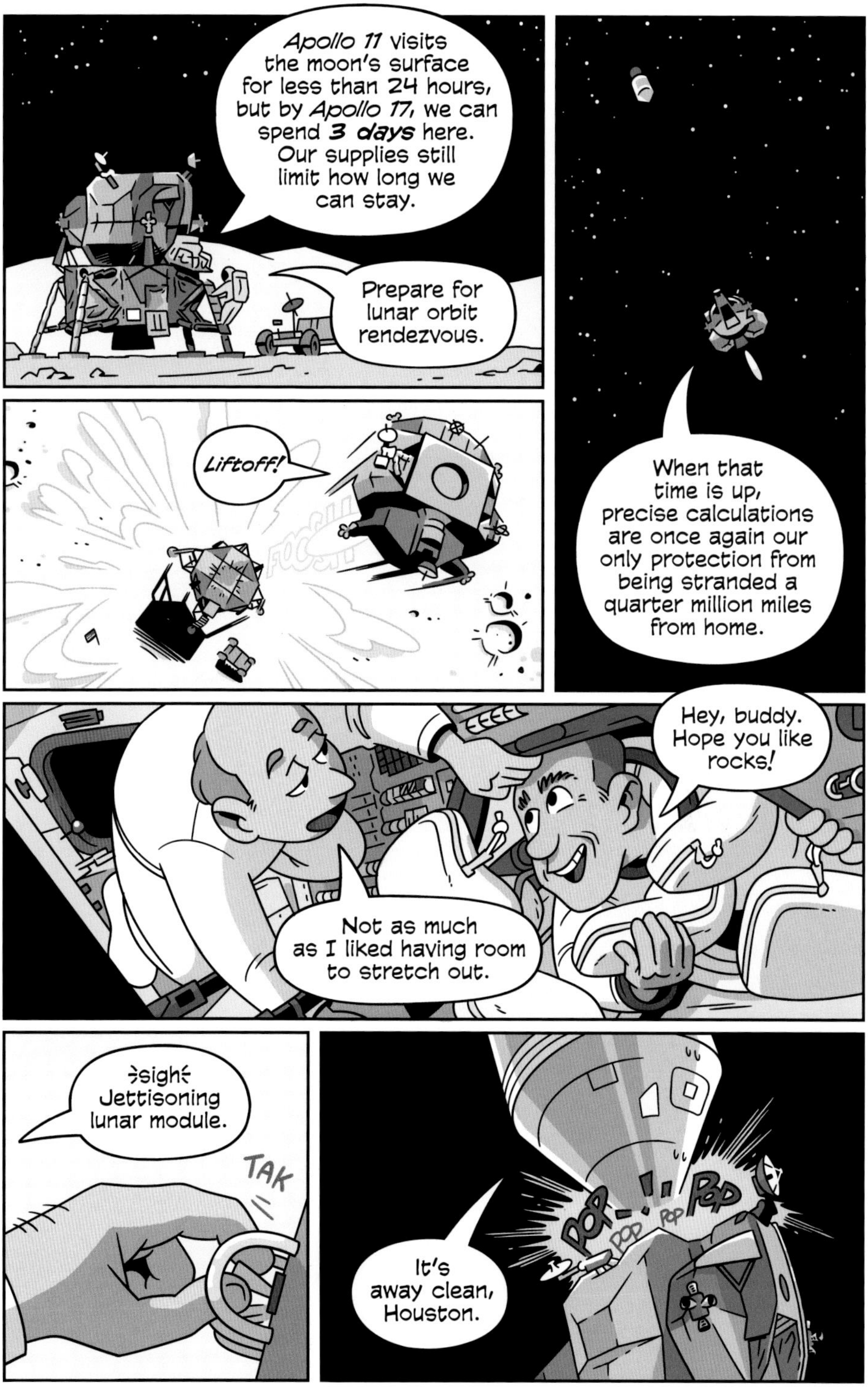
Apollo 11 visits the moon's surface for less than 24 hours, but by *Apollo 17*, we can spend ***3 days*** here. Our supplies still limit how long we can stay.
Prepare for lunar orbit rendezvous.
Liftoff!
When that time is up, precise calculations are once again our only protection from being stranded a quarter million miles from home.
Hey, buddy. Hope you like rocks!
Not as much as I liked having room to stretch out.
sigh Jettisoning lunar module.
TAK
POP
POP
POP
POP
It's away clean, Houston.

Each Apollo's return looks much like its departure. The command module's engine begins firing on the far side of the moon, accelerating enough to escape its gravitational pull and then follow a curving path back to Earth.

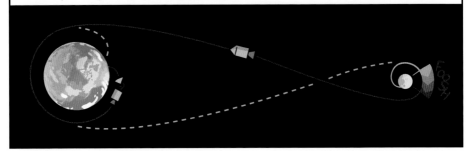

They don't pass any Soviets along the way. After a string of failed launches, the USSR has abandoned their crewed lunar program.

Bah, moon missions are a waste of resources anyway!

Despite the Americans' success, they're in a similar position. They have a lot of hardware and expertise but no immediate goal.

It'd be a shame to waste the stuff. It *was* really expensive.

Do you think...?

We *totally* should.

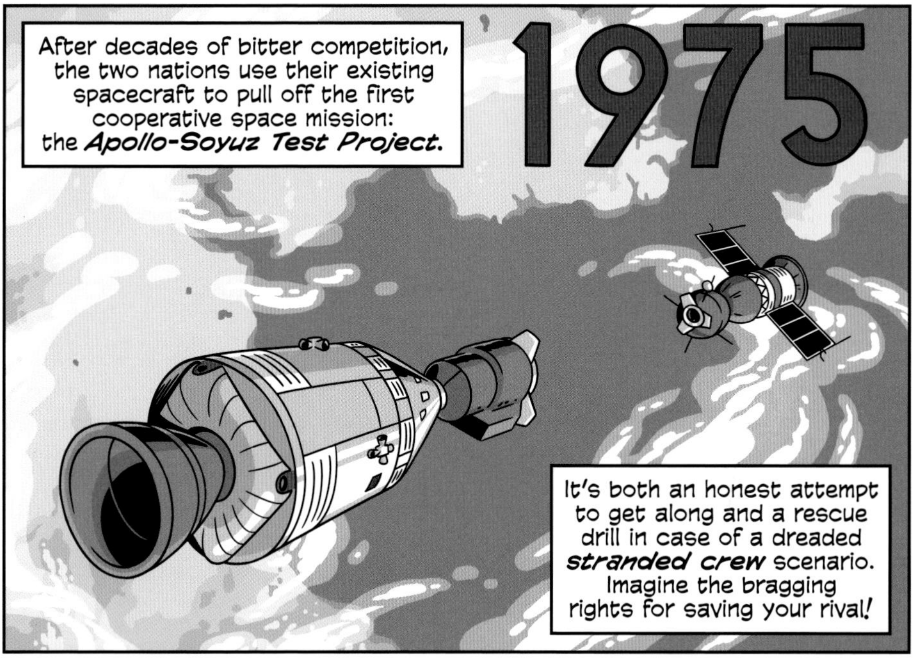
After decades of bitter competition, the two nations use their existing spacecraft to pull off the first cooperative space mission: the *Apollo-Soyuz Test Project*.
1975
It's both an honest attempt to get along and a rescue drill in case of a dreaded ***stranded crew*** scenario. Imagine the bragging rights for saving your rival!

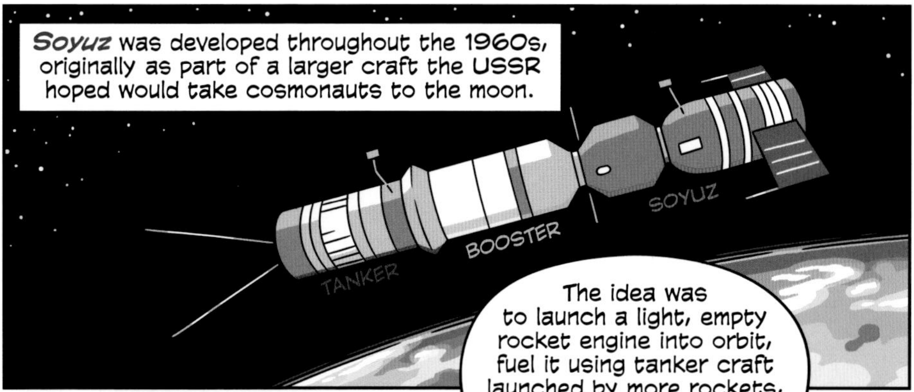
Soyuz was developed throughout the 1960s, originally as part of a larger craft the USSR hoped would take cosmonauts to the moon.
SOYUZ
BOOSTER
TANKER
The idea was to launch a light, empty rocket engine into orbit, fuel it using tanker craft launched by more rockets, and then dock the *Soyuz* to its freshly filled booster.

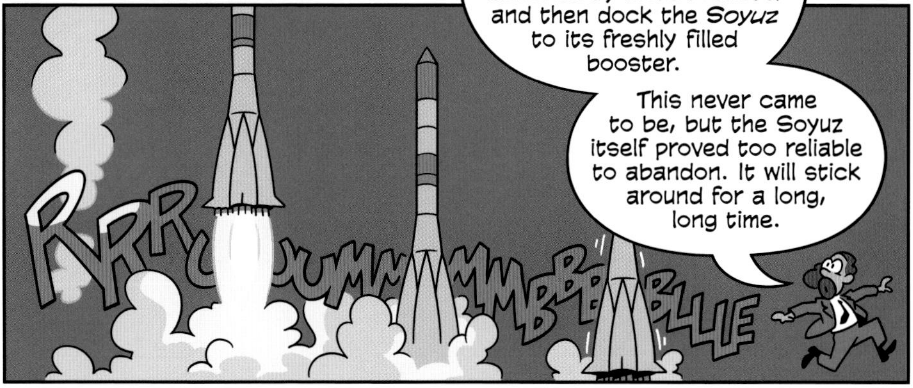
This never came to be, but the Soyuz itself proved too reliable to abandon. It will stick around for a long, long time.
RRRUUUMMMMBBBBLLLE

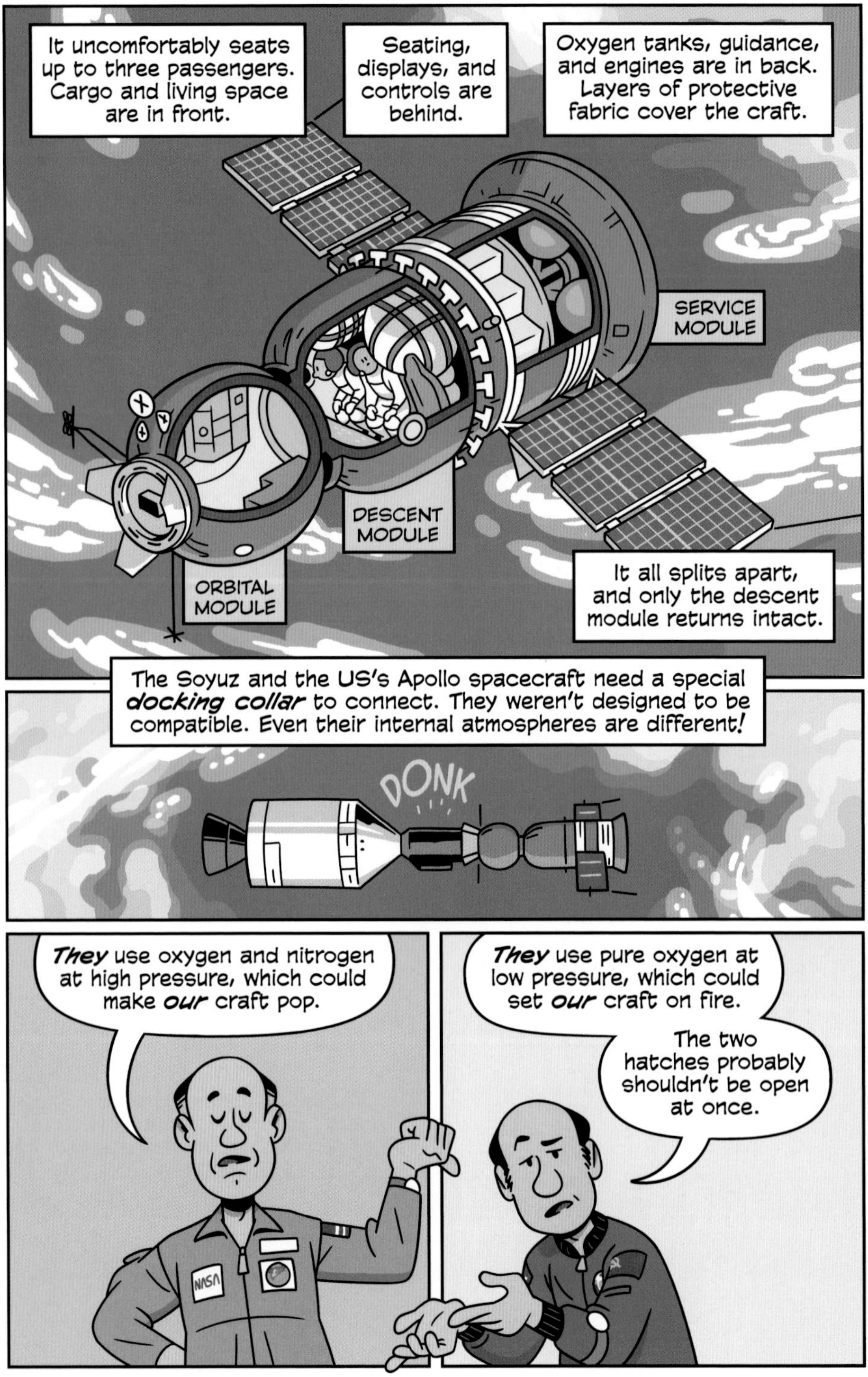

It uncomfortably seats up to three passengers. Cargo and living space are in front.
Seating, displays, and controls are behind.
Oxygen tanks, guidance, and engines are in back. Layers of protective fabric cover the craft.
SERVICE MODULE
DESCENT MODULE
ORBITAL MODULE
It all splits apart, and only the descent module returns intact.
The Soyuz and the US's Apollo spacecraft need a special *docking collar* to connect. They weren't designed to be compatible. Even their internal atmospheres are different!
DONK
They use oxygen and nitrogen at high pressure, which could make *our* craft pop.
They use pure oxygen at low pressure, which could set *our* craft on fire.
The two hatches probably shouldn't be open at once.
NASA

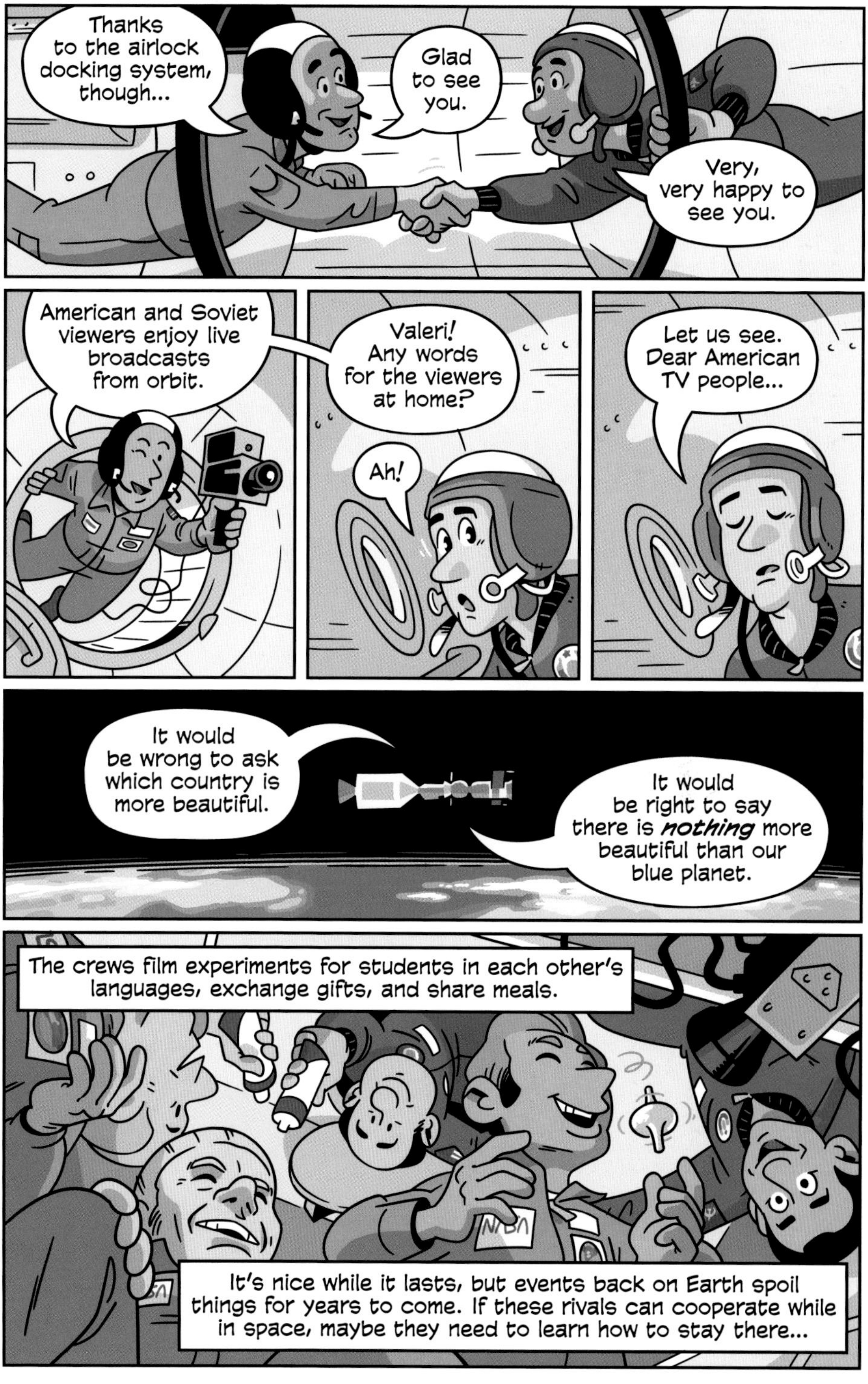
Thanks to the airlock docking system, though...
Glad to see you.
Very, very happy to see you.
American and Soviet viewers enjoy live broadcasts from orbit.
Valeri! Any words for the viewers at home?
Ah!
Let us see. Dear American TV people...
It would be wrong to ask which country is more beautiful.
It would be right to say there is *nothing* more beautiful than our blue planet.
The crews film experiments for students in each other's languages, exchange gifts, and share meals.
NASA
It's nice while it lasts, but events back on Earth spoil things for years to come. If these rivals can cooperate while in space, maybe they need to learn how to stay there...

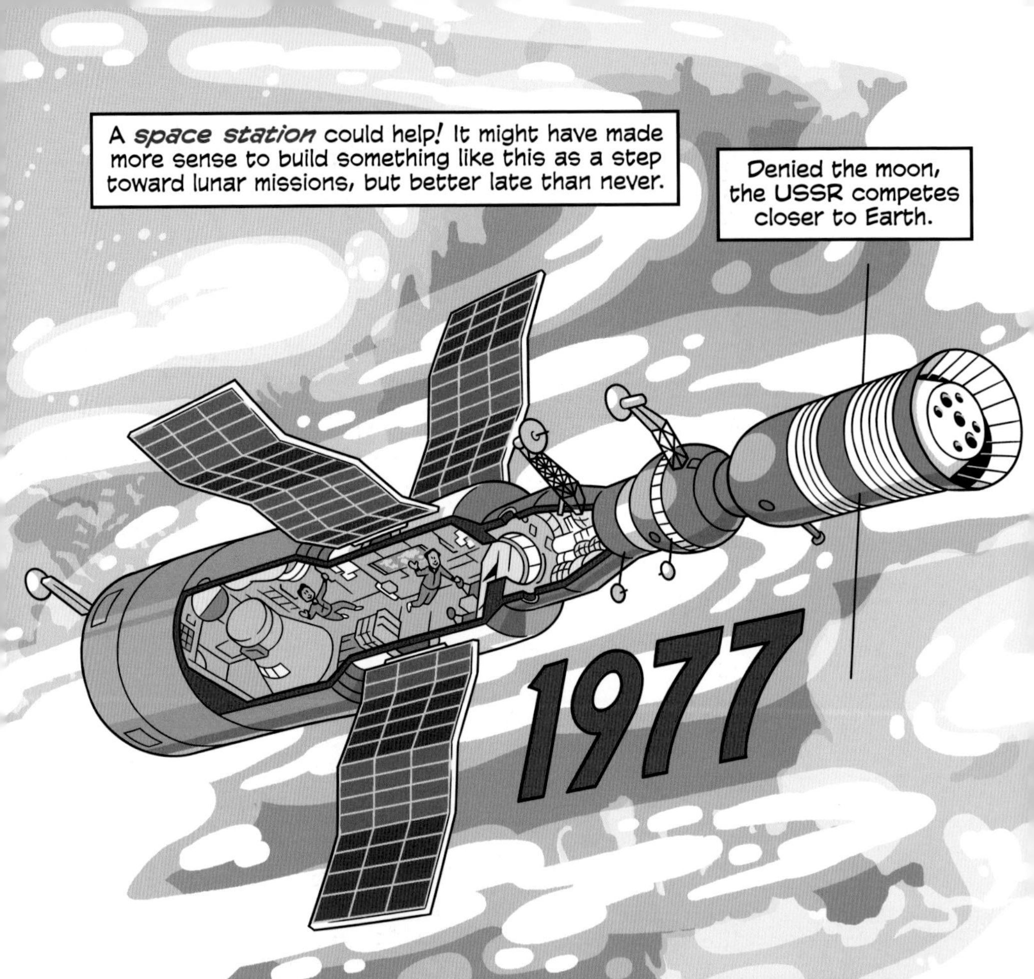

A *space station* could help! It might have made more sense to build something like this as a step toward lunar missions, but better late than never.
Denied the moon, the USSR competes closer to Earth.
1977

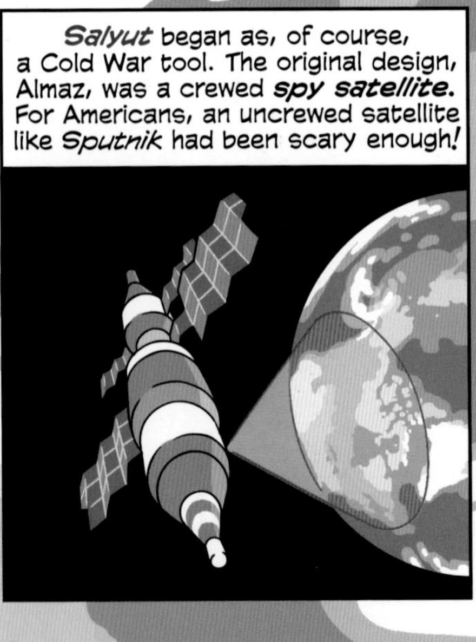

Salyut began as, of course, a Cold War tool. The original design, Almaz, was a crewed ***spy satellite.*** For Americans, an uncrewed satellite like *Sputnik* had been scary enough!

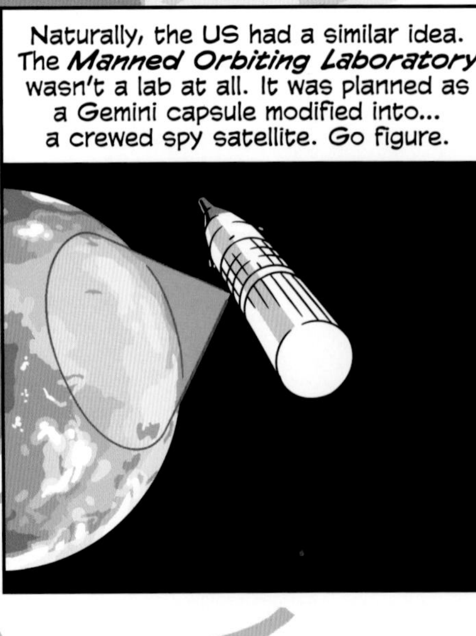

Naturally, the US had a similar idea. The ***Manned Orbiting Laboratory*** wasn't a lab at all. It was planned as a Gemini capsule modified into... a crewed spy satellite. Go figure.

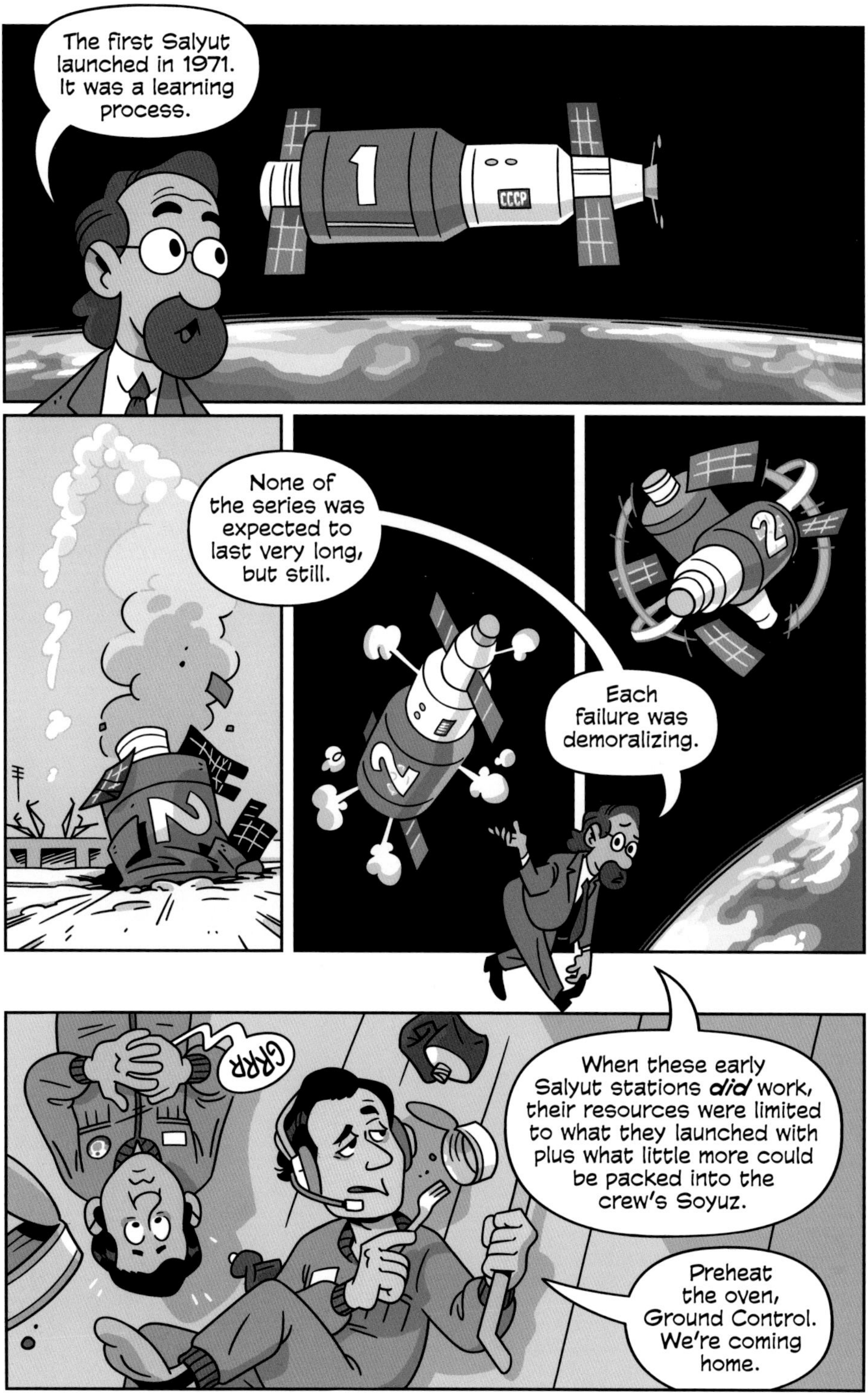
The first Salyut launched in 1971. It was a learning process.
CCCP
None of the series was expected to last very long, but still.
Each failure was demoralizing.
GRRR
When these early Salyut stations *did* work, their resources were limited to what they launched with plus what little more could be packed into the crew's Soyuz.
Preheat the oven, Ground Control. We're coming home.

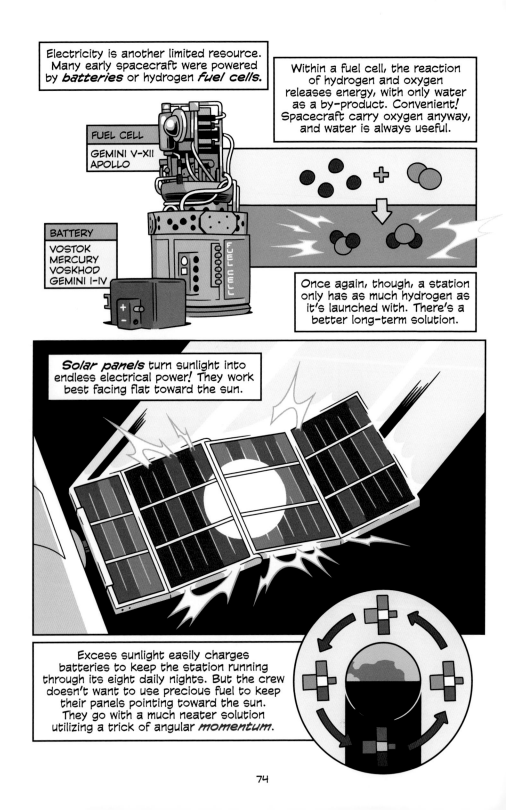

Electricity is another limited resource. Many early spacecraft were powered by *batteries* or hydrogen *fuel cells*.

Within a fuel cell, the reaction of hydrogen and oxygen releases energy, with only water as a by-product. Convenient! Spacecraft carry oxygen anyway, and water is always useful.

FUEL CELL

GEMINI V-XII
APOLLO

BATTERY

VOSTOK
MERCURY
VOSKHOD
GEMINI I-IV

Once again, though, a station only has as much hydrogen as it's launched with. There's a better long-term solution.

Solar panels turn sunlight into endless electrical power! They work best facing flat toward the sun.

Excess sunlight easily charges batteries to keep the station running through its eight daily nights. But the crew doesn't want to use precious fuel to keep their panels pointing toward the sun. They go with a much neater solution utilizing a trick of angular *momentum*.

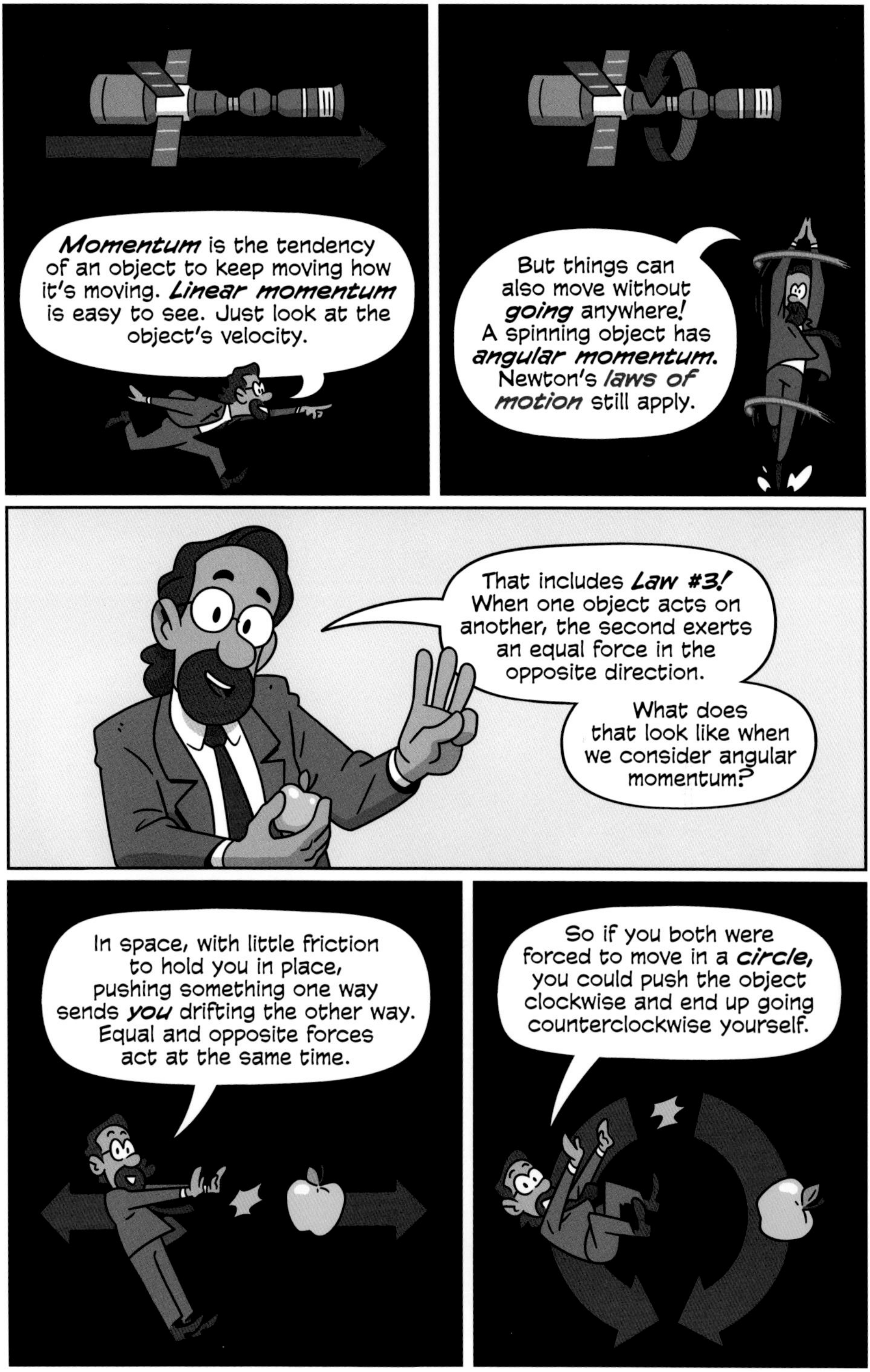
Momentum is the tendency of an object to keep moving how it's moving. Linear momentum is easy to see. Just look at the object's velocity.
But things can also move without going anywhere! A spinning object has angular momentum. Newton's laws of motion still apply.
That includes Law #3! When one object acts on another, the second exerts an equal force in the opposite direction.
What does that look like when we consider angular momentum?
In space, with little friction to hold you in place, pushing something one way sends you drifting the other way. Equal and opposite forces act at the same time.
So if you both were forced to move in a circle, you could push the object clockwise and end up going counterclockwise yourself.

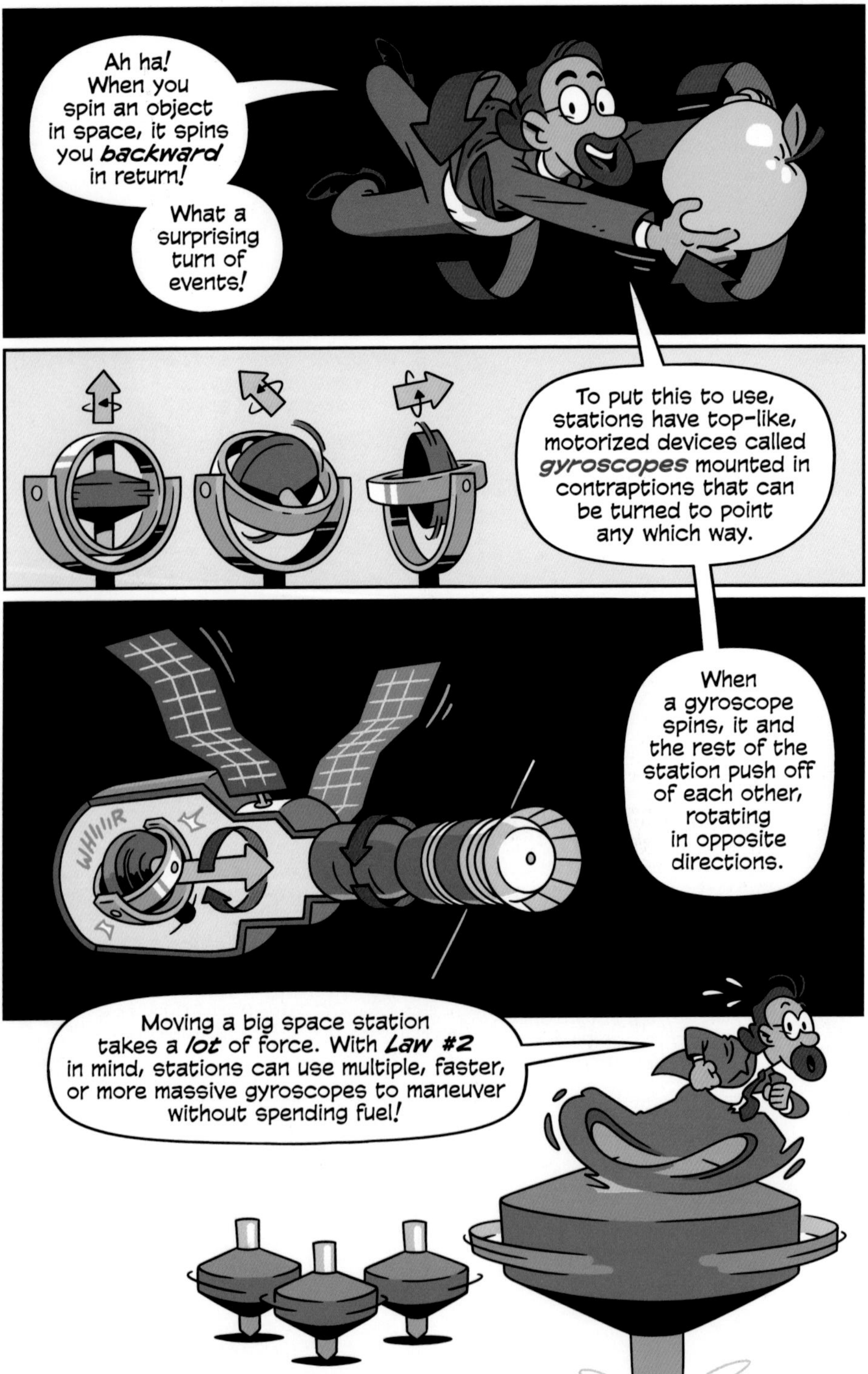
Ah ha! When you spin an object in space, it spins you *backward* in return!
What a surprising turn of events!
To put this to use, stations have top-like, motorized devices called *gyroscopes* mounted in contraptions that can be turned to point any which way.
When a gyroscope spins, it and the rest of the station push off of each other, rotating in opposite directions.
WHIIIRR
Moving a big space station takes a *lot* of force. With *Law #2* in mind, stations can use multiple, faster, or more massive gyroscopes to maneuver without spending fuel!

Gyroscopes need electricity to keep spinning, and solar panels depend on gyroscopes to point them toward the sun! They're both *essential* to a space station.

Even so, a station won't stay in orbit forever. This Salyut is very high up, but it's still within Earth's thermosphere.

The air is so, so, so thin, causing so, so, so little friction, but it all adds up!

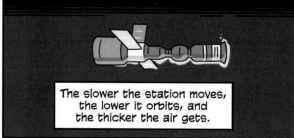

The slower the station moves, the lower it orbits, and the thicker the air gets.

The thicker the air, the more friction there is, and on and on until...uh-oh.

Salyuts have thrusters but only so much fuel.

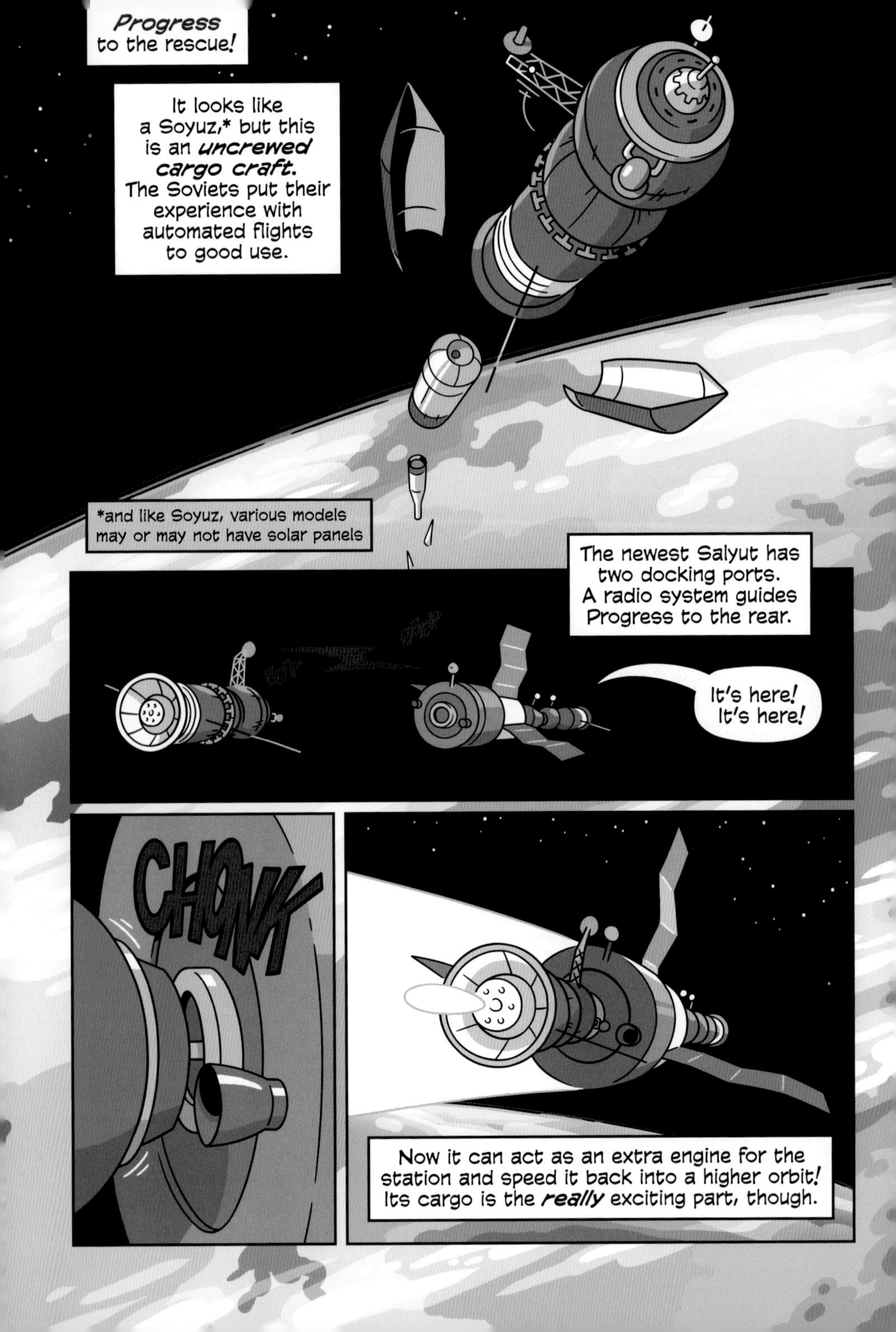

Progress to the rescue!
It looks like a Soyuz,* but this is an ***uncrewed cargo craft.*** The Soviets put their experience with automated flights to good use.
*and like Soyuz, various models may or may not have solar panels
The newest Salyut has two docking ports. A radio system guides Progress to the rear.
It's here! It's here!
CHONK
Now it can act as an extra engine for the station and speed it back into a higher orbit! Its cargo is the ***really*** exciting part, though.

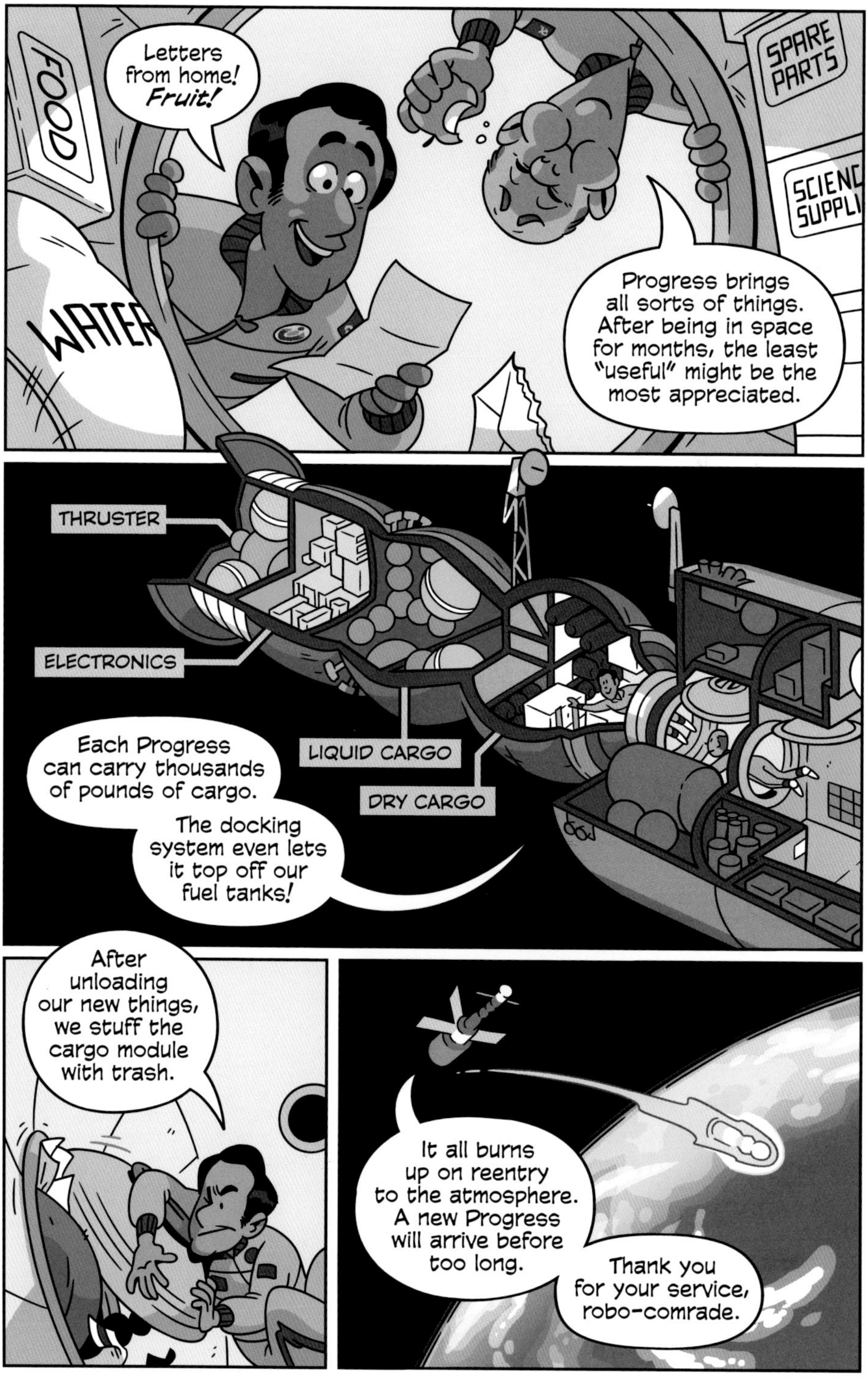
FOOD
Letters from home! *Fruit!*
SPARE PARTS
SCIENC SUPPLI
WATER
Progress brings all sorts of things. After being in space for months, the least "useful" might be the most appreciated.
THRUSTER
ELECTRONICS
LIQUID CARGO
DRY CARGO
Each Progress can carry thousands of pounds of cargo.
The docking system even lets it top off our fuel tanks!
After unloading our new things, we stuff the cargo module with trash.
It all burns up on reentry to the atmosphere. A new Progress will arrive before too long.
Thank you for your service, robo-comrade.

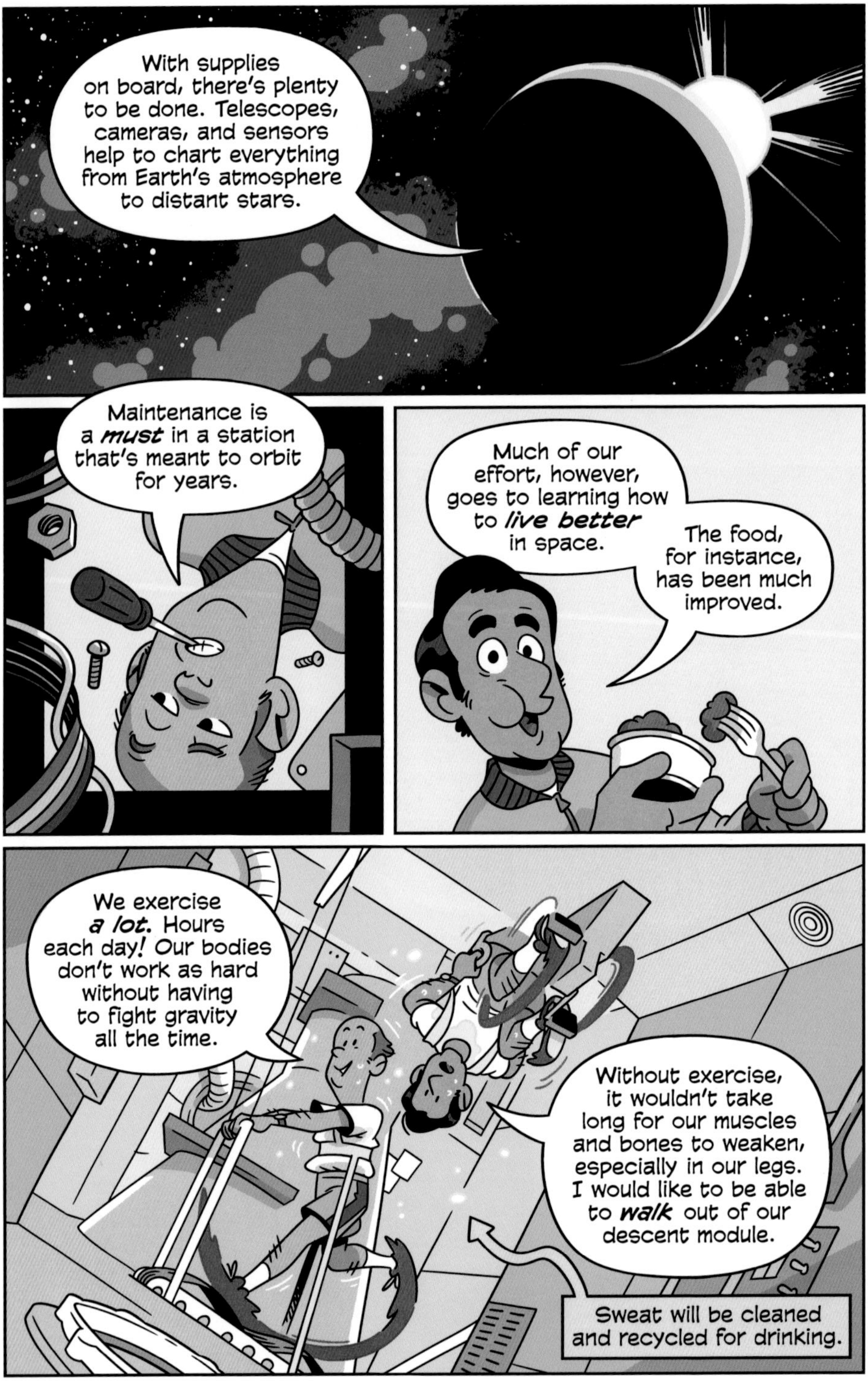

With supplies on board, there's plenty to be done. Telescopes, cameras, and sensors help to chart everything from Earth's atmosphere to distant stars.
Maintenance is a *must* in a station that's meant to orbit for years.
Much of our effort, however, goes to learning how to *live better* in space.
The food, for instance, has been much improved.
We exercise *a lot.* Hours each day! Our bodies don't work as hard without having to fight gravity all the time.
Without exercise, it wouldn't take long for our muscles and bones to weaken, especially in our legs. I would like to be able to *walk* out of our descent module.
Sweat will be cleaned and recycled for drinking.

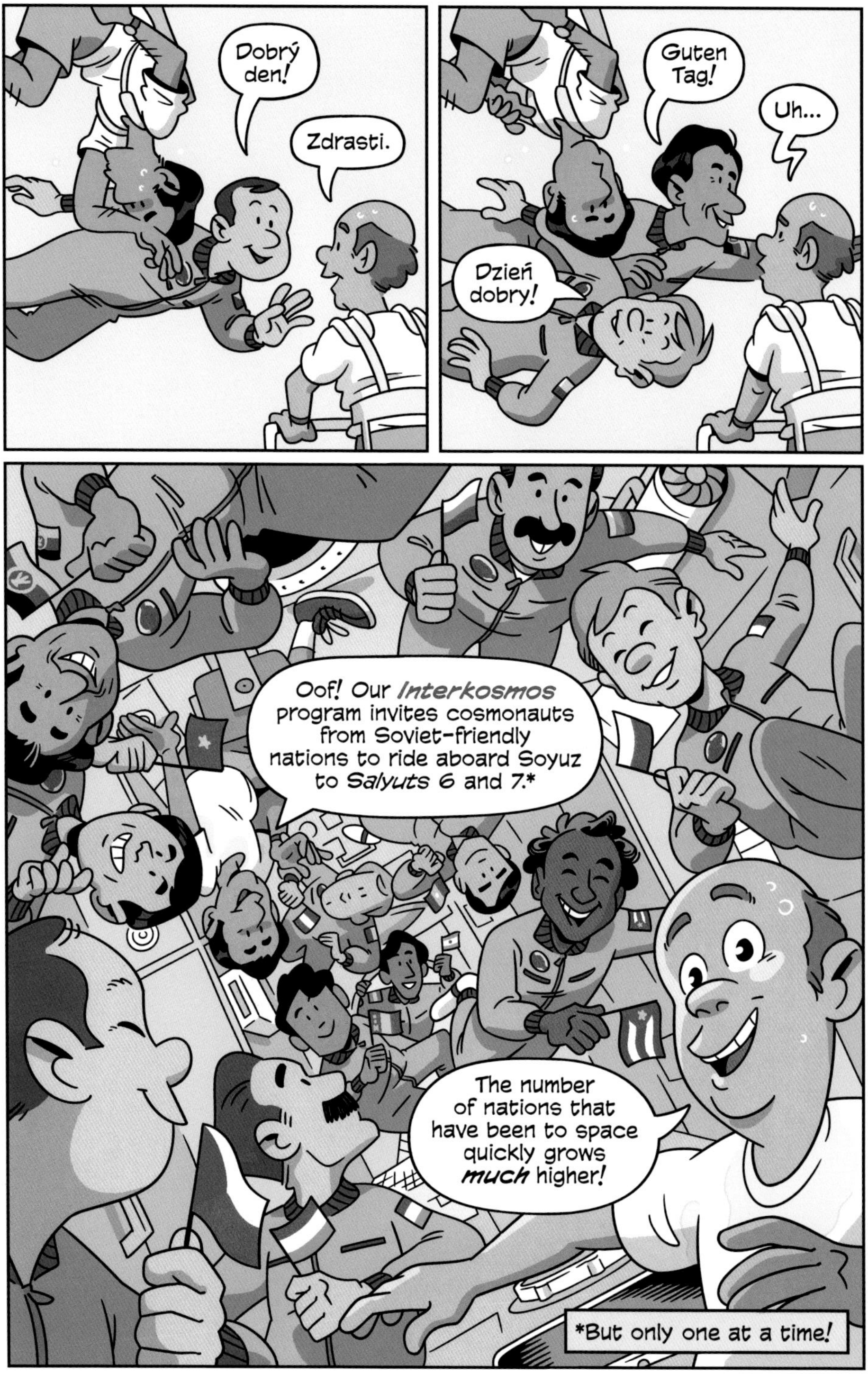
Dobrý den!
Zdrasti.
Guten Tag!
Uh...
Dzień dobry!
Oof! Our *Interkosmos* program invites cosmonauts from Soviet-friendly nations to ride aboard Soyuz to *Salyuts* 6 and 7.*
The number of nations that have been to space quickly grows ***much*** higher!
*But only one at a time!

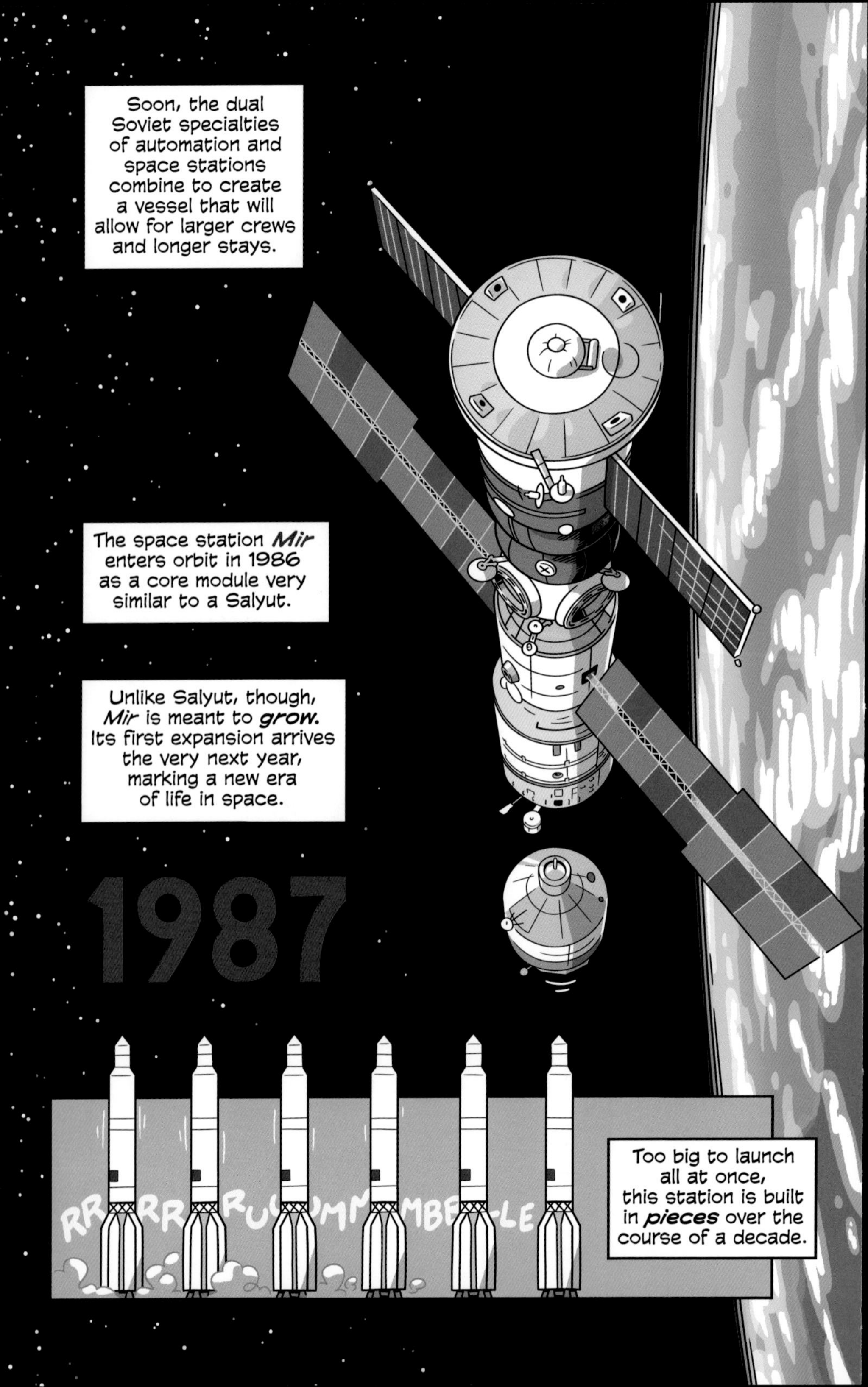
Soon, the dual Soviet specialties of automation and space stations combine to create a vessel that will allow for larger crews and longer stays.
The space station *Mir* enters orbit in 1986 as a core module very similar to a Salyut.
Unlike Salyut, though, *Mir* is meant to ***grow.*** Its first expansion arrives the very next year, marking a new era of life in space.
1987
RRRRRRUUMMMMBBLE-LE
Too big to launch all at once, this station is built in ***pieces*** over the course of a decade.

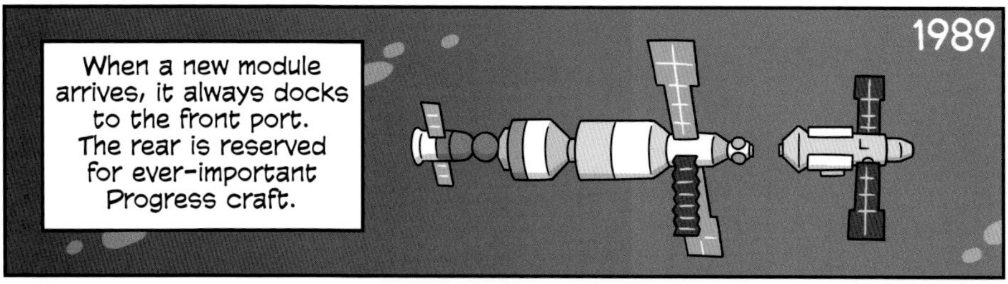
1989
When a new module arrives, it always docks to the front port. The rear is reserved for ever-important Progress craft.

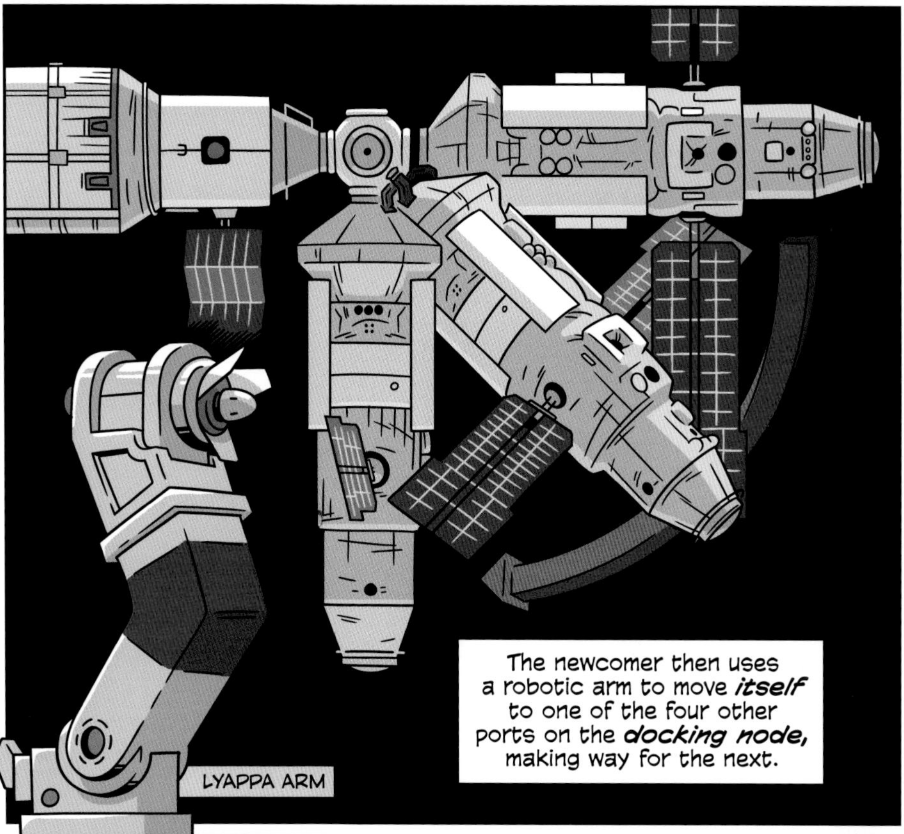
LYAPPA ARM
The newcomer then uses a robotic arm to move *itself* to one of the four other ports on the *docking node,* making way for the next.

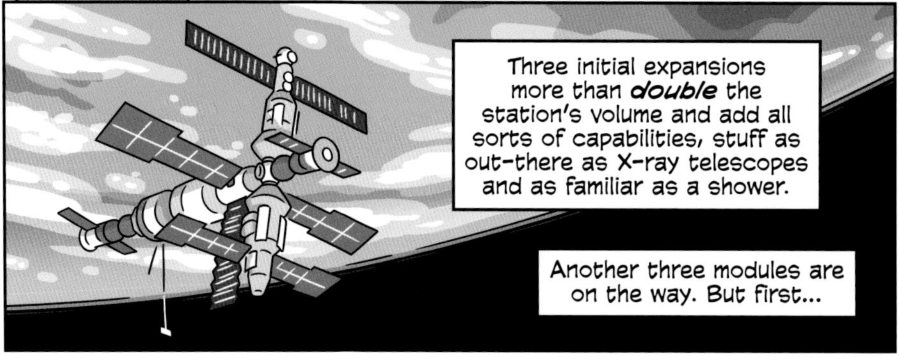
Three initial expansions more than *double* the station's volume and add all sorts of capabilities, stuff as out-there as X-ray telescopes and as familiar as a shower.
Another three modules are on the way. But first...

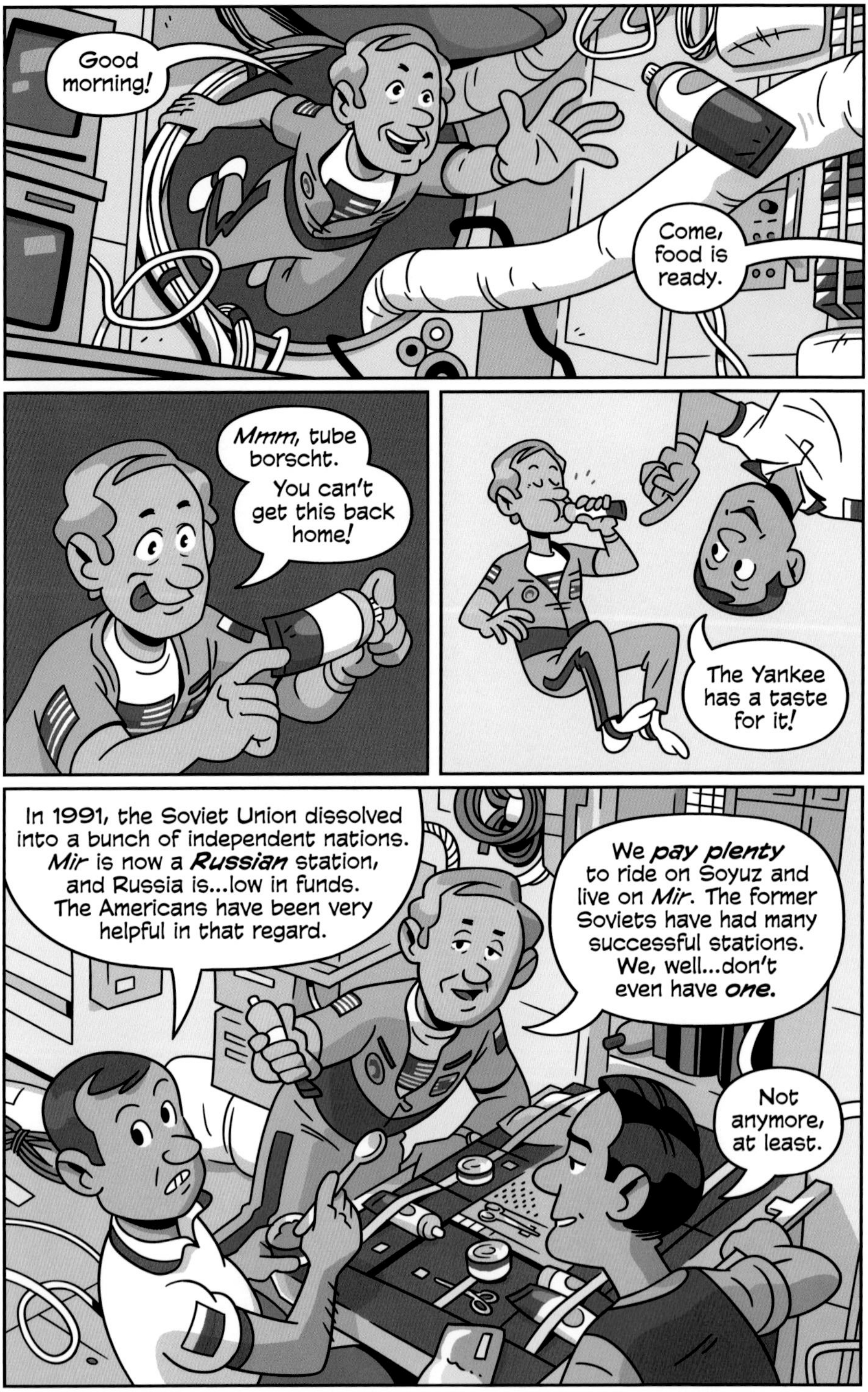
Good morning!
Come, food is ready.
Mmm, tube borscht.
You can't get this back home!
The Yankee has a taste for it!
In 1991, the Soviet Union dissolved into a bunch of independent nations. *Mir* is now a ***Russian*** station, and Russia is...low in funds. The Americans have been very helpful in that regard.
We ***pay plenty*** to ride on Soyuz and live on *Mir*. The former Soviets have had many successful stations. We, well...don't even have ***one.***
Not anymore, at least.

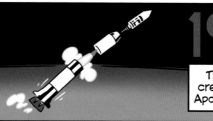

Ah, *Skylab*. Launched shortly after *Salyut 2*, it was made out of the third stage of the last remaining Saturn V rocket.

1973

That's some creative use of Apollo leftovers!

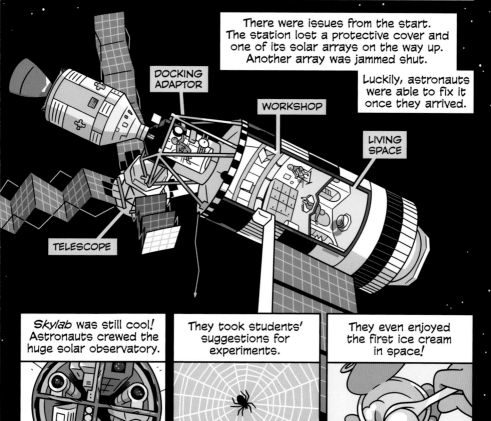

There were issues from the start. The station lost a protective cover and one of its solar arrays on the way up. Another array was jammed shut.

Luckily, astronauts were able to fix it once they arrived.

DOCKING ADAPTOR

WORKSHOP

LIVING SPACE

TELESCOPE

Skylab was still *cool!* Astronauts crewed the huge solar observatory.

They took students' suggestions for experiments.

They even enjoyed the first ice cream in space!

Because the US was behind schedule on building new craft to resupply and boost it, though, the station only hosted three missions before being abandoned and left to *deorbit*.

It was so big that it didn't burn up entirely. Luckily, no one got hurt.

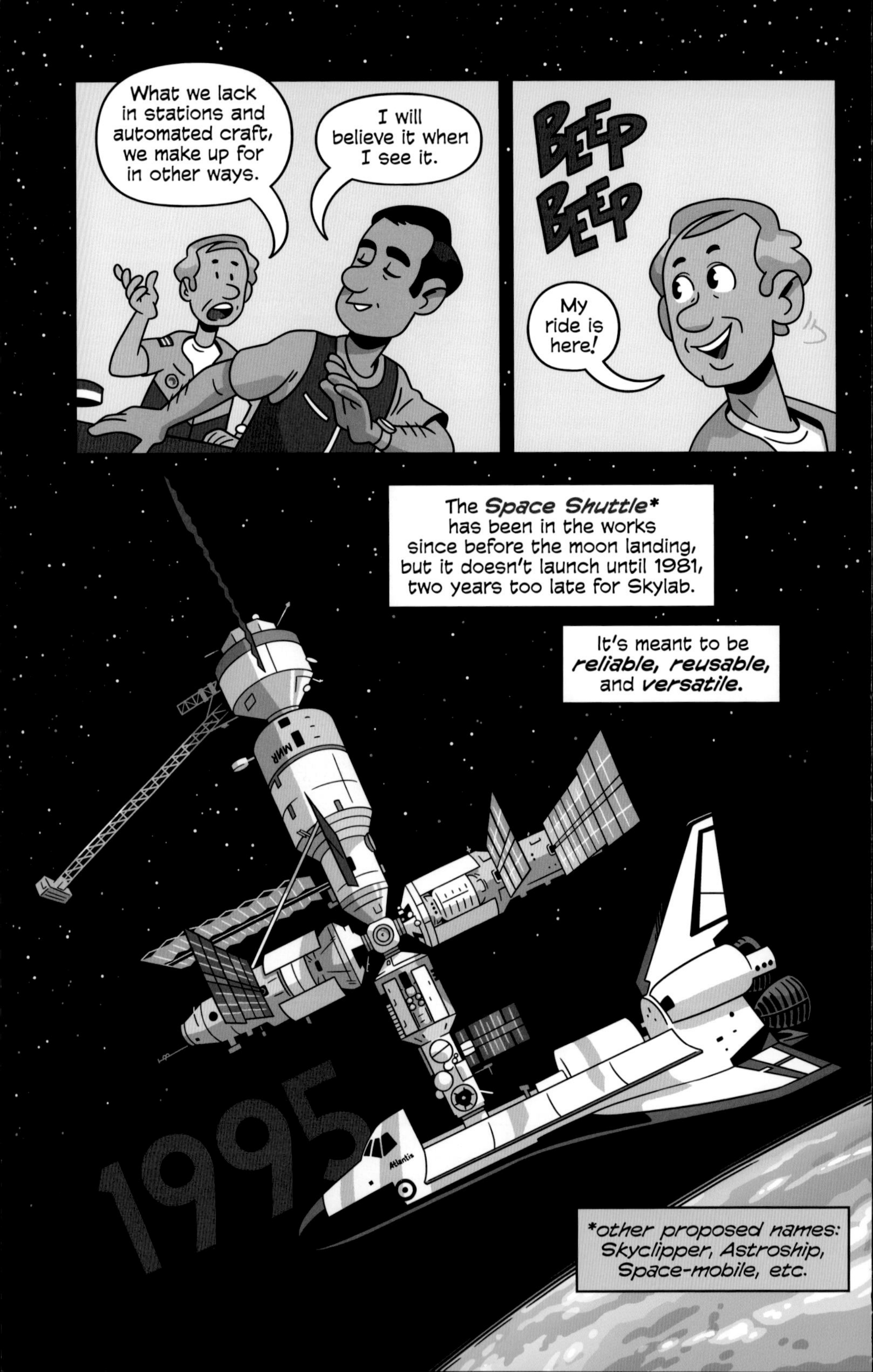
What we lack in stations and automated craft, we make up for in other ways.
I will believe it when I see it.
BEEP BEEP
My ride is here!
The *Space Shuttle** has been in the works since before the moon landing, but it doesn't launch until 1981, two years too late for Skylab.
It's meant to be ***reliable, reusable,*** and ***versatile.***
MIR
1995
Atlantis
*other proposed names: Skyclipper, Astroship, Space-mobile, etc.

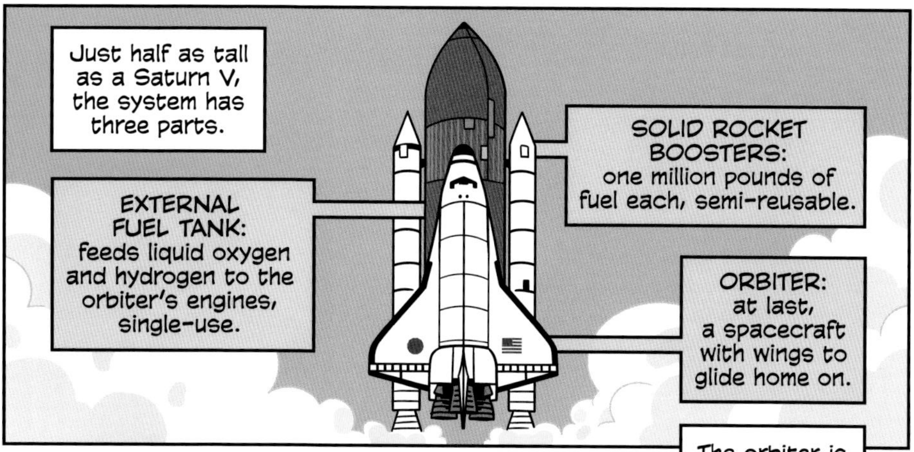
Just half as tall as a Saturn V, the system has three parts.
EXTERNAL FUEL TANK: feeds liquid oxygen and hydrogen to the orbiter's engines, single-use.
SOLID ROCKET BOOSTERS: one million pounds of fuel each, semi-reusable.
ORBITER: at last, a spacecraft with wings to glide home on.

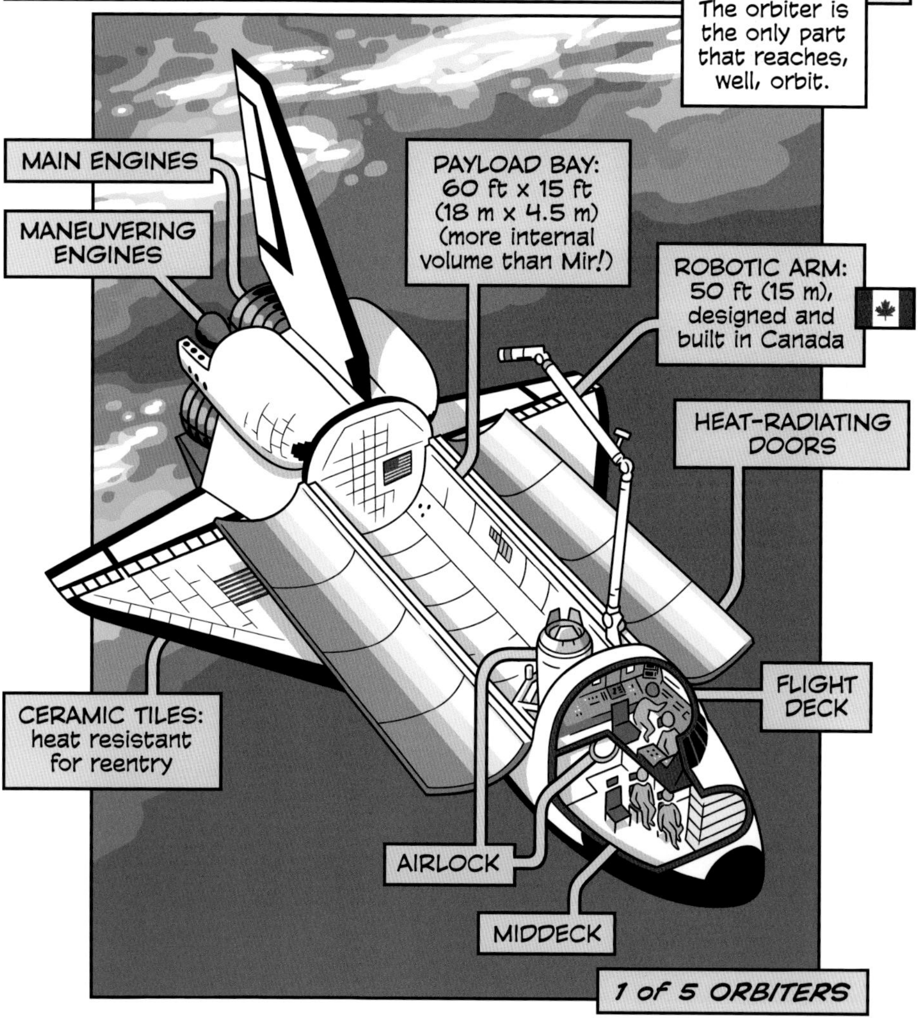
The orbiter is the only part that reaches, well, orbit.
MAIN ENGINES
MANEUVERING ENGINES
PAYLOAD BAY: 60 ft x 15 ft (18 m x 4.5 m) (more internal volume than Mir!)
ROBOTIC ARM: 50 ft (15 m), designed and built in Canada
HEAT-RADIATING DOORS
CERAMIC TILES: heat resistant for reentry
FLIGHT DECK
AIRLOCK
MIDDECK
1 of 5 ORBITERS

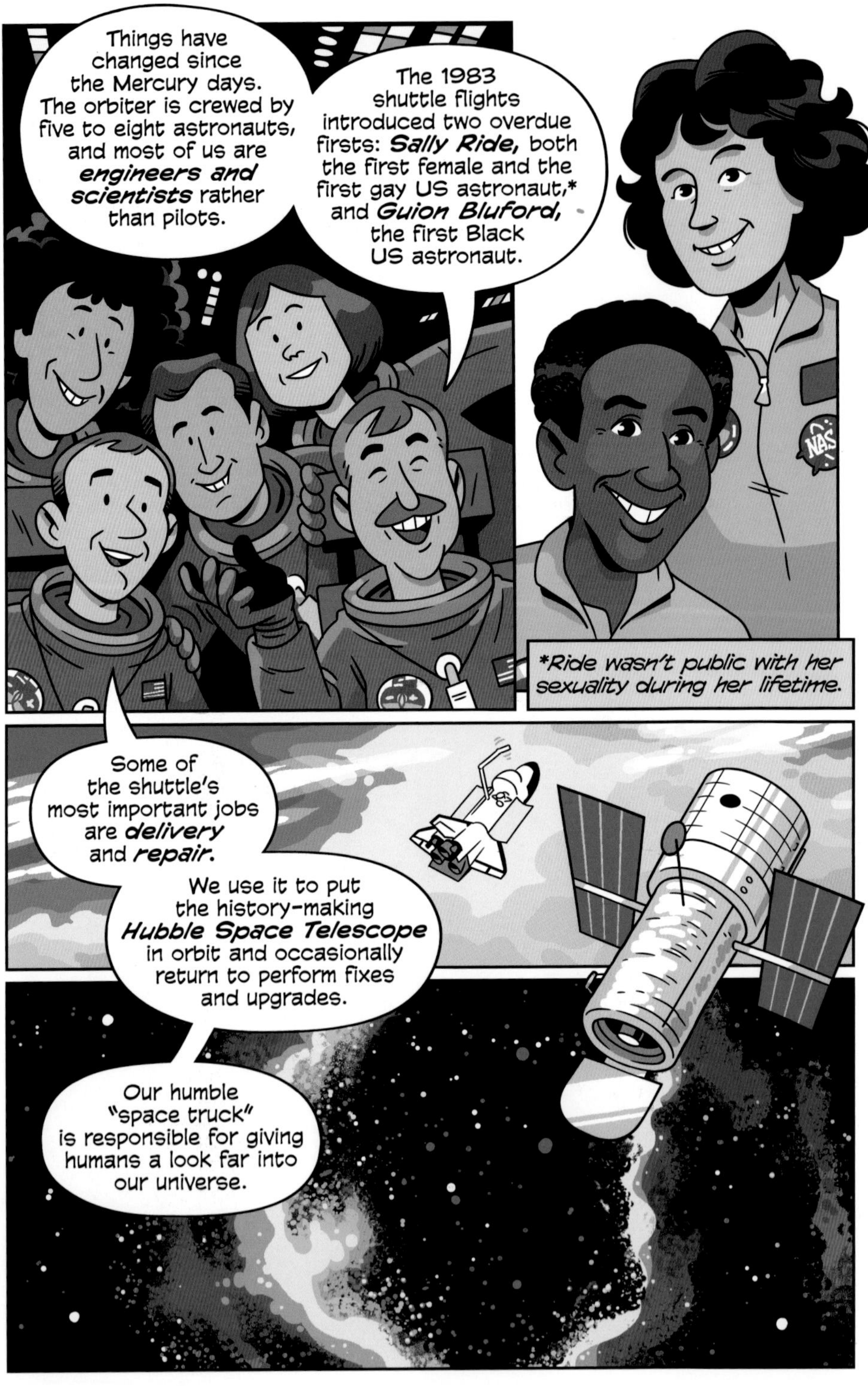
Things have changed since the Mercury days. The orbiter is crewed by five to eight astronauts, and most of us are *engineers and scientists* rather than pilots.
The 1983 shuttle flights introduced two overdue firsts: *Sally Ride,* both the first female and the first gay US astronaut,* and *Guion Bluford,* the first Black US astronaut.
Ride wasn't public with her sexuality during her lifetime.
NASA
Some of the shuttle's most important jobs are *delivery* and *repair.*
We use it to put the history-making *Hubble Space Telescope* in orbit and occasionally return to perform fixes and upgrades.
Our humble "space truck" is responsible for giving humans a look far into our universe.

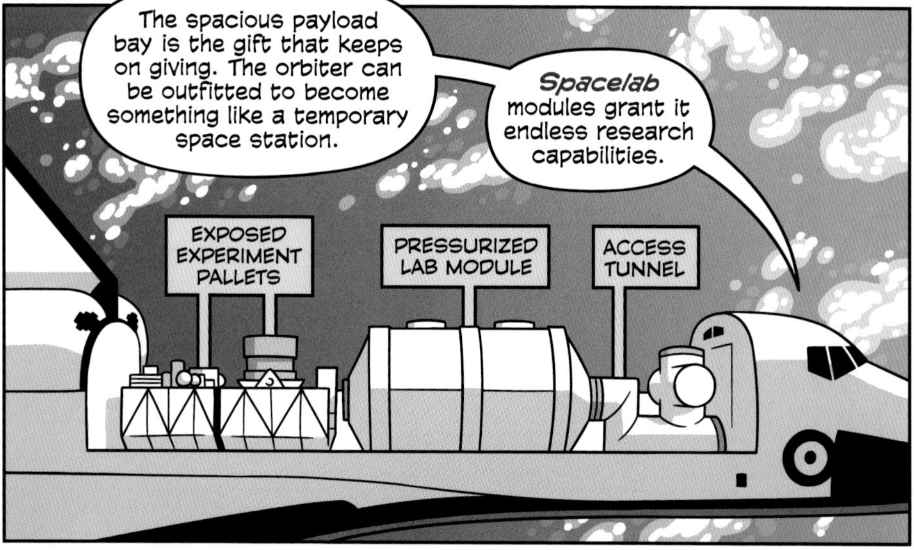
The spacious payload bay is the gift that keeps on giving. The orbiter can be outfitted to become something like a temporary space station.
Spacelab modules grant it endless research capabilities.
EXPOSED EXPERIMENT PALLETS
PRESSURIZED LAB MODULE
ACCESS TUNNEL

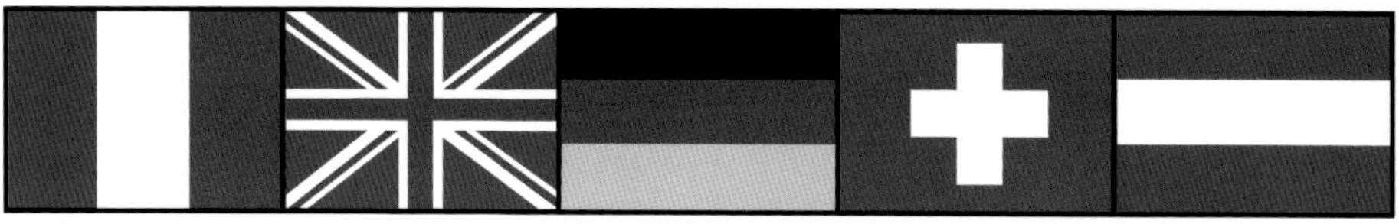

It's an international effort alongside the growing ***European Space Agency.*** Between Spacelab and Interkosmos, dozens of nations now participate in space.

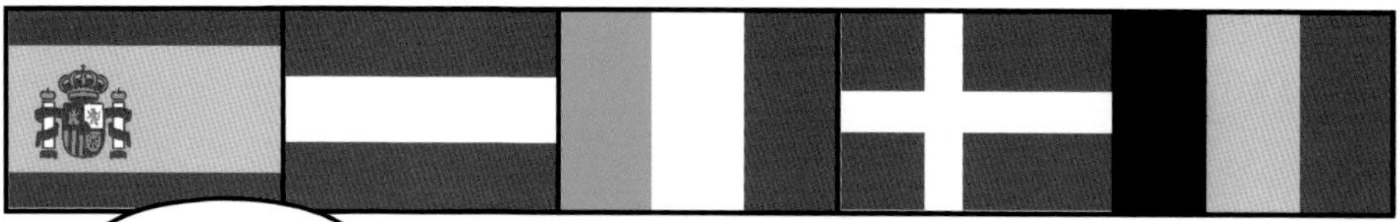

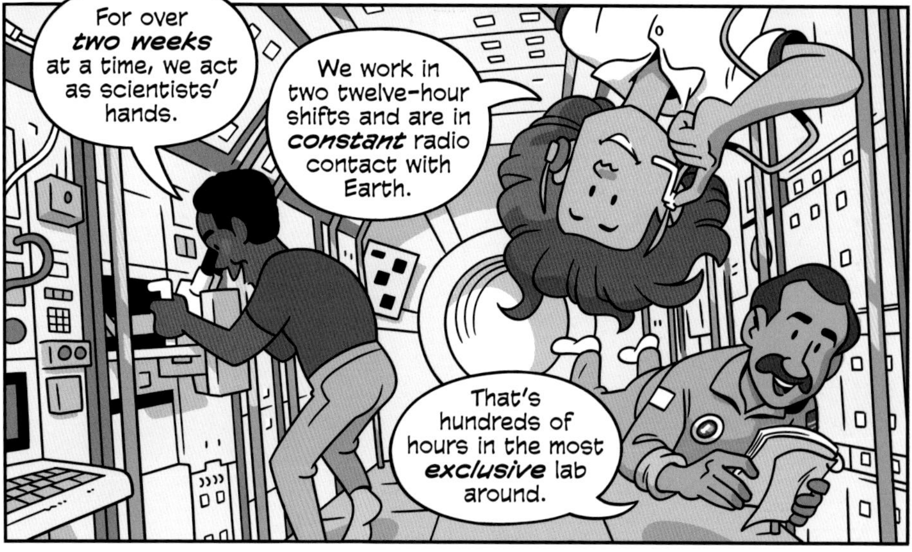
For over ***two weeks*** at a time, we act as scientists' hands.
We work in two twelve-hour shifts and are in ***constant*** radio contact with Earth.
That's hundreds of hours in the most ***exclusive*** lab around.

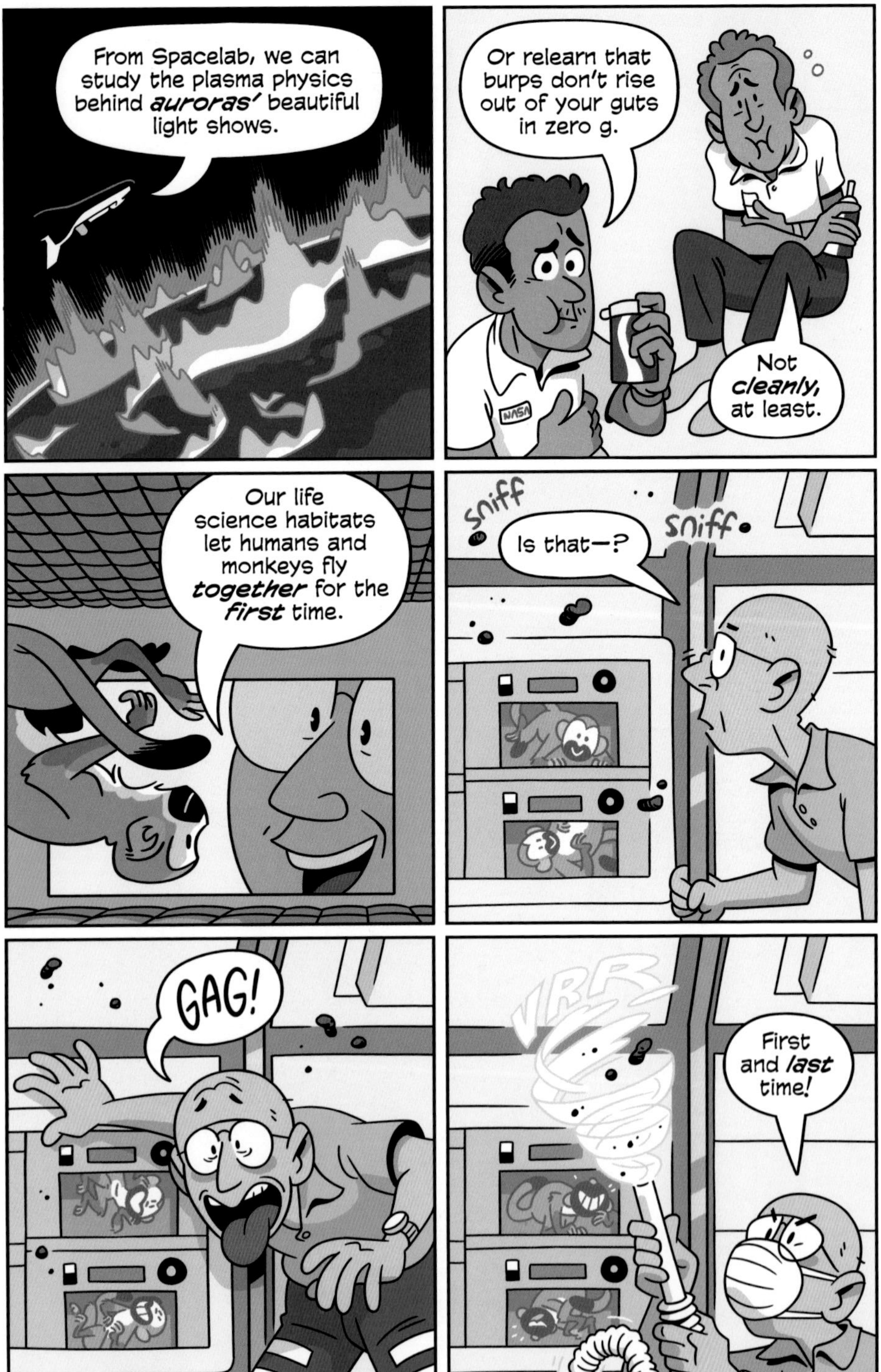
From Spacelab, we can study the plasma physics behind *auroras'* beautiful light shows.
Or relearn that burps don't rise out of your guts in zero g.
Not *cleanly,* at least.
NASA
Our life science habitats let humans and monkeys fly *together* for the *first* time.
sniff
Is that—?
sniff
GAG!
VRR-
First and *last* time!

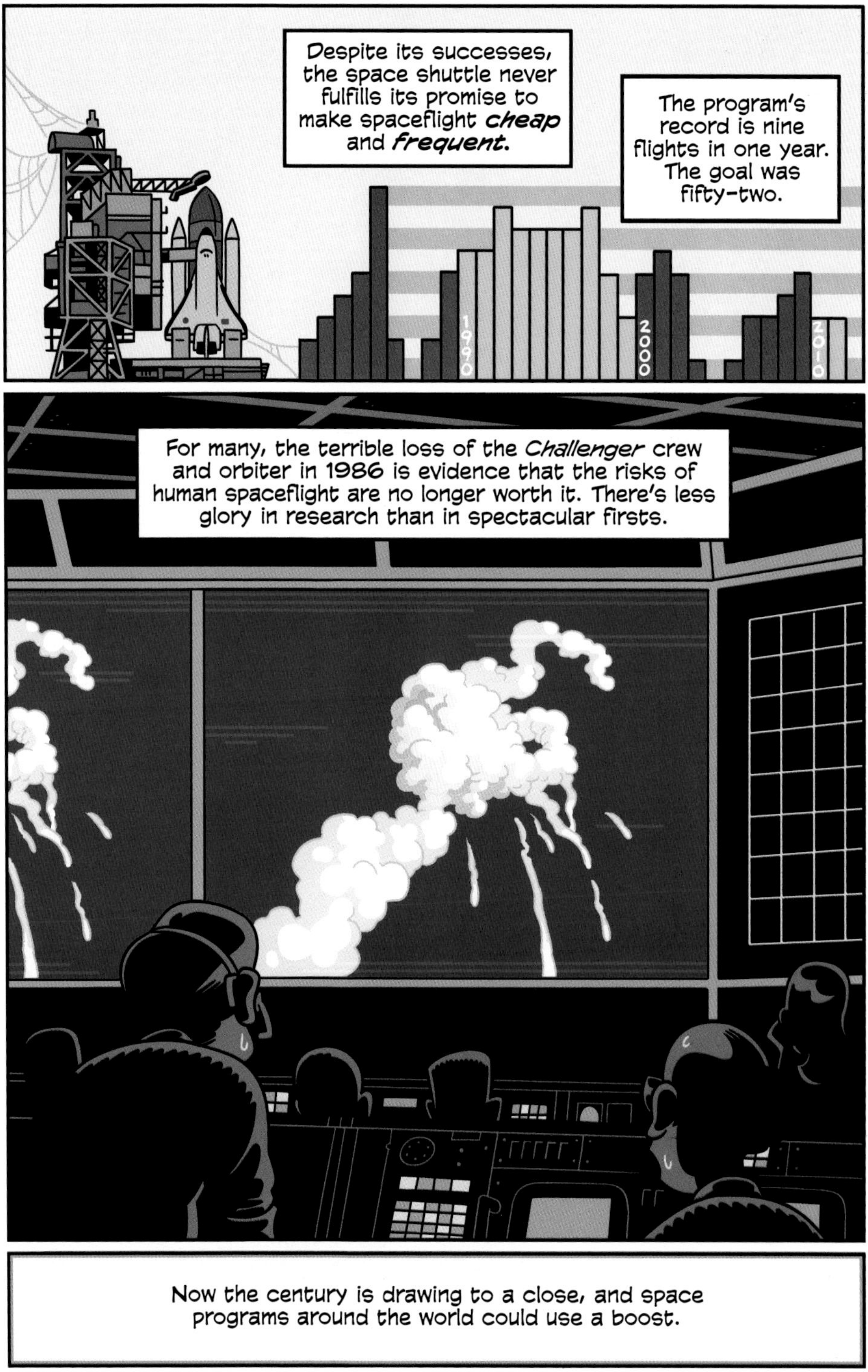
Despite its successes, the space shuttle never fulfills its promise to make spaceflight *cheap* and *frequent*.
The program's record is nine flights in one year. The goal was fifty-two.
1990
2000
2010
For many, the terrible loss of the *Challenger* crew and orbiter in 1986 is evidence that the risks of human spaceflight are no longer worth it. There's less glory in research than in spectacular firsts.
Now the century is drawing to a close, and space programs around the world could use a boost.

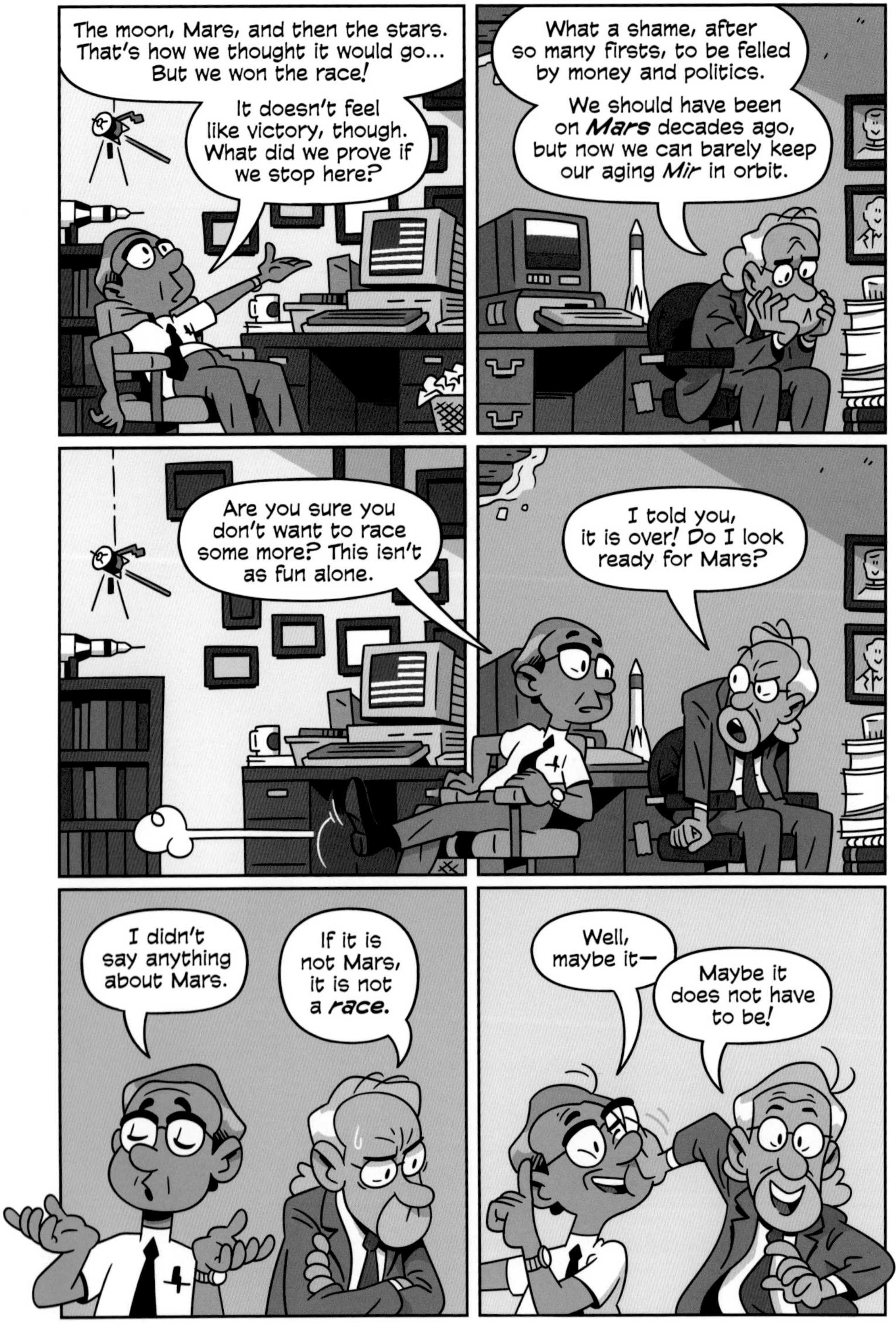

The moon, Mars, and then the stars. That's how we thought it would go... But we won the race!
It doesn't feel like victory, though. What did we prove if we stop here?
What a shame, after so many firsts, to be felled by money and politics.
We should have been on *Mars* decades ago, but now we can barely keep our aging *Mir* in orbit.
Are you sure you don't want to race some more? This isn't as fun alone.
I told you, it is over! Do I look ready for Mars?
I didn't say anything about Mars.
If it is not Mars, it is not a *race*.
Well, maybe it—
Maybe it does not have to be!

The US and Russia, the same nations that competed over rockets to obliterate one another, will combine their resources and know-how to *partner* on an ambitious new space station dedicated to scientific research. Neither could build it alone.

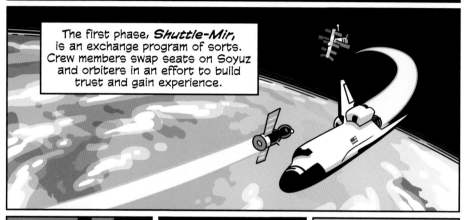

The first phase, *Shuttle-Mir,* is an exchange program of sorts. Crew members swap seats on Soyuz and orbiters in an effort to build trust and gain experience.

It doesn't always go smoothly, to say the least.

But gravity must have a strong hold on national differences.

Friendships grow quickly in space.

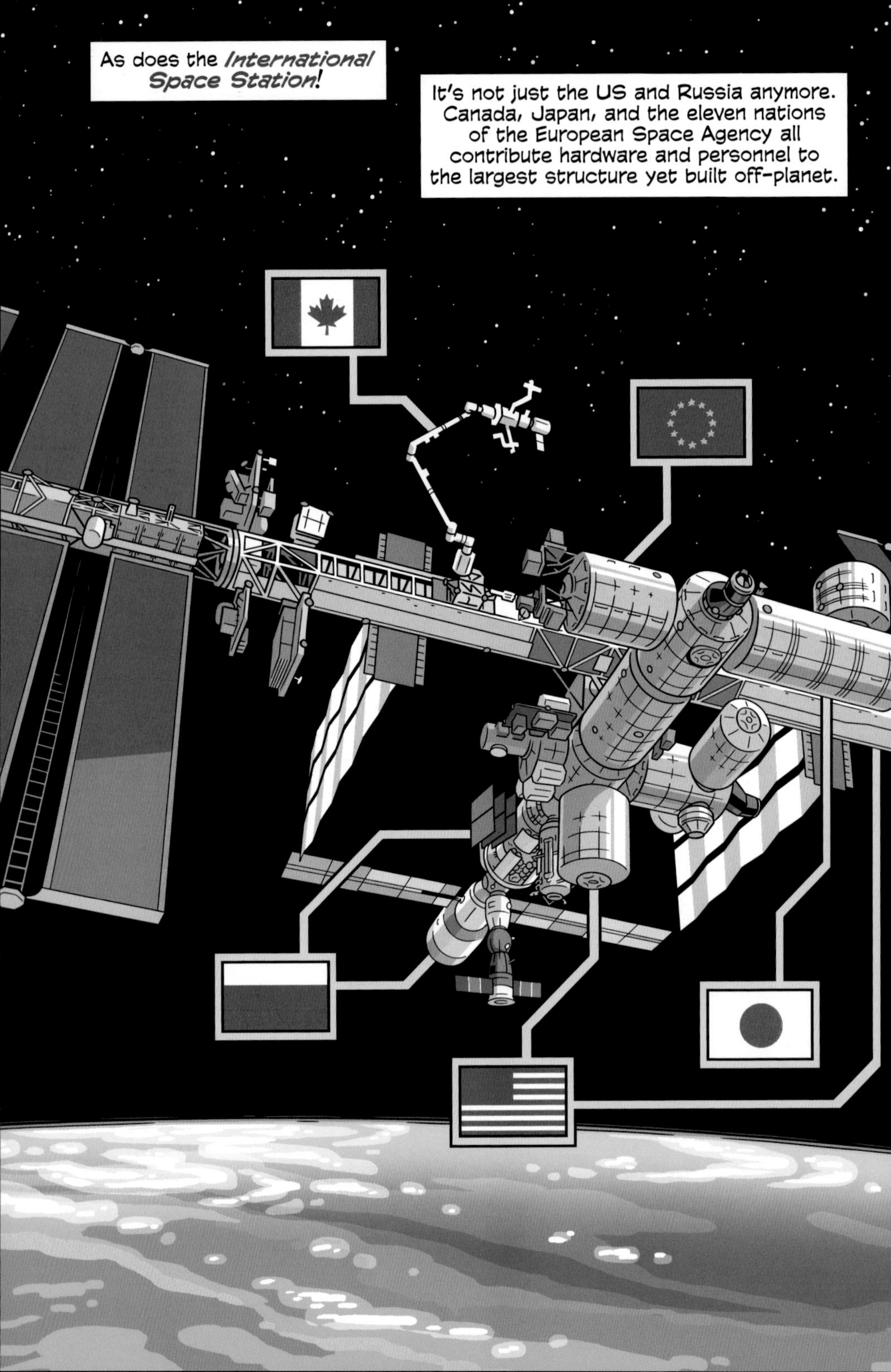
As does the *International Space Station*!
It's not just the US and Russia anymore. Canada, Japan, and the eleven nations of the European Space Agency all contribute hardware and personnel to the largest structure yet built off-planet.

2015

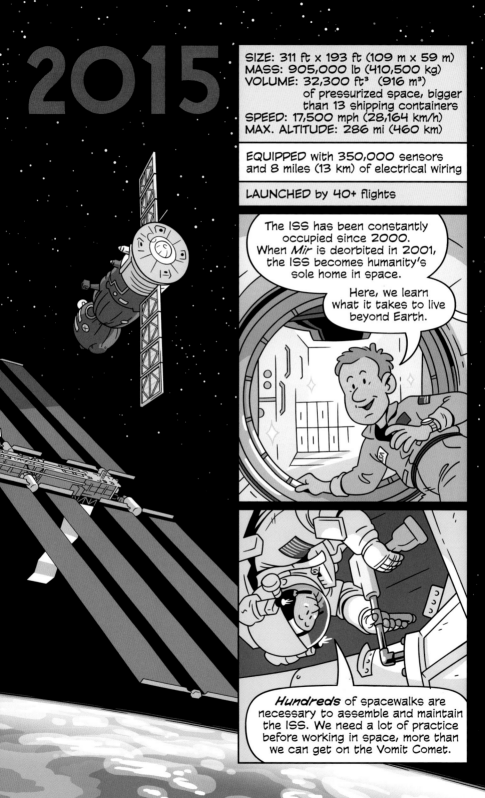

SIZE: 311 ft x 193 ft (109 m x 59 m)
MASS: 905,000 lb (410,500 kg)
VOLUME: 32,300 ft³ (916 m³)
of pressurized space, bigger
than 13 shipping containers
SPEED: 17,500 mph (28,164 km/h)
MAX. ALTITUDE: 286 mi (460 km)

EQUIPPED with 350,000 sensors
and 8 miles (13 km) of electrical wiring

LAUNCHED by 40+ flights

The ISS has been constantly occupied since 2000. When *Mir* is deorbited in 2001, the ISS becomes humanity's sole home in space.

Here, we learn what it takes to live beyond Earth.

Hundreds of spacewalks are necessary to assemble and maintain the ISS. We need a lot of practice before working in space, more than we can get on the Vomit Comet.

Welcome to the *Neutral Buoyancy Lab*, a 6.2-million-gallon (23.5-million-liter) pool filled with full-scale replicas of ISS modules! Even *this* place can't hold the whole station at once.
Whoops! A space suit is full of air, right? It should *float* in water.
We add extra weights until it's too heavy to float, but too light to sink: ***neutrally buoyant.***
It's pretty close to working in space, even though my body still feels gravity.
I train with ***four scuba divers.*** One to swap my neutrally buoyant practice tools and my heavy real ones, two to save me if I spring a leak, and another to film the whole thing.
You've gotta see the blooper reel.

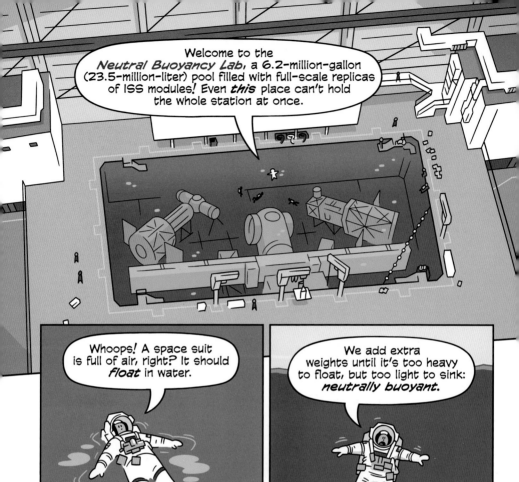

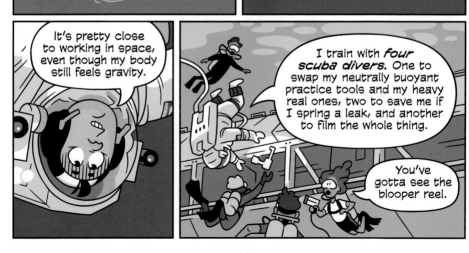

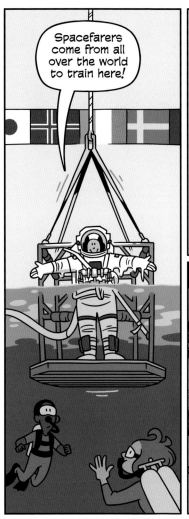

Spacefarers come from all over the world to train here!

Ciao!

Konnichiwa!

Hello!

Virtual reality is another great training tool. Spacewalking is dangerous, and you want to be as prepared as you can.

Let me try this.

≥Hrmf!≤

donk donk

Never mind.

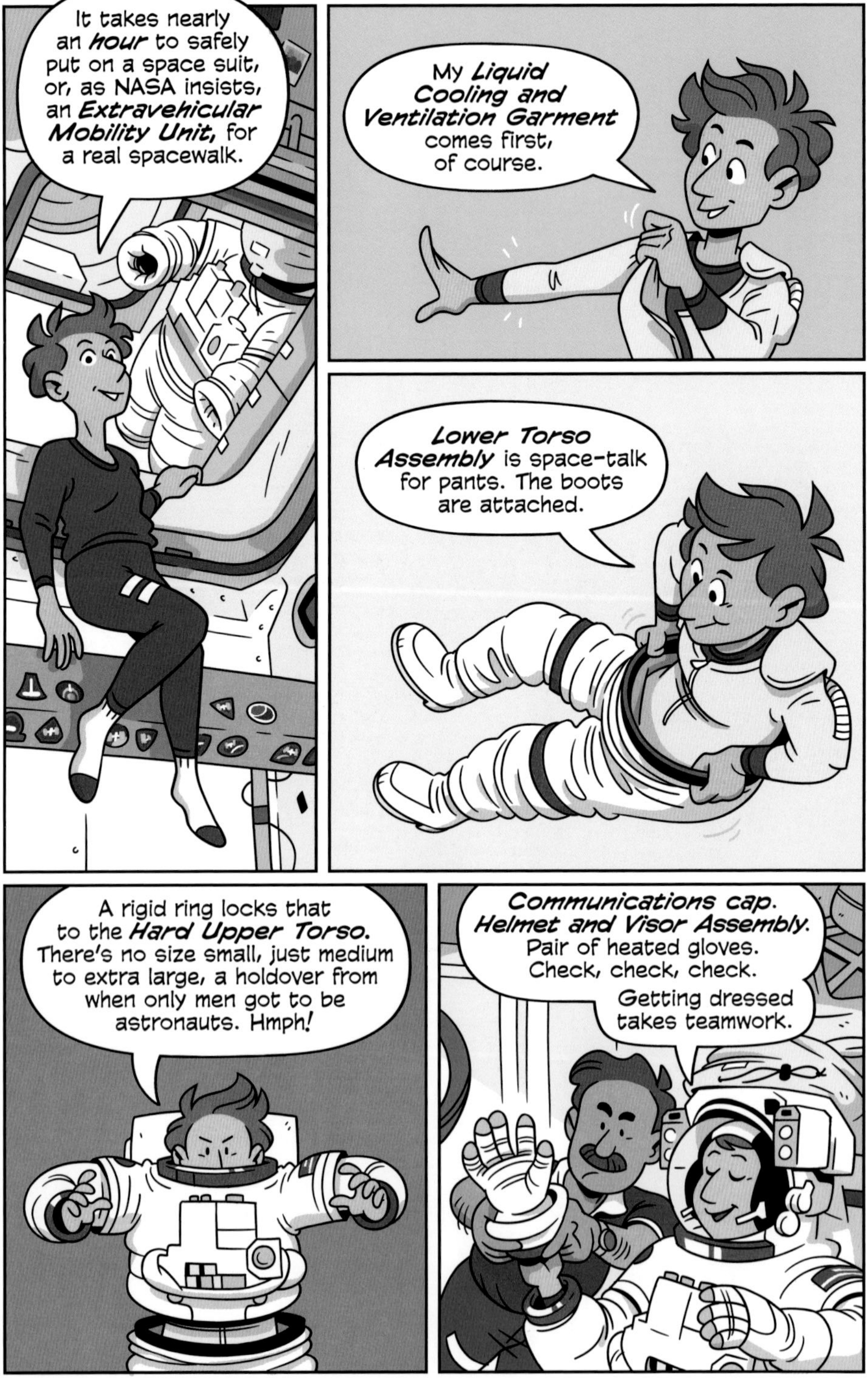
It takes nearly an *hour* to safely put on a space suit, or, as NASA insists, an ***Extravehicular Mobility Unit,*** for a real spacewalk.
My ***Liquid Cooling and Ventilation Garment*** comes first, of course.
Lower Torso Assembly is space-talk for pants. The boots are attached.
A rigid ring locks that to the ***Hard Upper Torso.*** There's no size small, just medium to extra large, a holdover from when only men got to be astronauts. Hmph!
Communications cap. Helmet and Visor Assembly. Pair of heated gloves. Check, check, check.
Getting dressed takes teamwork.

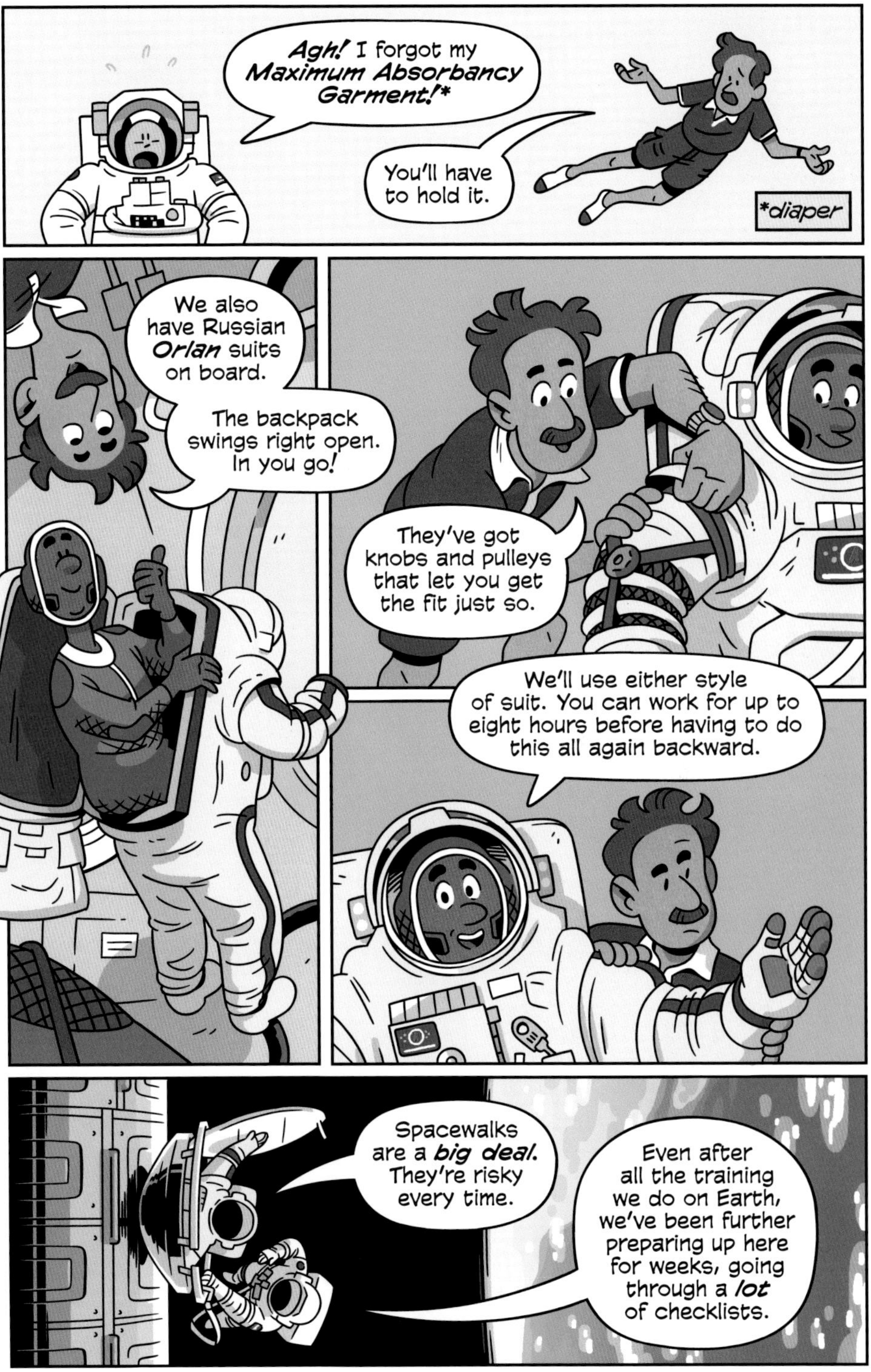

Agh! I forgot my ***Maximum Absorbancy Garment!****
You'll have to hold it.
*diaper
We also have Russian ***Orlan*** suits on board.
The backpack swings right open. In you go!
They've got knobs and pulleys that let you get the fit just so.
We'll use either style of suit. You can work for up to eight hours before having to do this all again backward.
Spacewalks are a ***big deal.*** They're risky every time.
Even after all the training we do on Earth, we've been further preparing up here for weeks, going through a ***lot*** of checklists.

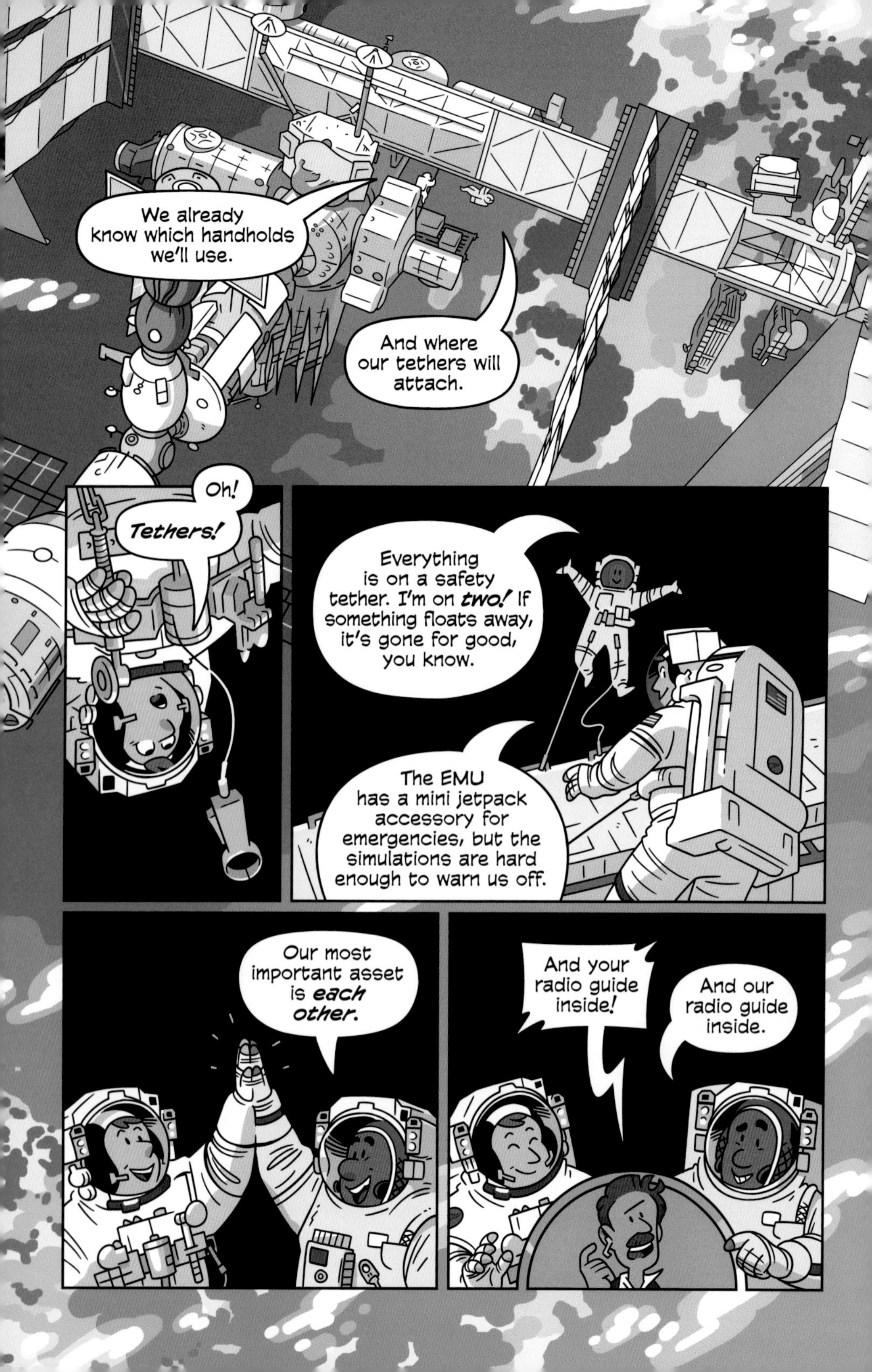
We already know which handholds we'll use.
And where our tethers will attach.
Oh!
Tethers!
Everything is on a safety tether. I'm on ***two!*** If something floats away, it's gone for good, you know.
The EMU has a mini jetpack accessory for emergencies, but the simulations are hard enough to warn us off.
Our most important asset is ***each other.***
And your radio guide inside!
And our radio guide inside.

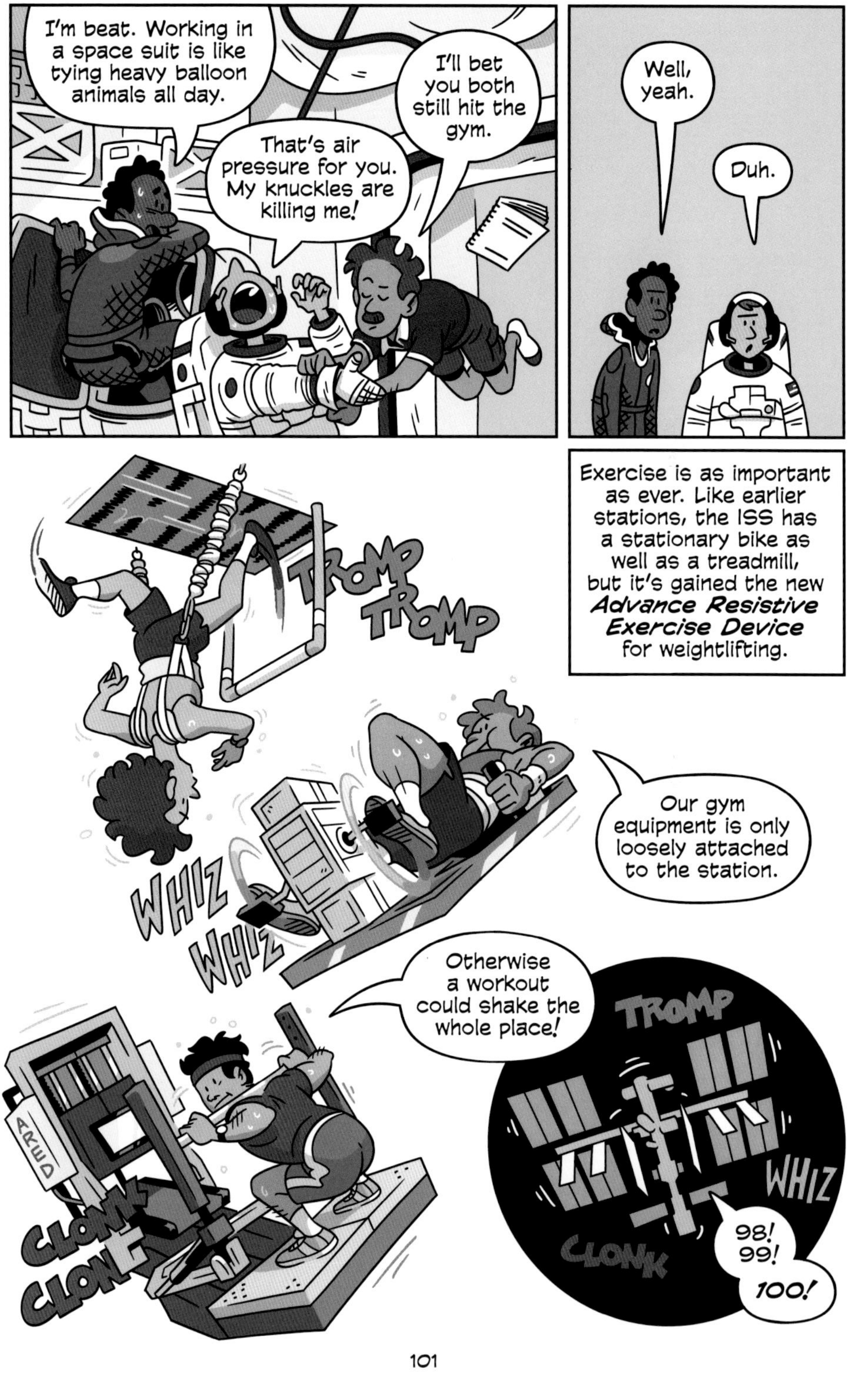

I'm beat. Working in a space suit is like tying heavy balloon animals all day.
That's air pressure for you. My knuckles are killing me!
I'll bet you both still hit the gym.
Well, yeah.
Duh.
Exercise is as important as ever. Like earlier stations, the ISS has a stationary bike as well as a treadmill, but it's gained the new *Advance Resistive Exercise Device* for weightlifting.
TROMP
TROMP
WHIZ
WHIZ
Our gym equipment is only loosely attached to the station.
Otherwise a workout could shake the whole place!
ARED
CLONK
CLONK
TROMP
WHIZ
CLONK
98!
99!
100!

Whew! You wouldn't expect astronauts to work out so much, would you? Time to unroll my *toiletry pouch* and clean up.

It's got the usual stuff. As with just about everything else on board, a little *Velcro* dot keeps items in place.

WATER

SOAP

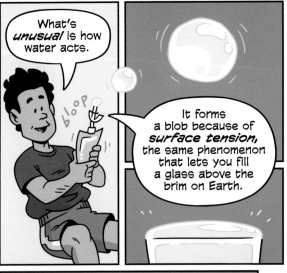

What's *unusual* is how water acts.

bloop

It forms a blob because of *surface tension*, the same phenomenon that lets you fill a glass above the brim on Earth.

This also makes it stick to whatever it lands on. I can add a squirt of soap and mix it in, or I can moisten a camp towel for a quick wipe-down.

Our no-rinse shampoo barely suds up, but it works.

≩sigh≩
I do miss running water.

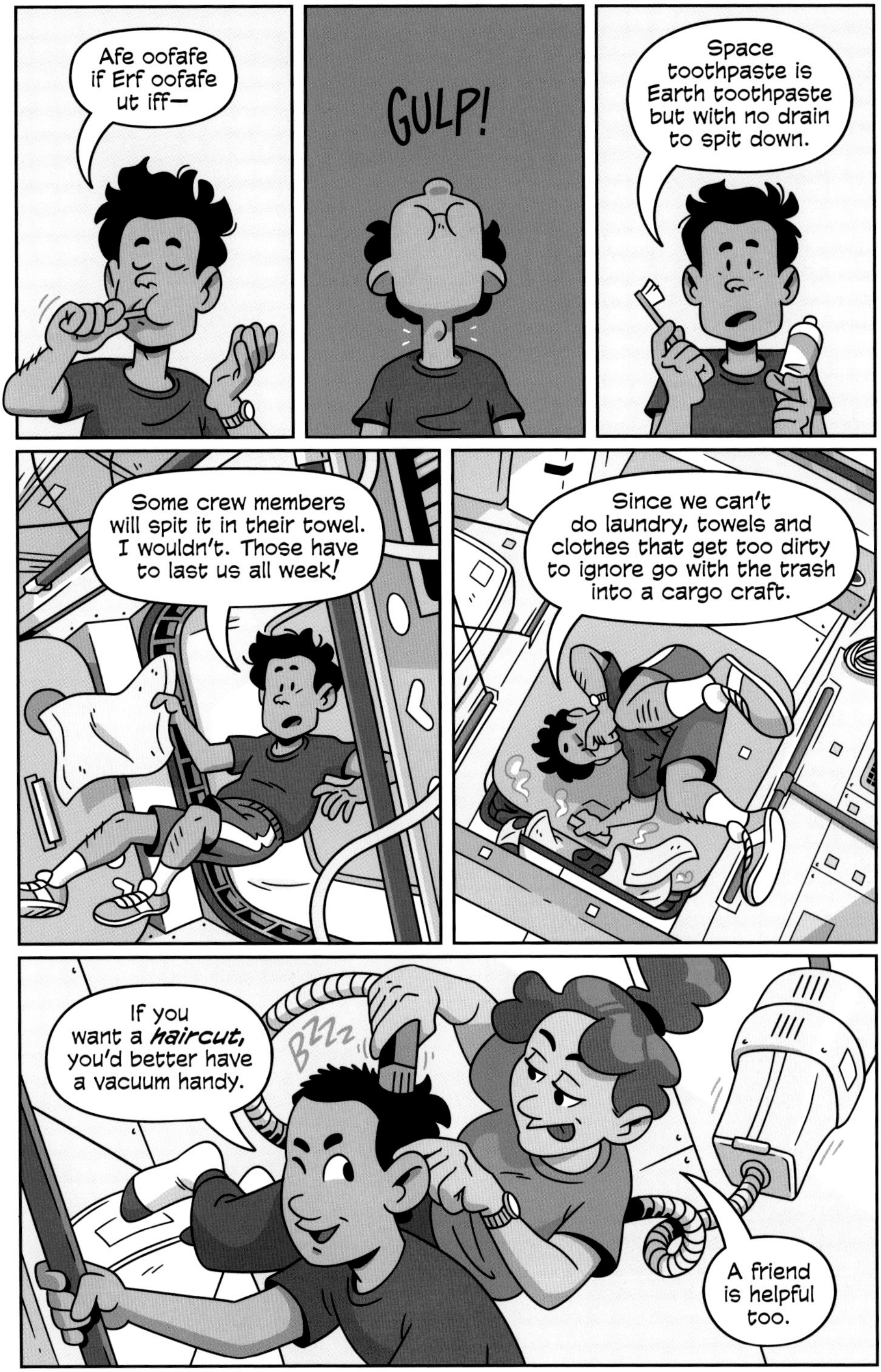
Afe oofafe if Erf oofafe ut iff—
GULP!
Space toothpaste is Earth toothpaste but with no drain to spit down.
Some crew members will spit it in their towel. I wouldn't. Those have to last us all week!
Since we can't do laundry, towels and clothes that get too dirty to ignore go with the trash into a cargo craft.
If you want a haircut, you'd better have a vacuum handy.
BZZz
A friend is helpful too.

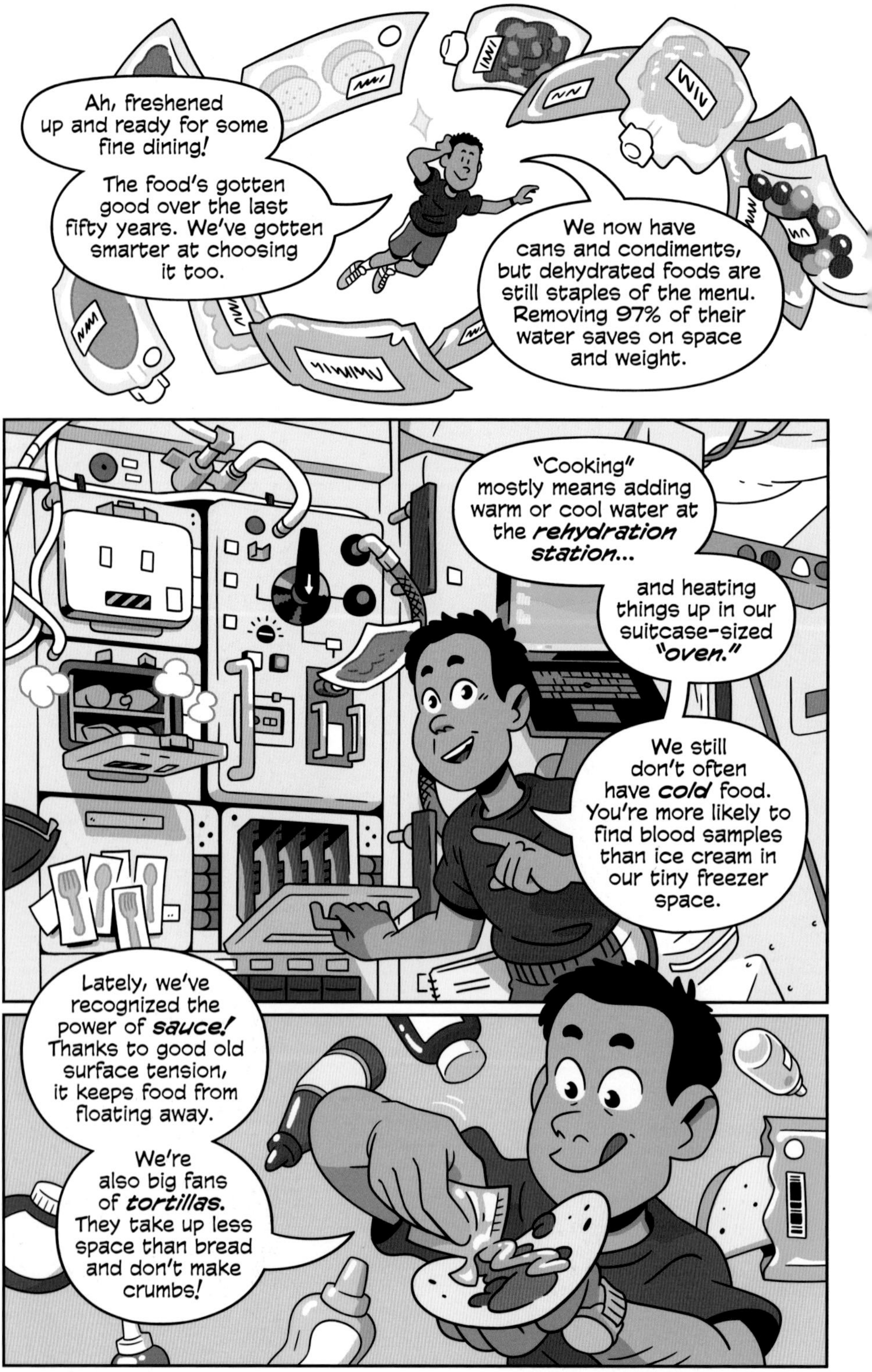
Ah, freshened up and ready for some fine dining!
The food's gotten good over the last fifty years. We've gotten smarter at choosing it too.
We now have cans and condiments, but dehydrated foods are still staples of the menu. Removing 97% of their water saves on space and weight.
"Cooking" mostly means adding warm or cool water at the ***rehydration station***...
and heating things up in our suitcase-sized ***"oven."***
We still don't often have ***cold*** food. You're more likely to find blood samples than ice cream in our tiny freezer space.
Lately, we've recognized the power of ***sauce!*** Thanks to good old surface tension, it keeps food from floating away.
We're also big fans of ***tortillas.*** They take up less space than bread and don't make crumbs!

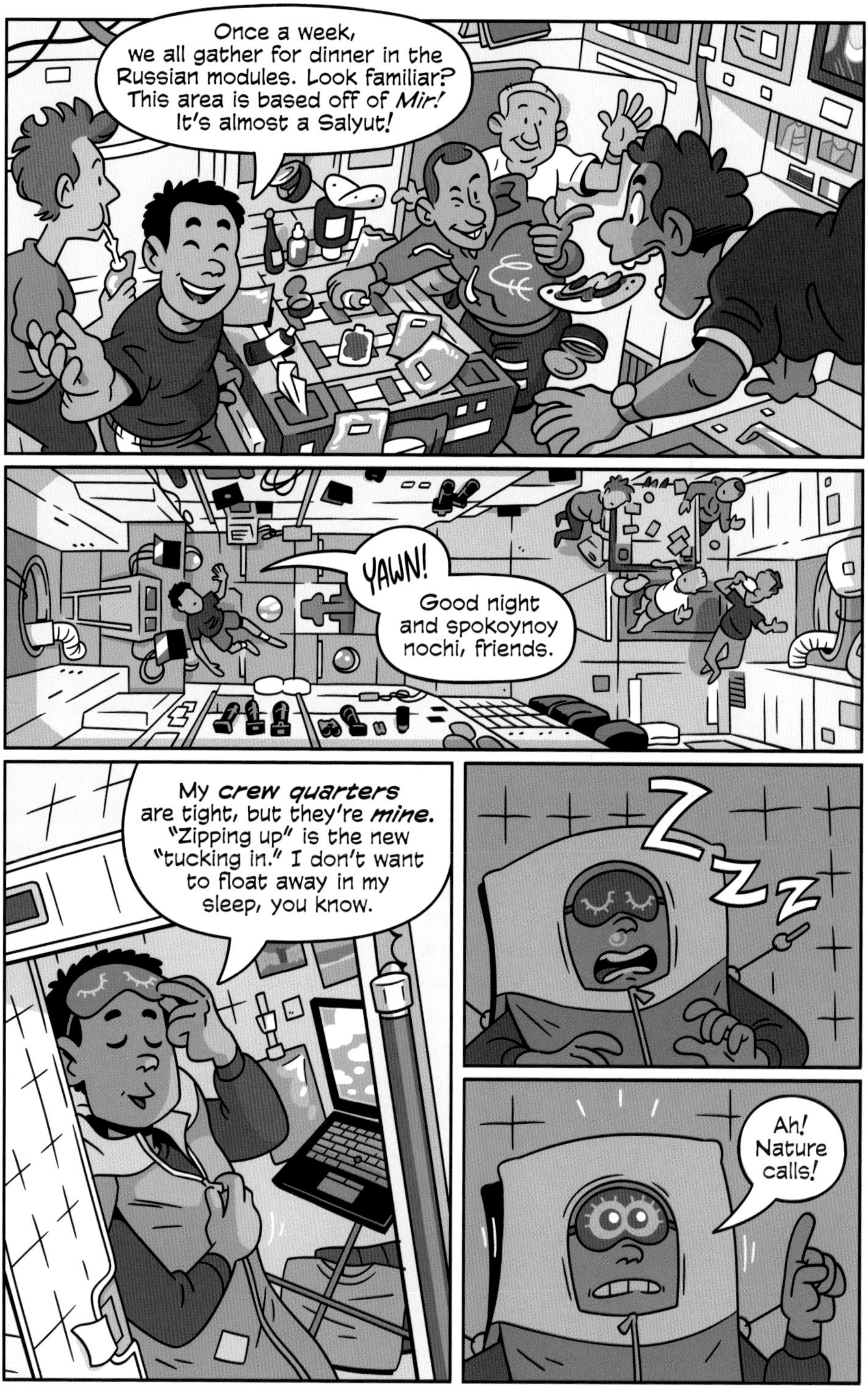
Once a week, we all gather for dinner in the Russian modules. Look familiar? This area is based off of *Mir!* It's almost a Salyut!
YAWN!
Good night and spokoynoy nochi, friends.
My ***crew quarters*** are tight, but they're ***mine.*** "Zipping up" is the new "tucking in." I don't want to float away in my sleep, you know.
Z z z
Ah! Nature calls!

Finally, what you've been waiting for! *Space toilet!* The toilet in space!
First things first. Switch on the *suction.*
CLICK
WHIRR
Solids go in this bag here.
PLORT
The opening is elastic, so you can seal the smell before pushing this down into the bucket.
Stuff it in the hole, and replace the bag for the next guest!
Liquids are sucked down this tube.
Please wipe it clean when you're done.
GLUG
WHIR
And, no. It doesn't vent into space.
The third law would turn the ISS into a pee rocket!

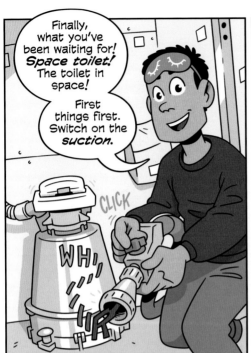

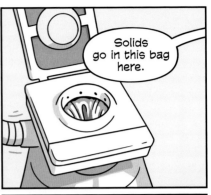

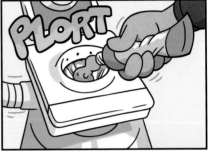

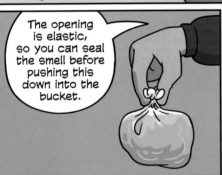

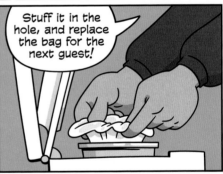

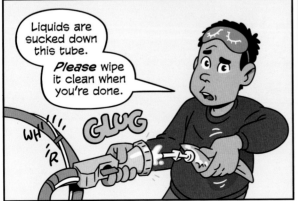

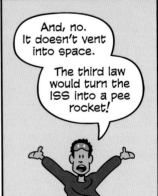

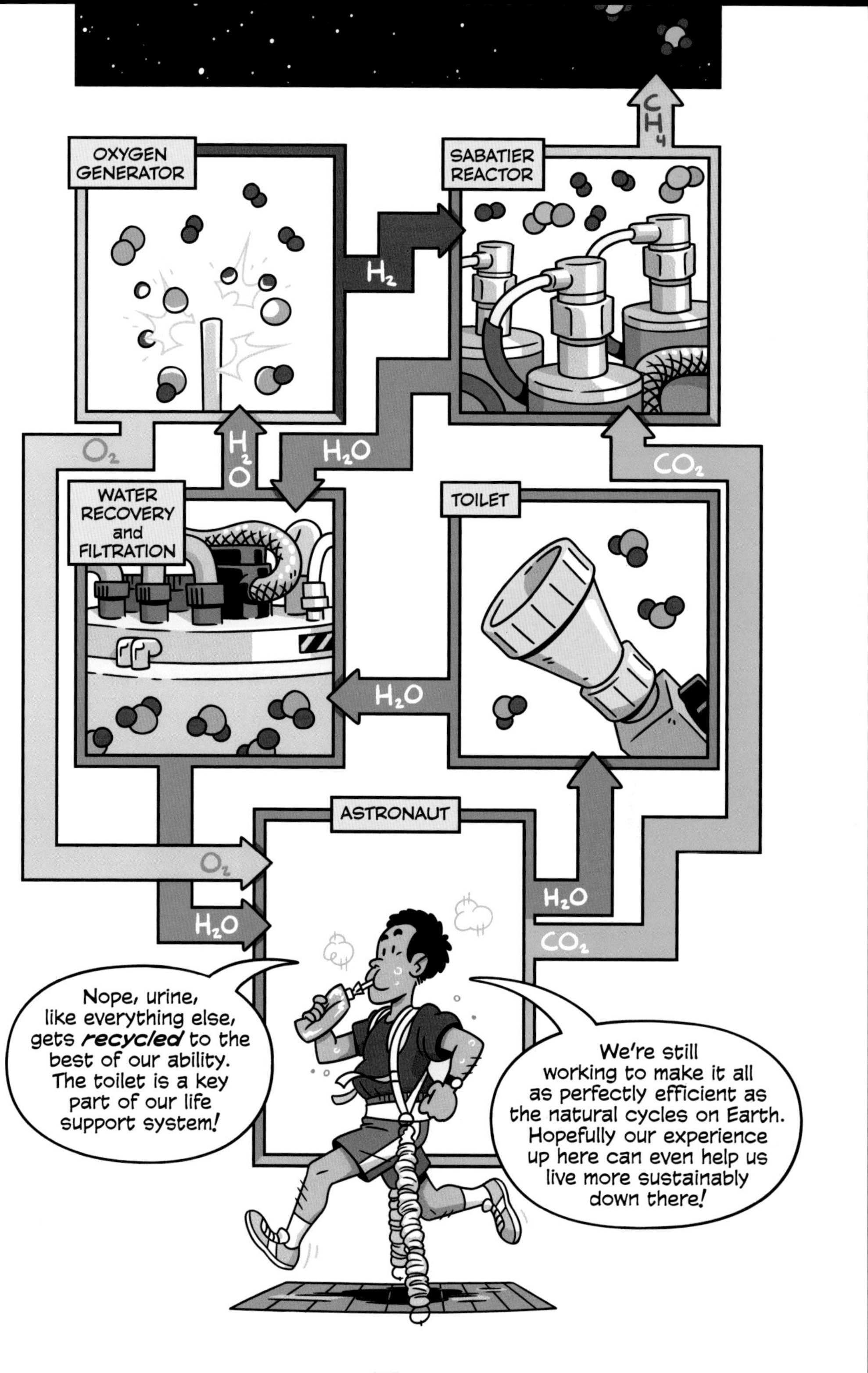
CH4
OXYGEN GENERATOR
SABATIER REACTOR
H2
O2
H2O
H2O
CO2
WATER RECOVERY and FILTRATION
TOILET
H2O
ASTRONAUT
O2
H2O
H2O
CO2
Nope, urine, like everything else, gets *recycled* to the best of our ability. The toilet is a key part of our life support system!
We're still working to make it all as perfectly efficient as the natural cycles on Earth. Hopefully our experience up here can even help us live more sustainably down there!

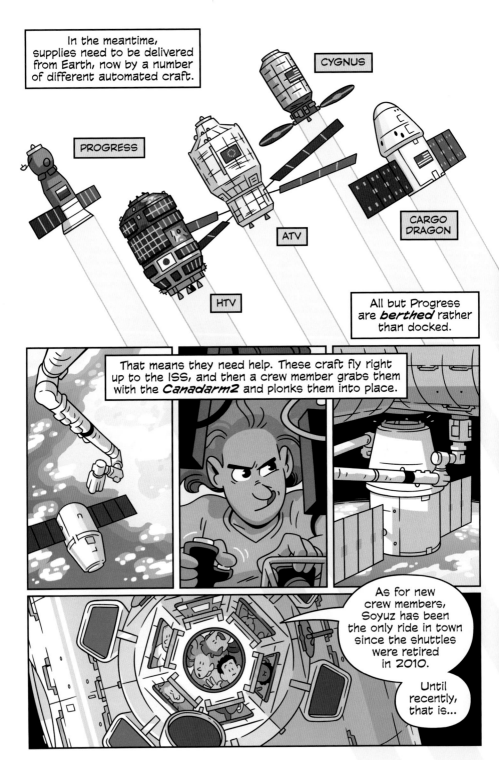

In the meantime, supplies need to be delivered from Earth, now by a number of different automated craft.

CYGNUS

PROGRESS

ATV

CARGO DRAGON

HTV

All but Progress are *berthed* rather than docked.

That means they need help. These craft fly right up to the ISS, and then a crew member grabs them with the *Canadarm2* and plonks them into place.

As for new crew members, Soyuz has been the only ride in town since the shuttles were retired in 2010.

Until recently, that is...

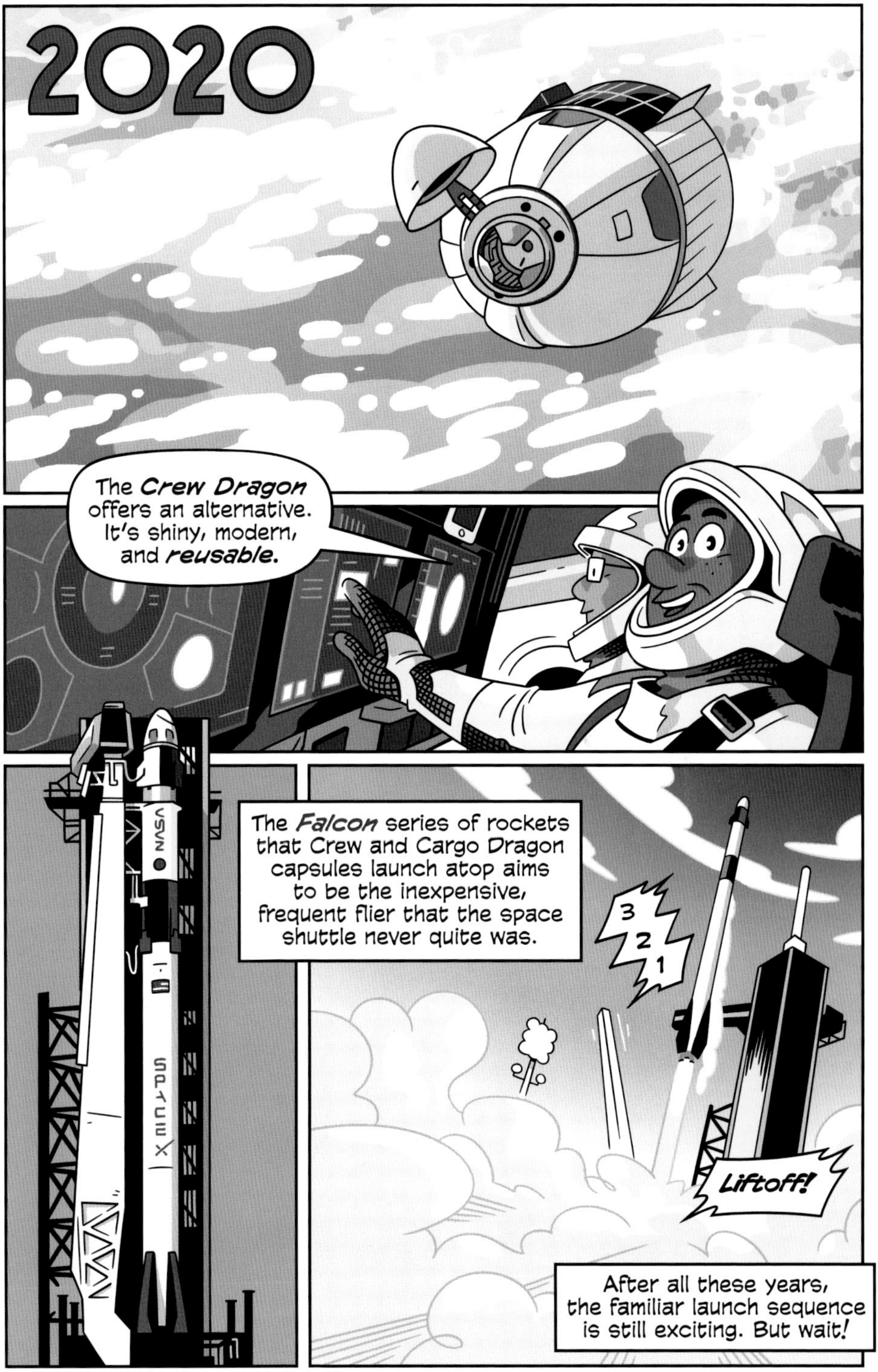
2020
The *Crew Dragon* offers an alternative. It's shiny, modern, and *reusable.*
NASA
The *Falcon* series of rockets that Crew and Cargo Dragon capsules launch atop aims to be the inexpensive, frequent flier that the space shuttle never quite was.
SPACEX
3
2
1
Liftoff!
After all these years, the familiar launch sequence is still exciting. But wait!

Once the upper stage rockets away, the spent booster doesn't sink into the ocean. No, no.

It does a flip!

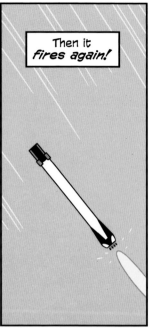

Then it *fires again!*

Using its fins to stay upright, it gently lowers itself to land on a floating pad.

In less than a month, this can be cleaned up and ready to fly again and again.

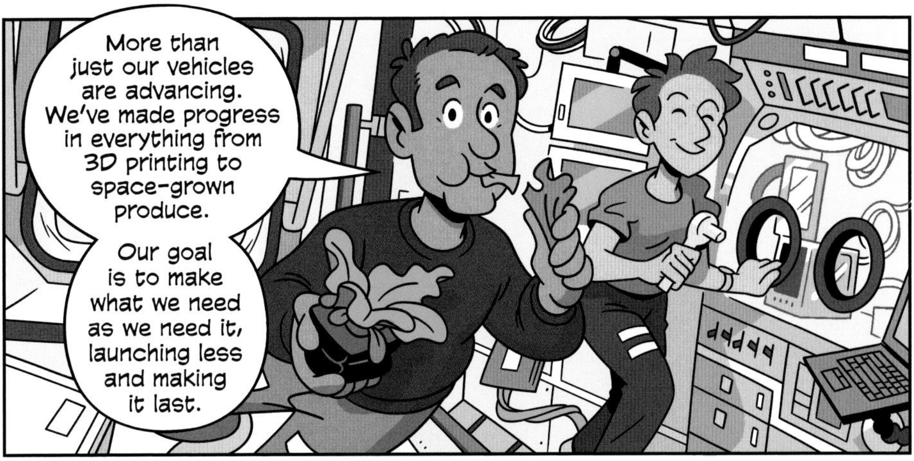
More than just our vehicles are advancing. We've made progress in everything from 3D printing to space-grown produce.
Our goal is to make what we need as we need it, launching less and making it last.

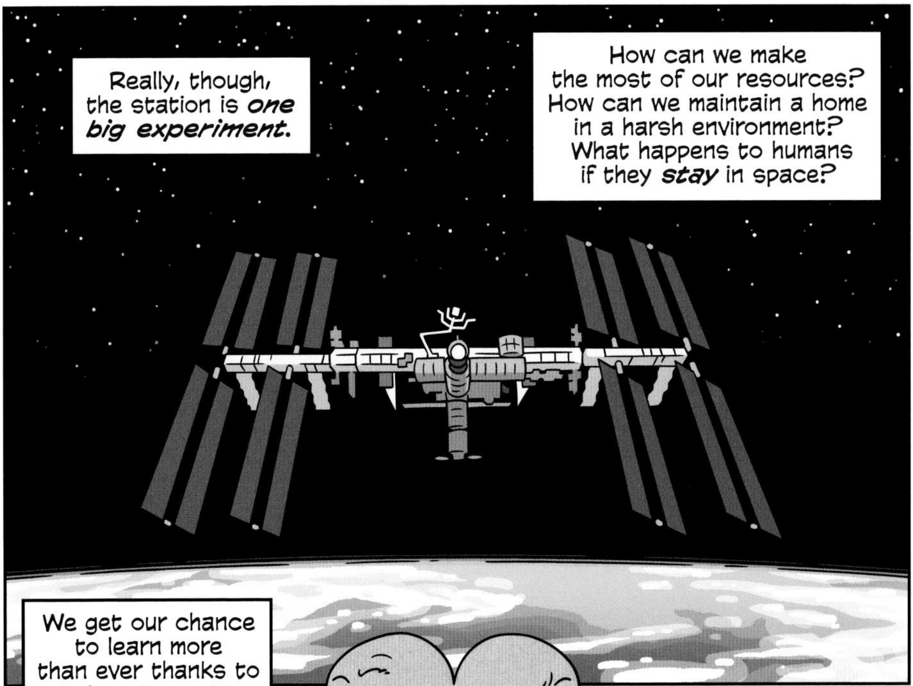
Really, though, the station is *one big experiment.*
How can we make the most of our resources? How can we maintain a home in a harsh environment? What happens to humans if they *stay* in space?
We get our chance to learn more than ever thanks to twin astronauts *Scott and Mark Kelly.*

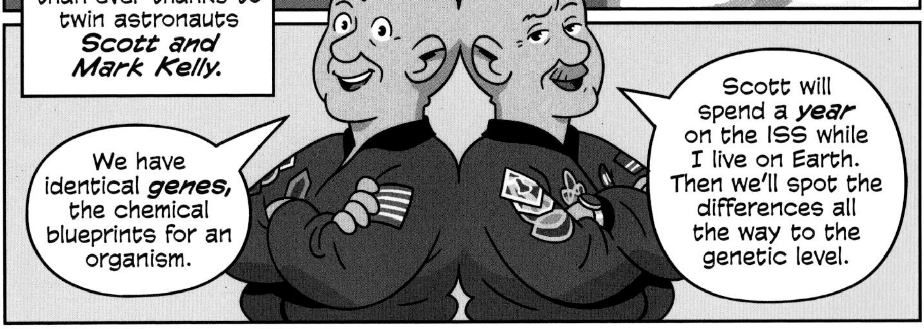
We have identical *genes,* the chemical blueprints for an organism.
Scott will spend a *year* on the ISS while I live on Earth. Then we'll spot the differences all the way to the genetic level.

Thanks to long-duration spaceflights from Project *Gemini* to *Mir*, we already know to expect changes in my muscles and bones.

Because of the way body fluids slosh around without gravity, my eyesight eventually changes too.

My brain stays sharp, though, thank you very much. No "space madness" here.

Checkmate, Mark!

Hey!

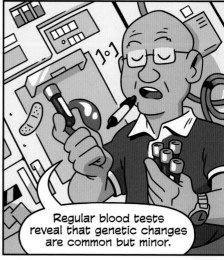

Regular blood tests reveal that genetic changes are common but minor.

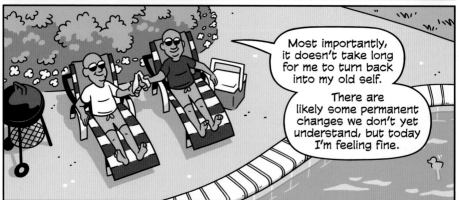

Most importantly, it doesn't take long for me to turn back into my old self.

There are likely some permanent changes we don't yet understand, but today I'm feeling fine.

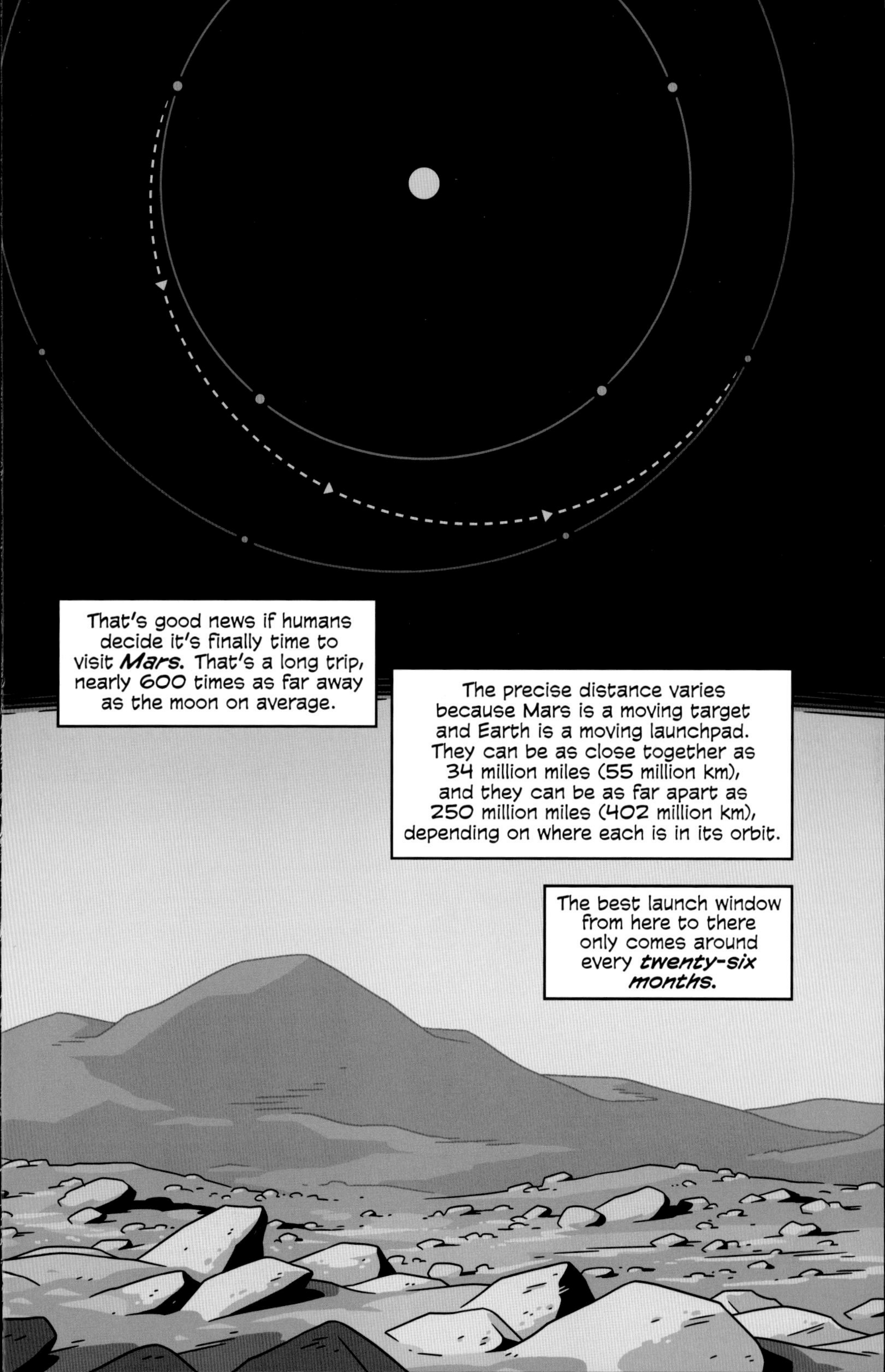
That's good news if humans decide it's finally time to visit *Mars*. That's a long trip, nearly 600 times as far away as the moon on average.
The precise distance varies because Mars is a moving target and Earth is a moving launchpad. They can be as close together as 34 million miles (55 million km), and they can be as far apart as 250 million miles (402 million km), depending on where each is in its orbit.
The best launch window from here to there only comes around every *twenty-six months*.

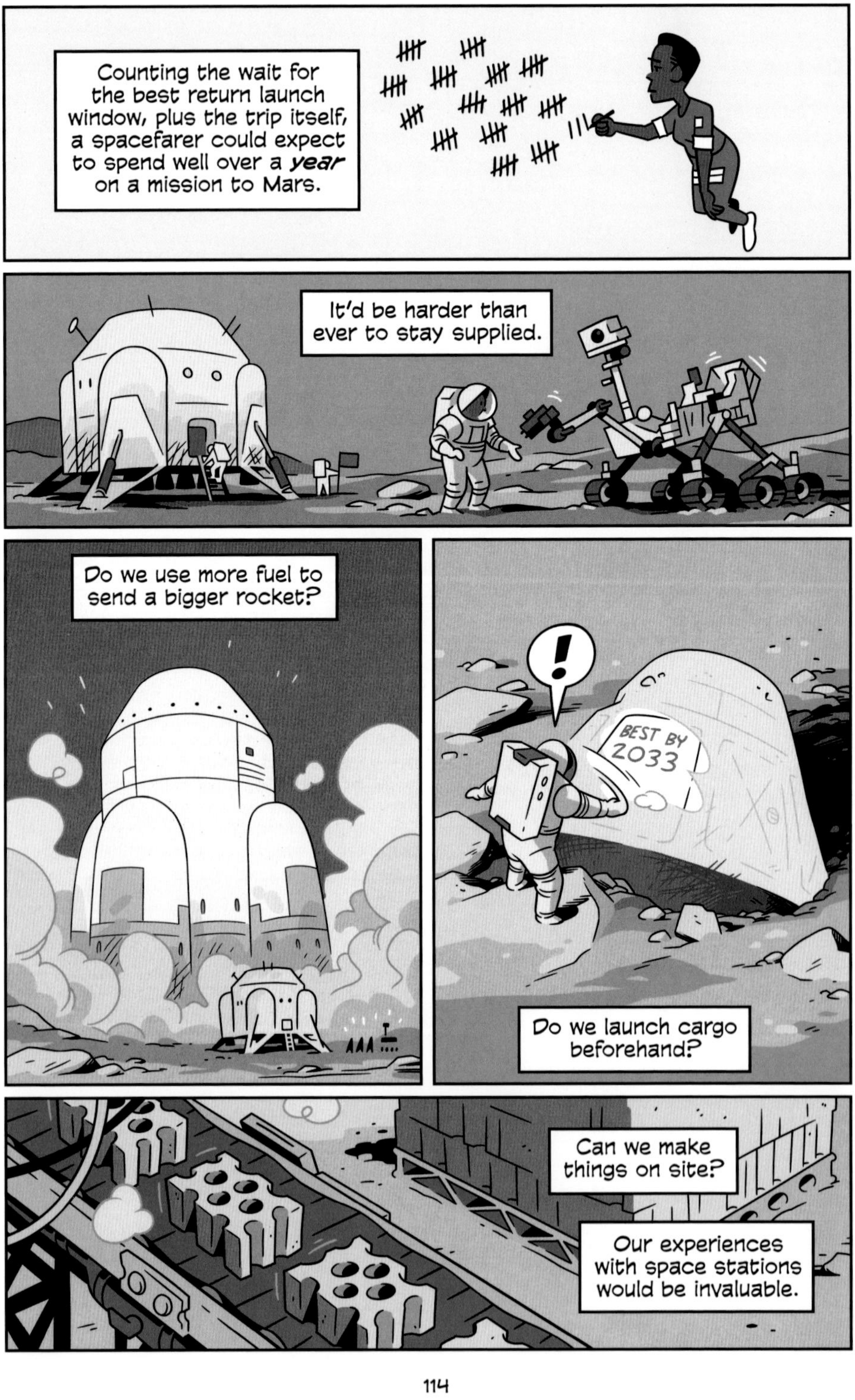
Counting the wait for the best return launch window, plus the trip itself, a spacefarer could expect to spend well over a ***year*** on a mission to Mars.
It'd be harder than ever to stay supplied.
Do we use more fuel to send a bigger rocket?
!
BEST BY 2033
Do we launch cargo beforehand?
Can we make things on site?
Our experiences with space stations would be invaluable.

Those experiences could also be short lived. The more connected the international space program becomes, the more relationships there are to fail.
WAR?
AKING — BREAKING — BREAKING — BREAKIN
With luck, the strength of cooperation in orbit can withstand conflicts on the surface.
Though the first Space Race is over, a *second* may yet follow. The world is full of nations eager to claim a place in the sky and the *status* that comes with it.
China is only the third nation to achieve human spaceflight. In 2003, *Yang Liwei* became the first taikonaut to orbit Earth and an instant hero at home. Within another decade, the *Tiangong* space station was in orbit.
The competitive spirit is alive and well. China, along with others sure to follow, pursues human spaceflight for the same reasons as the US and USSR a half-century ago.

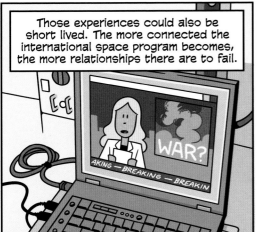

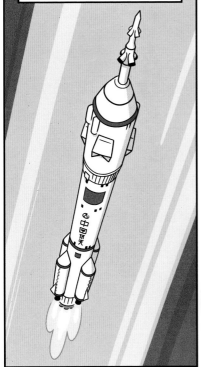

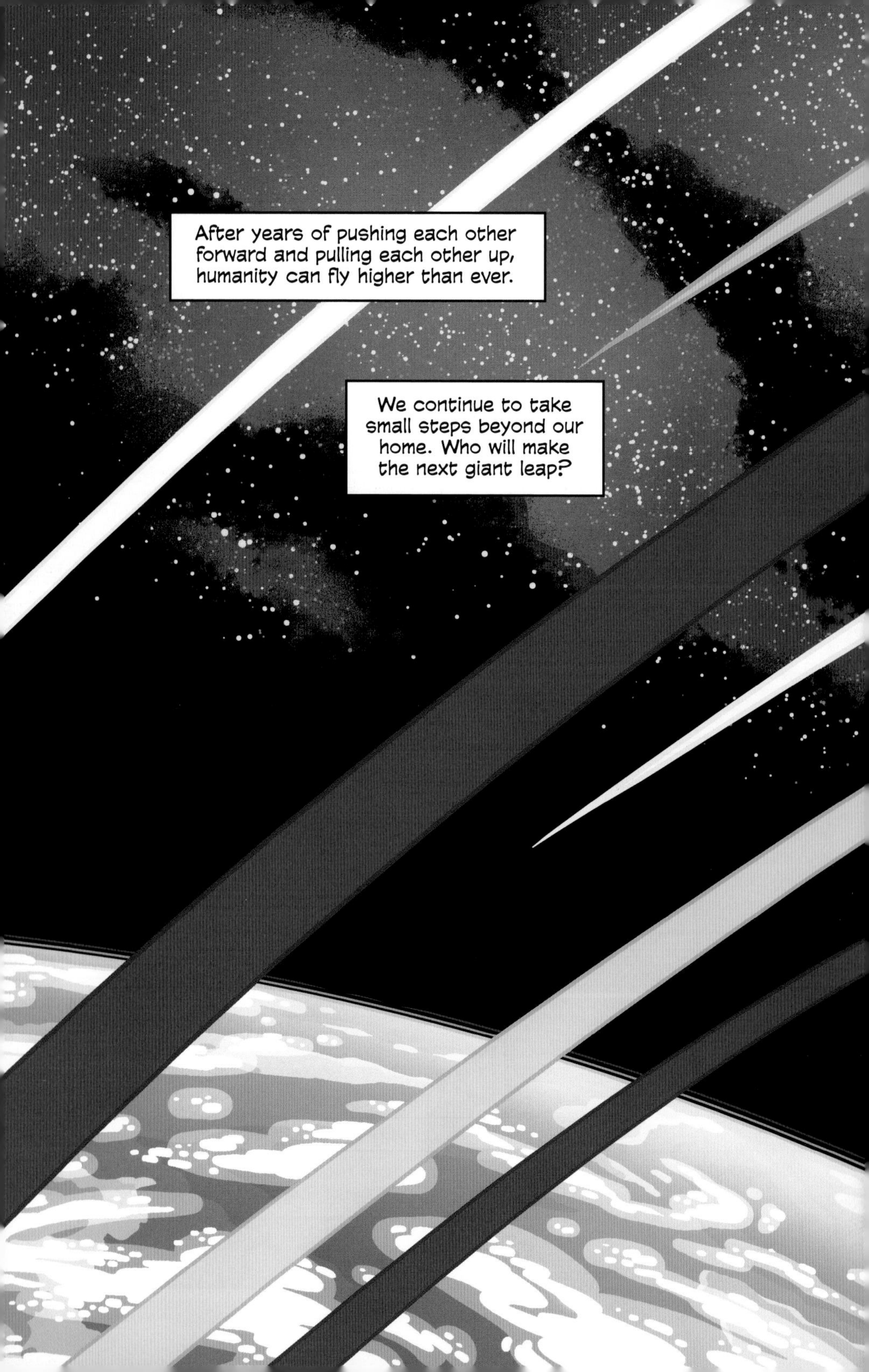
After years of pushing each other forward and pulling each other up, humanity can fly higher than ever.
We continue to take small steps beyond our home. Who will make the next giant leap?

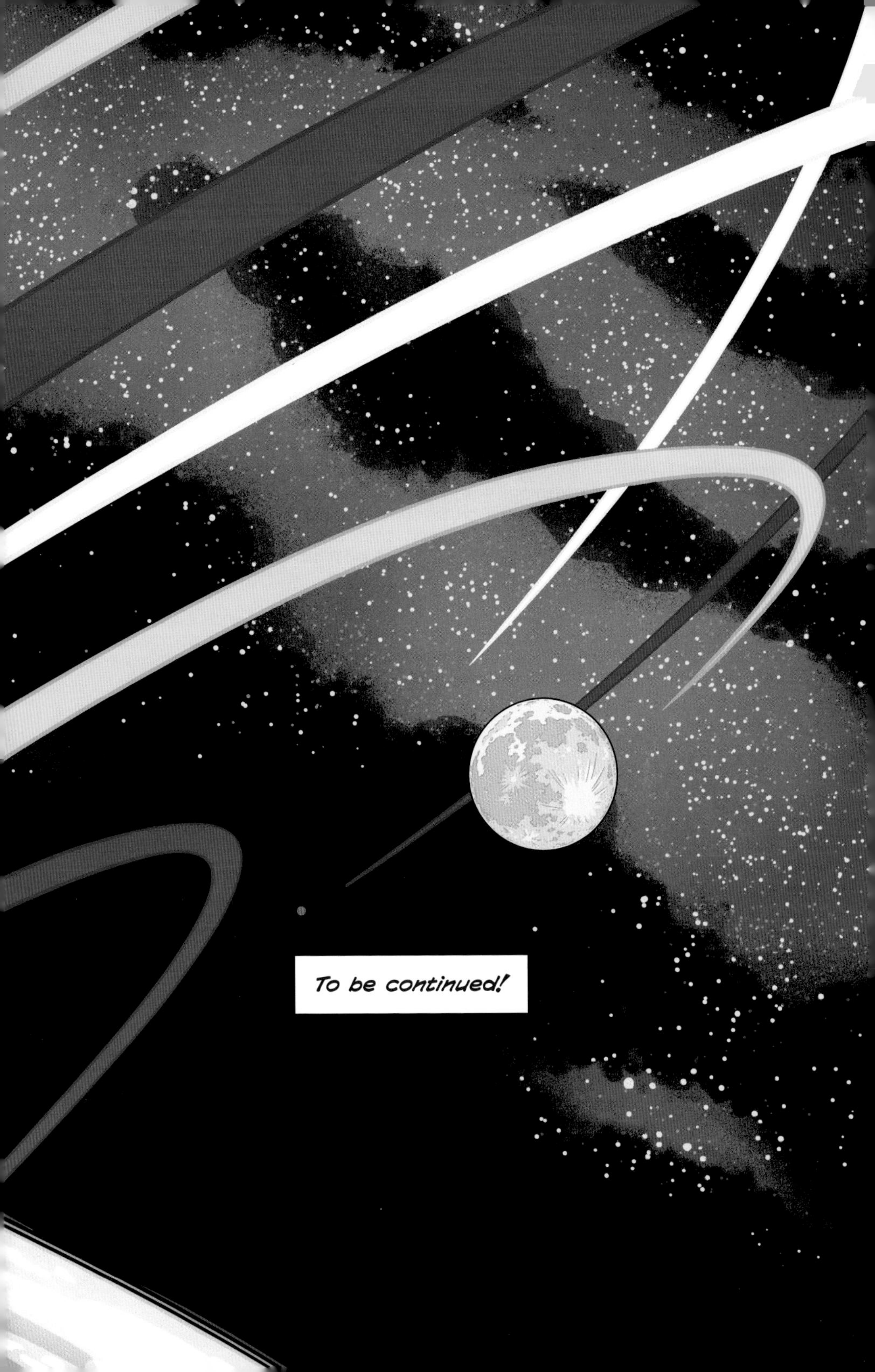
To be continued!

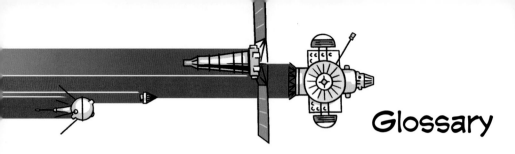

Glossary

Space programs are dated from the start of the program or design process to the end of its final mission.

Apollo (1961–1972)
The US program to send humans to the moon. On July 20, 1969, the commander of *Apollo 11*, Neil Armstrong, became the first person to walk on the moon.

Atmosphere
The layers of gas that surround and protect Earth. From lowest altitude to highest, these layers are the troposphere, stratosphere, mesosphere, thermosphere, and exosphere. Together, they are hundreds of miles thick, but humans can only survive unaided in the bottom 6.2 miles (10 km).

Computer
A term originally referring to human professionals tasked with solving the numerous complex mathematical equations necessary for successful spaceflight. They were eventually joined by, then superseded by, mechanical computers.

Falcon (2002–present)
A twenty-first century series of reusable rockets capable of landing intact after launch.

Friction
The force created by one object moving along another. It resists continuous movement and, even in small amounts, eventually slows and stops the objects while producing heat.

Gemini (1961–1966)
The US program to prepare for human spaceflight beyond Earth's orbit. The missions demonstrated two-person crews, extravehicular activity, spacecraft docking, and flights up to two weeks in duration.

Gravity
The attractive force between any two objects. On Earth's surface, the feeling of weight comes from the opposing force exerted by the ground against your body. This g-force is multiplied many times over in rapidly accelerating vehicles such as rockets.

Gyroscope
A spinning device that uses the conservation of angular momentum to reorient a spacecraft without expending fuel.

Interkosmos (1967–1994)
The Soviet program that flew crew members from allied nations to Salyuts and *Mir*.

International Space Station (1993–present)
A cooperatively designed, built, and operated space station that has grown to become the largest manmade object in space. It has been continuously occupied since the year 2000.

Laws of Motion
As described by Sir Isaac Newton, these state that first, an object in uniform motion will maintain that motion unless acted on by an outside force; second, force is the product of mass and acceleration; third, when one object acts on another, the two exert equal forces in opposite directions.

Mercury (1958–1963)
The US program to launch humans into space, consisting of both suborbital and orbital flights.

Mir (1986–2000)
A Soviet, then Russian, space station that was the first to be modularly constructed. New segments were launched years apart and autonomously attached to the core structure.

Momentum
The tendency of an object to maintain its motion, whether linear, as when moving through space, or angular, as when rotating in place.

Neutral Buoyancy Lab
A deep, artificial pool used to simulate spacewalks. By slightly weighing trainees down, they will neither sink nor float and are able to work as if in the microgravity of Earth's orbit.

Orbital flight
Achieved by moving perpendicular to the earth or another astronomical body so fast that the vehicle rises away from the body at the same rate it falls. At an altitude of around 150 miles (241 km), a spacecraft must travel 17,000 mph to maintain a circular trajectory. A suborbital flight reaches the upper atmosphere but does not travel fast enough to circle the globe.

Payload
Anything launched atop a rocket. This ranges from explosives to explorers, and its successful delivery is the purpose for which the rocket is built.

Progress (1973–present)
A series of robotic cargo vehicles used by the Soviet Union and Russia to resupply space stations. Such vehicles are essential for continuous life in orbit.

Rocket
A device or vehicle that achieves thrust by directing the exhaust of a chemical explosion opposite its motion. Staged rockets are assembled from multiple rockets stacked or bundled together to be discarded as their fuel is spent.

Salyut (1970–1986)
A series of Soviet space stations, the first in Earth's orbit. Their designs influenced future stations from *Mir* to the ISS.

Satellite
Any object orbiting an astronomical body. The moon is Earth's only natural satellite. Space stations and many devices for observation and communication are artificial satellites of Earth.

Skylab (1965–1974)
The first American space station. It was built from a Saturn V rocket, the launch vehicle for the Apollo missions.

Soyuz (1962–present)
A series of Soviet and Russian spacecraft, as well as associated rockets. These are the most used spacecraft to date, having been in service from the 1960s to the present.

Space
The virtually empty area beyond Earth's atmosphere and between astronomical bodies.

Space Shuttle (1968–2011)
Formally the Space Transportation System, this US spacecraft consists of an orbiter, an external fuel tank, and two booster rockets. It served a wide variety of mission types as the first crewed reusable spacecraft.

Space suit
A garment to help keep humans alive outside of Earth's atmosphere. These may allow space travelers to leave their vehicles for some amount of time, either with an umbilical cable to attach them to their spacecraft's life support systems or with the use of additional equipment for cooling, ventilation, and electrical power.

Space station
A spacecraft designed for long-term habitation in orbit around a particular body. Despite strict resource management, today's crews still depend on regular resupply missions from Earth.

Spacelab
A scientific laboratory composed of multiple modules to be carried in a space shuttle's payload bay. These were designed, built, and partially operated by crew members from the European Space Agency.

Tiangong (1992–present)
A twenty-first-century Chinese space station. China is the first nation to achieve human spaceflight since the Soviet Union and United States in the 1960s.

Voskhod (1964–1965)
The Soviet space program to fly two-person crews on long-duration flights, notable for the first spacewalk.

Vostok (1958–1963)
The Soviet space program responsible for sending the first human into space. Yuri Gagarin orbited Earth aboard *Vostok 1* on April 12, 1961.